D1429567

LIVERPOOL JMU LIBRARY

3 1111 01456 5897

Exhibiting Mormonism

RELIGION IN AMERICA

Harry S. Stout, General Editor

Recent Titles in the Series

EXHIBITING MORMONISM

*The Latter-day Saints and the
1893 Chicago World's Fair*

REID L. NEILSON

OXFORD
UNIVERSITY PRESS

OXFORD
UNIVERSITY PRESS

Oxford University Press, Inc., publishes works that further
Oxford University's objective of excellence
in research, scholarship, and education.

Oxford   New York
Auckland   Cape Town   Dar es Salaam   Hong Kong   Karachi
Kuala Lumpur   Madrid   Melbourne   Mexico City   Nairobi
New Delhi   Shanghai   Taipei   Toronto

With offices in
Argentina   Austria   Brazil   Chile   Czech Republic   France   Greece
Guatemala   Hungary   Italy   Japan   Poland   Portugal   Singapore
South Korea   Switzerland   Thailand   Turkey   Ukraine   Vietnam

Copyright © 2011 by Oxford University Press, Inc.

Published by Oxford University Press, Inc.
198 Madison Avenue, New York, New York 10016

www.oup.com

Oxford is a registered trademark of Oxford University Press
All rights reserved. No part of this publication may be reproduced,
stored in a retrieval system, or transmitted, in any form or by any means,
electronic, mechanical, photocopying, recording, or otherwise,
without the prior permission of Oxford University Press.

Library of Congress Cataloging-in-Publication Data
Neilson, Reid Larkin, 1972–
Exhibiting Mormonism : the Latter-day Saints and the 1893 Chicago
World's Fair / Reid L. Neilson.
p.   cm.—(Religion in America series)
Includes index.
ISBN 978-0-19-538403-1 (hardcover : alk. paper)
1. Church of Jesus Christ of Latter-day Saints—Public
relations—History—19th century.   2. Church of Jesus Christ of
Latter-day Saints—Public opinion—History—19th century.   3. Mormon
Church—Public relations—History—19th century.   4. Mormon
Church—Public opinion—History—19th century.   5. World's Columbian
Exposition (1893 : Chicago, Ill.)   I. Title.   II. Series: Religion in
America series (Oxford University Press)
BX8611.N43 2011
289.3'7731109034—dc22   2010041452

1 3 5 7 9 8 6 4 2

Printed in the United States of America
on acid-free paper

To my father Ralph Reid Neilson

Favourable publicity will open many doors now closed to the Gospel message. This explains why the [Mormon Tabernacle] Choir is going to Chicago. This explains why the Choir went to the great Columbian Exposition in Chicago in 1893—the first extensive trip it ever took and undertaken at a time too when prejudice against the [LDS] Church was very strong, but weakened from this time on.... This is the key to a variety of activities engaged in by officials and organizations of the Church. With what results?—a better understanding by the people generally of the principles and objectives of the Church. Evil-minded people had spread abroad so much intense prejudice against them that the delivery of the Gospel message through our missionary methods has been seriously handicapped. In defense the Church has been forced to use available publicity means, with excellent results.*

—Joseph F. Merrill, 1934

---

* Joseph F. Merrill, "Tabernacle Choir at Chicago Fair," *Millennial Star* 96, no. 36 (September 6, 1934): 569.

Contents

List of Illustrations

Acknowledgements

They say it takes a village to raise a child, and the same is true to write a book. I appreciate the many individuals and institutions that have enabled me to complete this historical project. I was fortunate to research, write, and teach at Brigham Young University in Provo, Utah, while writing this monograph. The leadership of the College of Religious Education and the Department of Church History and Doctrine, including Terry B. Ball, Arnold K. Garr, Steven C. Harper, Kent P. Jackson, Dennis L. Largey, John P. Livingstone, Paul H. Peterson, Brent L. Top, and Dennis A. Wright, provided much-needed research assistants, teaching reductions, and travel funding. My other colleagues and friends in Religious Education, including Ronald Bartholowmew, Alexander L. Baugh, Richard E. Bennett, Susan Easton Black, Richard O. Cowan, Richard Crookston, Scott C. Esplin, Lawrence R. Flake, J. Spencer Fluhman, Alonzo L. Gaskill, Linda Godfrey, Michael Goodman, Brian M. Hauglid, Andrew H. Hedges, Richard Neitzel Holzapfel, R. Devan Jensen, Ann Madsen, Craig K. Manscill, Robert L. Millet, Lloyd D. Newell, Camille Fronk Olson, Alan K. Parrish, Kip Sperry, Thomas A. Wayment, Mary Jane Woodger, and Fred E. Woods, made the Joseph Smith Building a wonderful place to write and teach about Mormon and American religious history. And Patty Smith and her student staff at the Faculty Support Center graciously fulfilled my many research and administrative requests.

Owing to the generosity of my university administration, I was fortunate to present several papers on the Mormon involvement in the 1893 Chicago World's Fair at a number of academic gatherings, including the L. Tom Perry Special Collections's 2005 Omnibus Lecture Series at Brigham Young University in Provo, Utah; the College of Religious Education's 2006 Faculty Forum Series at Brigham Young University in Provo, Utah; the 2007 Annual Illinois State History Conference in Springfield, Illinois; the American Historical Association's 2007 annual regional meeting in Honolulu, Hawaii; the American Academy of Religion's 2007 annual regional meeting in Omaha, Nebraska; the 2008 Utah State History Conference in Salt Lake City, Utah; the Women's Research Institute's 2008 Women's Studies Colloquia at Brigham

Young University in Provo, Utah; the American Historical Association's 2009 annual meeting in New York City, New York; and the Mormon History Association's 2009 annual meeting in Springfield, Illinois. In addition to the scholars who provided much appreciated feedback on my project at these gatherings, I am also grateful to the librarians and staff of the L. Tom Perry Special Collections, the Utah Valley Regional Family History Center, and the Harold B. Lee Library at Brigham Young University; the Church History Library and the Family History Library at The Church of Jesus Christ of Latter-day Saints; the Special Collections and the J. Willard Marriott Library at the University of Utah; the Special Collections and Archives at Utah State University; and the Research Library and Collections at the Utah State Historical Society.

A number of friends, colleagues, and family members, including Linda Hunter Adams, Richard Lyman Bushman, Seth A. Dowland, J. Spencer Fluhman, Terryl L. Givens, Matthew J. Grow, Steven C. Harper, Michael Hicks, Richard Jaffe, Laurie F. Maffly-Kipp, Ralph R. Neilson, Shelly A. Neilson, Susan Sessions Rugh, Richard Hughes Seager, Heather M. Seferovich, Thomas A. Tweed, Grant Wacker, and Benjamin Zeller, reviewed the manuscript at different stages and offered helpful critiques along the way, yet I alone am responsible for the finished product. My friend and editor Cynthia Read and her editorial and production staff at Oxford University Press were a delight to work with on this project. Long may she continue to "fish" for good books! The leadership of the Church History Department of The Church of Jesus Christ of Latter-day Saints, including Elder Marlin K. Jensen, Elder Paul K. Sybrowsky, and Richard E. Turley Jr. were likewise supportive of my project when I moved professionally to Salt Lake City.

Moreover, my wife Shelly and children John, Katherine, and Allyson were encouraging throughout the entire process. Shelly believed in this book and its future publication before I did, and for that early and ongoing vote of confidence, she merits my continual gratitude. And my late mother Katherine (1946–2010) continued her cheerleading despite her own health challenges. Finally, I dedicate this book to my father Ralph Reid Neilson who taught me by example the value of hard work and determination, two personal qualities that were instrumental for my completion of this study and for most of the happiness in my life. All of these persons and organizations deserve to be thanked and remembered for their generosity and contribution to the telling of this important chapter in Mormon and American religious history.

                                                      Reid L. Neilson
                                                      Bountiful, Utah
                                                      July 2010

Exhibiting Mormonism

Introduction

IN 1891, JOSIAH Strong, a renowned Congregationalist minister and general secretary of the Evangelical Alliance for the United States, published a revised edition of his best-selling book *Our Country: Its Possible Future and Its Present Crisis* (1885). Convinced that white Anglo-Saxon Protestant Americans were responsible for the Christian evangelization and spiritual redemption of the world, he again lifted up his warning shout that not all was well at home or abroad. Strong likened the final decade of the nineteenth century to other watershed moments in church history like the Incarnation of Christ and the German Reformation. "Many are not aware that we are living in extraordinary times. Few suppose that these years of peaceful prosperity, in which we are quietly developing a continent, are the pivot on which is turning the nation's future. And fewer still imagine that the destinies of mankind, for centuries to come, can be seriously affected, much less determined, by the men of this generation in the United States," he wrote.[1] Strong then shared what he perceived to be the biggest perils facing his chosen generation in white Protestant America: excessive and continuing immigration, the influence of Romanism (Catholicism), the infiltration of the public school system by Catholics and secularists, the destructive influence of intemperance, the growing political power of socialism, the public fixation on wealth, and the corrosive effects of urbanization.[2]

Given the religious and political tenor of America's overlapping Gilded Age and Progressive Era, it is not surprising that Strong also railed against the seemingly homegrown evils of The Church of Jesus Christ of Latter-day Saints (hereafter referred to as the church), popularly known as the LDS or

---

1. Josiah Strong, *Our Country: Its Possible Future and Its Present Crisis*, rev. ed. (New York: American Home Missionary Society, [1885] 1891), 15.

2. Strong, *Our Country*, vii–x.

Mormon Church or simply Mormonism.[3] "The civilized world wonders that such a hideous caricature of the Christian religion should have appeared in this most enlightened land; that such an anachronism should have been produced by the most progressive civilization," Strong lamented the rise of the Latter-day Saint religion in the midst of the Protestant Establishment.[4] Between the publication of Strong's first (1885) and second editions (1891) of *Our Country*, however, church President Wilford Woodruff had publicly issued the "Manifesto" in September 1890, declaring that he and his fellow church leaders were no longer teaching plural marriage, that he had overseen the flattening of the Endowment House where plural marriages were previously solemnized, and that he and his church were now committed to sustaining the laws of the land.[5] Although Strong, like many non-Mormon

------

3. Believing that that all religions have the right to name themselves, I deferred to the church's official style guide, posted on its "Newsroom" website, which states: "The official name of the Church is The Church of Jesus Christ of Latter-day Saints. This full name was given by revelation from God to Joseph Smith in 1838. While the term 'Mormon Church' has long been publicly applied to the Church as a nickname, it is not an authorized title, and the Church discourages its use." Accordingly, I used the full name of the church as the first reference in each chapter and employed "the church" as a shortened reference thereafter. Moreover, the church's style guide clarifies that: "the term 'Mormonism' is acceptable in describing the combination of doctrine, culture and lifestyle unique to The Church of Jesus Christ of Latter-day Saints." But I was careful to delineate "Mormonism" from the institutional "church." When referring to church members I used "Latter-day Saints" and "Mormons" interchangeably. I also used the term "Mormon" in proper names (like Book of Mormon, Mormon Tabernacle Choir, or Mormon Trail) or as an adjective (like Mormon pioneers) per the Newsroom style guide. To avoid confusion, I did not apply the term "Mormon" to the hundreds of schismatic groups that followed the 1844 martyrdom of Joseph Smith, including The Reorganized Church of Jesus Christ of Latter Day Saints (renamed the Community of Christ in 2001), as instructed by the *Associated Press Stylebook*. ("Style Guide—The Name of the Church," Newsroom, The Church of Jesus Christ of Latter-day Saints, accessed February 21, 2011, http://newsroom.lds.org/style-guide; "Church of Jesus Christ of Latter-day Saints," in Diane Connolly and Debra L. Mason, *Reporting on Religion: A Primer on Journalism's Best Beat* (Westerville, Ohio: Religion Newswriters Association, 2006), 74–75; and "The Church of Jesus Christ of Latter-day Saints," in *Associated Press Stylebook* (New York: Associated Press, 2004), 48, 215.)

4. Strong, *Our Country*, 111. See also Strong's pamphlet *Political Aspects of Mormonism* (New York: League for Social Services, 1898) for an example of his continued tirade against the church.

5. For the best biography of Wilford Woodruff, see Thomas G. Alexander, *Things in Heaven and Earth: The Life and Times of Wilford Woodruff, A Mormon Prophet* (Salt Lake City: Signature Books, 1991). For more details on the 1890 Manifesto, see Thomas G. Alexander, "The Odyssey of a Latter-day Prophet: Wilford Woodruff and the Manifesto of 1890," *Journal of Mormon History* 17 (1991): 169–206; Kenneth W. Godfrey, "The Coming of the Manifesto," *Dialogue: A Journal of Mormon Thought* 5 (Autumn 1970): 11–25; E. Leo Lyman, "The Political Background of the Woodruff Manifesto," *Dialogue: A Journal of Mormon Thought* 24 (Fall 1991): 21–39; and Jan Shipps, "The Principle Revoked: A Closer Look at the Demise of Plural Marriage," *Journal of Mormon History* 11 (1984): 65–77.

observers, was skeptical that polygamy ("the most striking feature of the Mormon monster") had truly come to an end, he expressed concern that Mormonism's gravest threat to the United States still remained: that of Latter-day Saint "ecclesiastical despotism." He declared Mormonism not merely a misguided religious movement, but a political-economic monolith "ruled by a man who is prophet, priest, king and pope, all in one." Mormon prophets from Joseph Smith to Wilford Woodruff, Strong believed, "out-pope[d] the Roman by holding familiar conversation with the Almighty, and getting, to order, new revelations direct from heaven," including the audacity to begin and end the practice of plural marriage on American soil.[6]

Josiah Strong was not a lone voice crying against the Latter-day Saints in the spiritual wilderness of the United States. Common American perceptions of the Mormons were extremely negative between 1830 and 1890 and would only begin to improve once the church relinquished future plural marriages.[7] Moreover, by the final decade of the nineteenth century, most of Strong's fellow countrymen likewise censured the Latter-day Saints for the way they bundled religious, social, economic, and political control in their Great Basin Kingdom. Mormonism had become the "viper on the hearth"[8] of American Protestantism. As historian Matthew J. Grow summarizes, nineteenth-century Protestant leaders lumped the Latter-day Saints with the reviled Catholics and Masons, and they condemned all three groups with invective rhetoric and sporadic violence. Americans living in the Age of Jackson believed that the trio threatened their national ideals, including republicanism and morality. "Depictions of Catholicism and Mormonism generally rested on a sharp dichotomy between a group of unscrupulous leaders and the deceived rank-and-file members, who, though innocent, would unquestioningly obey the evil commands of their superiors. The per-

---

6. Strong, *Our Country*, 112–113.

7. Regarding Mormonism's strained relationship with American culture, see Klaus J. Hansen, *Mormonism and the American Experience* (Chicago: University of Chicago Press, 1981); Thomas G. Alexander, *Mormonism in Transition: A History of the Latter-day Saints, 1890–1930* (Urbana: University of Illinois Press, 1986); E. Leo Lyman, *Political Deliverance: The Mormon Quest for Utah Statehood* (Urbana: University of Illinois Press, 1986); Edwin Brown Firmage and Richard Collins Mangrum, *Zion in the Courts: A Legal History of The Church of Jesus Christ of Latter-day Saints, 1830–1900* (Urbana: University of Illinois Press, 1988); Marvin S. Hill, *Quest for Refuge: The Mormon Flight from American Pluralism* (Salt Lake City: Signature Books, 1989); and Kenneth H. Winn, *Exiles in a Land of Liberty: Mormons in America, 1830–1846* (Chapel Hill: University of North Carolina Press, 1989).

8. See Terryl L. Givens, *The Viper on the Hearth: Mormons, Myths, and the Construction of Heresy* (New York: Oxford University Press, 1997).

ception of group cohesion led to charges of bloc voting, and the frequently raised specter of the temporal ambitions of the religious hierarchies evoked fears of theocracy," Grow explains. "The description of secret and sinister rituals performed by Mormons and Catholics further defined the groups as un-American. Their reliance on immigrants also provoked fears of an influx of foreigners who would bring their autocratic religious principles to subvert American democracy. Finally, using the venerable American genre of the captivity narrative, authors described the sexual and economic exploitation of women in convents and in polygamy."[9] Mormonism and Americanism were thus depicted as mutually exclusive concepts.

While a great deal of ink has been spilt to document the popular representations of Mormonism during the ante- and postbellum periods, much less has been written on how the Latter-day Saints themselves were participants in the construction and contestation of their own image in America. The Mormons were historical actors with agency of their own and must shoulder some of the responsibility, for better or worse, for how they were perceived by outsiders during the nineteenth century. Whereas American Protestants viewed the Latter-day Saints as pseudo-Christians, sexual deviants, disloyal subjects, and economic misfits, the Latter-day Saints believed themselves to be, and represented themselves as, the polar opposite: legitimate Christians (Restoration versus flawed Reformation), chaste adherents (polygamy versus unfaithful monogamy), patriotic Americans (theocracy versus majority-rule democracy), and economic beacons (cooperation versus unbridled individualism) in the United States.

In other words, it was as if Protestant and Mormon Americans were looking at the same photographic film, but with one group viewing the positive image and the other the negative image. The polar-opposite representations of Mormonism derived from LDS and non-LDS perspectives may be likened to a fanciful figure drawn by a generation of nineteenth-century artists, but popularized by psychologists during the early twentieth century. In the case of the "young girl–old woman illusion," subjects are presented with a black-and-white line drawing and then asked what they see on the page. Through artistic trickery, images of a girl or a grandmother are present in the drawing, but viewers cannot perceive them both concurrently. Once the

---

9. Matthew J. Grow, "The Whore of Babylon and the Abomination of Abominations: Nineteenth-Century Catholic and Mormon Mutual Perceptions and Religious Identity," *Church History* 73, no. 1 (March 2004): 141–142. See also David Brion Davis, "Some Themes of Counter-Subversion: An Analysis of Anti-Masonic, Anti-Catholic, and Anti-Mormon Literature," *Mississippi Valley Historical Review* 47 (September 1960): 205–224.

viewers discover the optical illusion they can shift their gaze back and forth between the visage of the young girl and the old woman, two competing yet present interpretations of the same image. This same dichotomy seems illustrative of the competing representations of nineteenth-century Mormonism.[10]

The 1893 Chicago World's Fair, an American cultural celebration commemorating the four-hundredth anniversary of Christopher Columbus's "discovery" of the New World, marked the dramatic reengagement of the church with the non-Mormon world after decades of relative isolation in the Great Basin valleys of the American West. Since 1847, when the Mormon pioneer companies first colonized the Great Salt Lake region, church members were geographically restricted in their personal interactions with non-Mormons, with the exception of those few hundred Latter-day Saint men and women who ventured beyond the Mormon cultural region as missionaries, politicians, and business leaders. As a result, Latter-day Saints were more or less confined to asserting their doctrinal stances and moral positions through the printed word. But this changed in 1890, a year marked by the Manifesto and the formal announcement of the pending 1893 Chicago World's Fair. Between May and October 1893, over seven thousand Latter-day Saints from the Utah Territory, together with their fellow Americans, attended the international spectacle popularly known as the Columbian Exposition. Church members from Utah Territory embraced this opportunity to increase interpersonal contacts and to tell their own story in person in Chicago to the outside world. They wanted to rehabilitate their battered image in America, and no greater stage could have been provided than that at the 1893 Columbian Exposition.[11]

Chicago's "White City," the city built on the fairgrounds, became the catalyst of Mormonism's emerging transformation from a nineteenth-century missionary-minded people to a twentieth-century evangelistic *and* public relations juggernaut. As the Latter-day Saints continued to participate in a number of American world's fairs and expositions, including those held in San Francisco (1894), Omaha (1898), St. Louis (1904), Portland (1905), Jamestown (1907), Seattle (1909), San Francisco (1915), and San Diego (1915),

---

10. Edmund Wright, "The Original of E. G. Boring's 'Young Girl/Mother-in-Law' Drawing and Its Relation to the Pattern of a Joke," *Perception* 21 (1992): 273–275; and Gerald Fisher, "Mother, Father, and Daughter: A Three-Aspect Ambiguous Figure," *American Journal of Psychology* 81 (1968): 274–277. Psychologists today label this phenomenon "perceptual ambiguity."

11. Andrew Jenson, *Church Chronology: A Record of Important Events Pertaining to the History of the Church of Jesus Christ of Latter-day Saints* (Salt Lake City: Deseret News, 1899), 201.

church leaders readjusted their own insular worldviews and sought to engage in both missionary and public relations activities, in order to make both converts and allies to their cause. Their efforts resulted in unprecedented self-promotion success during the Century of Progress International Exposition (1933–1934) in Chicago. "Participation in these fairs and expositions made friends for the Church, introduced people to its message, dispelled misconceptions, and developed technologies that could be used in proclaiming the gospel to the world," one historian points out.[12] Official church involvement in these cultural celebrations also caused many Americans to readjust their views on Mormonism and its believers. No longer did they routinely mock the Latter-day Saints. Some Americans began to actually admire certain aspects of the church and its adherents, particularly its Mormon Tabernacle Choir and its ongoing contributions to the colonization and growth of the American West. Moreover, the Latter-day Saints grew into favor because of their strong traditional families, internal welfare program, and contributions to American conservative politics. Even the distinctive theological tenets of the church were increasingly overlooked by most of the Mormons's fellow countrymen and women. Thus, the 1893 Columbian Exposition and the 1933–1934 Century of Progress International Exposition, both held in Chicago, act as bookends to tell a larger story of accommodation and assimilation on the part of the Mormons into the American religious mainstream.

Two years after the Century of Progress International Exposition closed its doors to the public, Latter-day Saints participated in the 1936 Texas Centennial Exposition in Dallas, Texas, a fair commemorating the centennial of Texas's independence from Mexico. Under the direction of Professor E. H. Eastman, head of the church-operated Brigham Young University's art department, the church prepared promotional exhibits for the Texas exposition. Owing to the overcrowded conditions in the Hall of Religions, where most ecclesiastical organizations were headquartered, Eastman and his exhibit crew set up their displays, which included a film projector and viewing screen, artifacts from Utah's pioneer experience, and photographs of the founding figures and places from nineteenth-century Mormonism, in the neighboring Hall of Varied Industries. All of this was set to music, making it an impressive exhibit for visitors. Just as the 1933–1934 Chicago exposition had been staffed by young missionary elders, the Texas exhibit was manned by missionaries from the Texas Mission, under the direction of its president. During the months that the exhibit

12. Brent L. Top, "World's Fairs," in *Encyclopedia of Latter-day Saint History*, ed. Arnold K. Garr, et al. (Salt Lake City: Deseret Book, 2000), 1367.

was up and running, missionaries distributed 15,000 evangelistic tracts, 10,000 pamphlets, 7,000 postcards, and sold 60 copies of the Book of Mormon, in addition to engaging in 7,500 extended gospel discussions with fairgoers. Based on the viewer feedback, the church would continue to utilize projection technologies in future fairs.[13]

Because of its public relations and evangelistic success in both Chicago and Dallas, the church participated in the Golden Gate International Exposition (1939–1940) held at San Francisco, California, on the man-made Treasure Island. The church had enjoyed great publicity during the 1894 California Midwinter Exposition and the 1915 Panama-Pacific Exposition, both of which were held in the San Francisco area, which Mormon pioneers had helped colonize beginning in 1846. By 1939, there were Mormon stakes (akin to Catholic dioceses) in both San Francisco and Oakland, signaling the strength of the church in that area. Once again the church constructed its own exhibit area to tell to fairgoers the story of Mormonism, but unlike the Illinois and Texas expositions that were administered by the local mission presidency, the California exhibit was overseen by the Church Radio and Publicity Committee under the direction of Chairman Apostle Stephen L Richards and his staff secretary Gordon B. Hinckley, working from church headquarters in Salt Lake City. They determined to draw upon the best components of past fair exhibits, reusing the popular model of the Salt Lake Tabernacle from the 1909 world's fair in Seattle and an updated projection show from the Texas exposition. They also organized multiple performances of the Mormon Tabernacle Choir in San Francisco, in addition to a series of historical lectures centered on the pioneering feats of Mormons in the American West. The results were impressive: over 1.25 million fairgoers passed through the Mormon exhibit, and 230,000 of these visitors listened to a thirty-minute missionary presentation. Under Apostle Richards's direction, the church created a new evangelistic tract for the fair, "Joseph Smith's Own Story," which missionaries from the California Mission and members of the Oakland and San Francisco stakes distributed to over two hundred thousand guests. Nearly one-fifth of all visitors to the Golden Gate International Exposition passed through the Mormon exhibit during these two years.[14]

Following the 1941 Japanese bombing of Pearl Harbor, Hawaii, which ushered the American involvement in the Second World War, Mormon leaders

---

13. Gerald J. Peterson, "History of Mormon Exhibits in World Expositions" (Master's thesis, Brigham Young University, 1974), 53–56.

14. Peterson, "History of Mormon Exhibits," 56–61.

contracted its global missionary program in the war-torn nations of Europe, Asia, and the isles of the Pacific. They also limited church public relations efforts both at home and abroad. Two decades passed before the church got involved in another world's fair. Finally, church leaders determined to participate in the 1962 Century 21 Exposition, popularly known as the Seattle World's Fair, by sending the Salt Lake Mormon Tabernacle Choir to showcase Mormonism in the Pacific Northwest, just as it had during the 1909 Alaska-Yukon Exposition. The celebrated choir performed two major concerts to sold-out crowds that August in Seattle. Moreover, during the Century 21 Exposition, local church members also presented a musical production in a series of shows to over fifty thousand spectators in Seattle. *Promised Valley* told the story of the Mormon pioneer exodus. And Latter-day Saints from the University of Utah's dance team performed "The Mormon Pioneer Woman," a visual and musical celebration of Mormon women during the Utah pioneer era. As historian Gerald J. Peterson notes, the 1962 Seattle cultural celebration reaffirmed to Mormon decision makers that "carefully planned, impressively constructed exhibits, with qualified missionary guides, were an exceptional means for bringing the restored Gospel to the attention of many souls."[15]

The 1964 New York World's Fair ushered in an unprecedented level of official church support. The First Presidency, led by President David O. McKay, selected a committee charged with exhibiting Mormonism in America's most populous metropolitan region. Previously, the church had limited its expenditures at world's fairs and exhibitions to under $100,000. The Mormon Pavilion (figure 1), as the church's enclosed extravaganza came to be known, cost the church $1.65 million dollars to construct and operate. Its displays showcased the leading doctrines of the church, including the purpose of life, value of families, and centrality of Jesus Christ to humankind's eternal salvation. Between 1964 and 1965, almost six million visitors toured the Mormon Pavilion at the New York World's Fair. Not surprisingly, the success of this Latter-day Saint exhibit impacted the way that Mormons evangelized in the public sphere thereafter. In the decades following the New York World's Fair, Mormon leaders and laity continued to participate in both domestic and international expositions.[16] Church leaders subsequently repurposed much of the exhibits' content at later world's fairs held in the United States, Canada, and Japan. Ultimately, many of these same materials used to temporarily exhibit

15. Peterson, "History of Mormon Exhibits," 61–65.

16. Peterson, "History of Mormon Exhibits," 69–129.

FIGURE 1 The Mormon Pavilion at the New York World's Fair in New York City, 1964–1965, courtesy of the Church History Library, The Church of Jesus Christ of Latter-day Saints, Salt Lake City, Utah.

Mormonism at twentieth-century world's fairs ended up providing the framework and content for the permanent exhibits displayed in visitors' centers on Temple Square in Salt Lake City. Lessons learned through active involvement in over a dozen American world's fairs and expositions paved the way for the church's twentieth-century visitors' center and exhibits program.[17]

A decade into the twenty-first century, Latter-day Saints continue to showcase dozens of rotating exhibits and historic sites, for both Mormons and non-Mormons alike. And church leaders and members are eager to exhibit their faith to anyone who might show interest. "Whether you're taking a break on a business trip or vacationing with family and friends, there are many opportunities to learn about the rich history and teachings of The

17. Top, "World's Fairs," 1367.

Church of Jesus Christ of Latter-day Saints," an official church website suggests of the breadth of its public offerings and attempts to exhibit Mormonism.[18] Tours of formal visitors' centers are open to the interested public at a number of domestic temple complexes in Arizona, California, Hawaii, Idaho, Utah, and Washington, D.C., as well as international temple sites in Mexico and New Zealand. Additional visitors' centers are located near church historic sites and important cultural locations, including Carthage Jail (Carthage, Illinois), the Hill Cumorah (Palmyra, New York), Historic Kirtland (Kirtland, Ohio), Old Town Independence (Independence, Missouri), Joseph Smith's Birthplace (South Royalton, Vermont), the Kanesville Tabernacle (Council Bluffs, Iowa), Liberty Jail (Liberty, Missouri), Mormon Handcart Center (Alcova, Wyoming), Mormon Trail Center (Omaha, Nebraska), Nauvoo (Nauvoo, Illinois), the Peter Whitmer Farm (Waterloo, New York), the Polynesian Cultural Center (Laie, Hawaii), Mormon Battalion Site (San Diego, California), and Temple Square (Salt Lake City, Utah).[19]

18. "The Church of Jesus Christ of Latter-day Saints: Places to Visit," http://www.lds.org/placestovisit/0,7484,1603-1-1,00.html (accessed December 23, 2009).

19. "The Church of Jesus Christ of Latter-day Saints: Visitors' Centers," http://www.lds.org/placestovisit/alphabetical/0,10659,1614-1-1-3,00.html (accessed December 23, 2009). Other historic locations with extensive exhibits and church missionary staffing include the following: in Palmyra, New York, historic sites include the Book of Mormon Historic Publication Site: Grandin Building, Martin Harris Farm, Sacred Grove, and the Smith Family Farm. Kirland, Ohio, historic sites include the Ashery, Isaac Morley Farm, John Johnson Inn Resource Center, Newel K. Whitney Store, Newel K. and Elizabeth Ann Whitney Home, Sawmill, and Schoolhouse. In nearby Hiram, Ohio, is the Historic Johnson Home. Heavily visited historic sites and exhibits in Nauvoo, Illinois, Mormonism's own version of Colonial Williamsburg, Virginia, include the Brigham Young Home, Cultural Hall, Heber C. Kimball Home, John Taylor Home, Jonathan Browning Home and Gun Shop, Land and Records Office, Lucy Mack Smith Home, Lyon Drug and Variety Store, Nauvoo Temple, Pendleton Log Home and School, Printing Office, Riser Home and Boot Shop, Sarah Granger Kimball Home, Scovil Bakery, Seventies Hall, Stoddard Home and Tin Shop, Webb Blacksmith Shop, and the Wilford Woodruff Home. In Salt Lake City the following sites are located on or near historic Temple Square: the Assembly Hall, Beehive House, Brigham Young Monument and Eagle Gate, Deuel Pioneer Log Home, Mormon Pioneer Memorial Monument, Salt Lake Temple, Seagull Monument, Social Hall Heritage Museum, and Tabernacle. In the St. George, Utah, region in Southern Utah are the Brigham Young Winter Home, Jacob Hamblin Home, St. George Tabernacle, and Pine Valley Chapel. A number of outdoor pageants, including the Castle Valley Pageant (Castle Dale, Utah), Clarkston Pageant (Clarkston, Utah), Hill Cumorah Pageant (Palmyra, New York), Manti Pageant (Manti, Utah), Mesa Pageant (Mesa, Arizona), Nauvoo Pageant (Nauvoo, Illinois), and Oakland Temple Pageant (Oakland, California), are hosted by the church. There is no question that Mormon visitors' centers, historic site, and pageants have proliferated in the decades since, and as a direct result of, church efforts in Chicago in 1893. "The Church of Jesus Christ of Latter-day Saints: Historic Sites," http://www.lds.org/placestovisit/alphabetical/0,10659,1614-1-1-1,00.html (accessed December 23, 2009).

The church's century-long involvement in domestic and international world's fairs and expositions has had far-reaching effects on both outsiders who have reexamined their views of the church as a result of exposure at these events, and on church insiders who have rethought the way they exhibit Mormonism. "The impact of the Church's world's fair experience has extended far beyond the durations or localities of the expositions themselves. Not only have impressive returns been reaped by way of public impression, receptivity and referrals to aid missionary work, but the exhibits have also extensively influenced the Church's public relations programs," Gerald Peterson concludes on the influence of world's fairs upon the church. "Art pieces, sculpture, audio visual presentations, dioramas, and most of the other successful methods used to win friends and converts at the world's fairs, are now widely used where Mormon tourist attractions draw large numbers of visitors annually. The fairs have added a new art dimension to the church and have had a noticeable influence upon its audio-visual and teaching libraries."[20]

Elder Joseph F. Merrill of the Quorum of the Twelve Apostles was correct in suggesting that the positive promotion of the church and its cultural contributions to American society would ultimately result in increased opportunities to share the theological message of Mormonism. "Evil-minded people had spread abroad so much intense prejudice against them that the delivery of the Gospel message through our missionary methods has been seriously handicapped. In defense the Church has been forced to use available publicity means, with excellent results," the apostle suggested in 1934.[21] The original Chicago World's Fair, held in 1893, helped Latter-day Saints learn how to represent the faith as well as to appreciate the benefits of exhibiting Mormonism.

20. Peterson, "History of Mormon Exhibits," 170.

21. Joseph F. Merrill, "Tabernacle Choir at Chicago Fair," *Millennial Star* 96, no. 36 (September 6, 1934): 569.

I

Before the Chicago World's Fair

EXHIBITING MORMONISM IN AMERICA, 1830–1892

It is better to represent ourselves than to be represented
by others.*
—MASTHEAD OF *The Mormon*, 1855

The press is a powerful lever or agency through which
the Lord can reach the minds of the people.**
—BRIGHAM YOUNG, 1856

DURING THE NINETEENTH CENTURY, members of The Church of Jesus
Christ of Latter-day Saints were viewed by their fellow Americans with suspicion and concern, especially once they cloistered themselves in their Great
Basin Kingdom centered in Salt Lake City. "The frenzied disquiet with which
many members of the American public regarded the Saints was not of short
duration, as alarms about various groups sometimes have been when they
were based mainly on second- and third-hand information subsequently
countered by direct experience with members of the group," religious studies
scholar Jan Shipps describes. The Saints' geographical and social isolation
west of the Rocky Mountains allowed them to flourish as a religious minority,
something they struggled to do in New York, Ohio, Missouri, and Illinois,
due to anti-Mormon opposition, some of which was of their own making.
"The peaks of the Rockies kept the United States (U.S., 'us') and 'them' apart.
The result was a situation that may be compared with the descent of the iron
curtain that kept the United States and the Soviet Union apart for so long,"
Shipps explains. After the saber rattling of the Utah War (1857–1858), the
issues of Mormon polygamy and theocracy were set on America's political

---

* *The Mormon* [New York City] (1855–1857).

** Brigham Young to George Q. Cannon, January 30, 1856, Church History Library, The
Church of Jesus Christ of Latter-day Saints, Salt Lake City, Utah, as quoted in Davis Bitton,
George Q. Cannon: A Biography (Salt Lake City: Deseret Book, 1999), 75.

backburner, as Americans east of the Rocky Mountains fought to divide or unify the United States. With the Civil War and African slavery were behind them, the U.S. government and the Protestant establishment determined to deal with the longstanding "Mormon problem" once and for all: the Latter-day Saints must submit to U.S. law and integrate into American culture.[1]

During these morality-charged years of late Victorian America, Latter-day Saints alternated between the urge to separate from and the necessity to assimilate into U.S. society. Literary scholar Terryl L. Givens describes this ongoing battle as one of the church's internal tensions between competing exile and integration impulses.[2] Sociologist Armand L. Mauss depicts the struggle of the church with assimilation as a pendulum swinging between the angel (spiritual) and the beehive (temporal).[3] During the preceding decades, the geographically isolated Mormons had shunned America's pluralistic vision; instead, they intertwined their religious, political, social, and economic life. Over time, however, the American Protestant establishment coerced the Latter-day Saints to move toward the American mainstream, nearly dismantling the church in the process. By the final decades of the nineteenth century, the Latter-day Saints, who were in legal and financial dire straits, were forced to jettison this earlier way of life in the "Kingdom of God" and accelerated their absorption into American culture, ushering in the greatest era of transition and transformation in Mormon history. Josiah Strong, as described in the introduction, and other American Protestants bent on the destruction of the theocratic church seemed to have gained the upper hand by the late 1880s.

Internal Latter-day Saint efforts to exhibit Mormonism in the United States between 1830 and 1890 were limited to narrow personal interactions between Mormons and their fellow Americans together with extensive church publishing labors. Moreover, this hard work of showcasing their new religious tradition was rooted in, and grew out of, a Latter-day Saint preoccupation with evangelism or missionary work, not public relations activities. In other words, millenarian Latter-day Saints, during most of the nineteenth century,

---

1. Jan Shipps, "From Satyr to Saint," in *Sojourner in the Promised Land: Forty Years among the Mormons* (Urbana: University of Illinois Press, 2000), 52, 62–66. See also Leonard J. Arrington, "Mormonism: Views from Without and Within," *BYU Studies* 14, no. 2 (Winter 1974): 143–148.

2. Terryl L. Givens, *People of Paradox: A History of Mormon Culture* (New York: Oxford University Press, 2007).

3. Armand L. Mauss, *The Angel and the Beehive: The Mormon Struggle with Assimilation* (Urbana: University of Illinois Press, 1994).

were obsessed with converting the world, not befriending its peoples and institutions. And when the much-anticipated and prayed-for Second Coming of Christ did not occur, even when the Protestant establishment had its boot on the church's neck in the 1880s, Mormon leaders were preassured to abandon some of what made their church unique on the American religious landscape. From henceforth they would be both in America *and* of America, to turn a biblical phrase. Friendshipping efforts by mormons beyond their religious ranks would become nearly as important to the survival and growth of the church in the United States and beyond as their ongoing evangelistic efforts. Although success or failure in both evangelization and public relations efforts is often conflated in the popular perception of a religious organization, the two activities are often at odds with one another. What works as a missionary tool does not always engender goodwill and improve relations with the public. For every new convert who entered the fold of the church, there were thousands who were repulsed by the Mormon message, especially polygamy.

Contesting the Mormon Image in Nineteenth-Century America

The church's strained relationship with American culture and its contested image can be divided into three major eras. The Founding period began with the coming forth of the Book of Mormon and the organization of the church in 1830, and it was characterized by strong outsider opposition, including sporadic violence, expulsion edicts, and the eventual assassination of founding leader Joseph Smith in Nauvoo, Illinois. Following the 1844 martyrdom, Brigham Young and the Quorum of the Twelve Apostles led a majority of the Latter-day Saints across the borders of the United States and into the mountain deserts of Mexico where they hoped to establish a Great Basin Kingdom in the valleys of modern-day Utah, Colorado, Idaho, Arizona, Wyoming, and Nevada. Next, the Pioneer period spanned from the 1847 Mormon colonization of the Salt Lake Valley until the 1890 Manifesto that began the process of jettisoning plural marriage from among the Latter-day Saints in America. Jan Shipps describes this era as a more peaceful ("non-violent") phase between Mormonism and American culture, the major exception being the Utah or Mormon War, which burned hotly in 1857–1858 but was then extinguished almost overnight. The resulting "cold war" during the 1860s, 1870s, and 1880s pitted the Latter-day Saints against non-Mormons for control of the pioneer economy and politics, in addition to old religious antagonisms. This stalemate was eventually broken as the American Protestant establishment brought the church to its knees financially and church president

Wilford Woodruff, led by inspiration, finally relented on the practice of plural marriage, ushering in what Shipps sees as the beginnings of third stage, that of accommodation and assimilation, extending from 1890 well into the twentieth century.[4]

During all three of these nineteenth- and twentieth-century phases, Mormons and non-Mormons were complicit in the representation and exhibition of the Latter-day Saints. Both sides actively contested the place of the church in America according to their own theological and social constructions. While some historians have suggested that Mormon leaders and laity did not engage in orchestrated public relations efforts (promotions calculated to generate public goodwill) during most of the nineteenth century, there is no question that the missionary-minded Latter-day Saints struggled mightily from an image-management perspective. Throughout the tumultuous 1880s, for instance, Mormon leaders focused their lobbying efforts on influencing territorial and national politicians in an attempt to achieve statehood for Utah, secure legal reprieves for former polygamists, and regain their organization's confiscated assets. "In general, public relations seems to have been furthest from the mind of church leaders as they systematically excluded Gentiles from participation in the economic and political life of Utah Territory, flaunted the practice of polygamy, and preached unusual and anathematic doctrines like blood atonement and the Adam-God theory," historian Thomas G. Alexander argues.[5]

As a result, American perceptions of the Latter-day Saints were extremely negative and hostile in the years leading up to the 1890 Manifesto and only began improving once the church relinquished future polygamous marriages. "Discontinuing the practice of plural marriage did more for the Saints than make statehood for Utah possible," Jan Shipps explains. "As long as men married multiple wives simultaneously, Latter-day Saint culture was the epitome of Otherness in America." In time, however, the now-monogamist Mormons would become the epitome of Americana, much to the chagrin of their evangelical Protestant counterparts.[6]

Throughout both the Founding (1830–1846) and Pioneer (1847–1890) periods of Mormonism, a majority of non-Mormon Americans viewed the

4. Shipps, "From Satyr to Saint," 53.

5. Thomas G. Alexander, *Mormonism in Transition: A History of the Latter-day Saints, 1890–1930* (Urbana: University of Illinois Press, 1986), 239. See also chapter 11, "The Church and Its Mission," 212–238.

6. Shipps, "From Satyr to Saint," 62–66. See also William R. Hutchison, *Religious Pluralism in America: The Contentious History of a Founding Ideal* (New Haven, Conn.: Yale University Press, 2003), 51–58.

church and its adherents with suspicion and disdain. The church, quite simply, suffered from an overall negative image in the United States. Scholars have chronicled the rise of anti-Mormonism in popular American culture, including literature, and analyzed how and why the Latter-day Saints were caricatured and constructed as the "Other" during the antebellum, Civil War, and postbellum eras. Historian R. Laurence Moore argues that early Latter-day Saints paradoxically sought to present themselves as persecuted religious deviants to survive in the crowded American religious marketplace, which rewarded the "new new" thing.[7] While no scholarly consensus exists on Moore's thesis, there is little question that antebellum Latter-day Saints were careful about what they wrote in tracts, how they evangelized both domestically and internationally, and why they sought to remain in deliberate tension with their fellow Americans. Rather than trying to join hands with other Christians, Latter-day Saints sought to emphasize the "Restoration," or return, of Christ's primitive church through Joseph Smith, and thereby highlight what they believed was the deficient character of other forms of Christianity. Hardly a public relations strategy, this nevertheless proved quite an effective evangelization approach, at least in their printed material. But this does not mean that Latter-day Saints were unconcerned with their public image or ignorant about the way outsiders viewed them.

Yet these well-documented studies of American popular thought raise a number of issues: How did the average U.S. citizen during the nineteenth century come in contact with the Latter-day Saints and their much-maligned religion? To what degree did the Mormons themselves engage in self-representation efforts and image making? Just how well known were the Mormons in the nineteenth century, and what did people truly know about them? Although Americans had strong opinions about the Mormons, they likely had little knowledge of them prior to the mid-twentieth century. Public ignorance, not necessarily bigotry, seems to have been the church's biggest public relations challenge by the 1890s. Not surprisingly, Latter-day Saints fought an uphill battle during the nineteenth century to represent themselves and to project their desired image on their fellow Americans. One can only imagine the limited amount of factual information that the typical American had access to or took the time to read during the nineteenth century when Mormonism was a hiss and a byword. And the church still suffers from a surprising lack of public awareness in the United States.

---

7. R. Laurence Moore, *Religious Outsiders and the Making of Americans* (New York: Oxford University Press, 1986), chapter 1.

In 2007, the Pew Forum on Religion and Public Life conducted and published a study of American public attitudes toward Mormonism and Islam. "The Muslim and Mormon religions have gained increasing national visibility in recent years. Yet most Americans say they know little or nothing about either religion's practices, and large majorities say that their own religion is very different from Islam and the Mormon religion," the report's authors summarize in their opening paragraph. Over half of the Americans surveyed said they knew little or nothing about the teachings and practices of the church; still nearly two-thirds felt that their spiritual backgrounds were radically different from that of Mormons. These findings grew out of the twenty-first century's Internet age, a time when information about Latter-day Saints and their religion has never been more accessible to the American public. As troubling as these findings are on a number of levels to scholars of religion in America, they illuminate one of the central longstanding difficulties for Mormons: that of getting their message out to the general public of who they are and, perhaps even more importantly, who they are not.[8]

First- and second-generation Latter-day Saints labored to represent themselves and exhibit their religion by means of interpersonal contacts and publishing initiatives, nearly all of which were evangelism—not public relations—oriented. To begin with, hundreds of nineteenth-century Latter-day Saints fanned out across the nation and throughout the world as personal witnesses of what insiders called the Restoration. By the early twenty-first century, young male and female volunteer representatives—dressed in white shirts and dark suits or conservative dresses—had become the public face of the church. More than *one million* Latter-day Saints have served as full-time missionaries (eighteen to twenty-four-month commitments) since the church's 1830 founding. In 2010 alone, over fifty thousand full-time Latter-day Saint volunteer representatives are evangelizing around the world in nearly three hundred and fifty missions. These missionaries receive intensive evangelistic and language training (fifty languages taught) at one of the church's seventeen Missionary Training Centers located around the globe. "There is no other religious denomination in the world—Catholic, Protestant, or non-Christian—whose full-time evangelizing force is even close in size to

8. "Public Expresses Mixed Views of Islam, Mormonism," Pew Forum on Religion and Public Life, September 25, 2007. This report came out during Mitt Romney's 2008 presidential campaign. For more on how Romney's faith adversely impacted his campaign, see Craig L. Foster, *A Different God? Mitt Romney, the Religious Right, and the Mormon Question* (Draper, Utah: Greg Kofford Books, 2008).

that recruited, trained, and supported by the LDS Church," two sociologists assert.[9] Given the ubiquity of Mormon missionaries on the streets and doorsteps of the United States today, many Americans assume that elders and sisters (formal missionary titles) have always been around in comparable numbers. Yet the average nineteenth-century American would have had little, if any, interpersonal contact with a flesh-and-blood Latter-day Saint. "Ordinary association between Mormons and non-Mormons was statistically unlikely. Being approached by an LDS missionary would have been a reasonably novel experience," Jan Shipps contends.[10] How could this be?

Simply put, there were not that many Mormon missionaries evangelizing in the United States during the Founding and Pioneer periods (1830–1890), especially when compared with the number of non-Mormon citizens. Whereas the church was the fourth largest church in America by 2010, it was a fledgling religious minority group throughout the nineteenth century.[11] Data culled from church missionary ledgers help explain the paucity of contacts between "real-live" Latter-day Saints and their fellow Americans. During the first six decades of the church, Mormon leaders assigned a total of just under 3,300 church members to evangelize full time in the United States and Canada: 1830s—502 missionaries; 1840s—879 missionaries; 1850s—177 missionaries; 1860s—220 missionaries; 1870s—603 missionaries; and 1880s—914 missionaries. General authorities also called 2,415 members to proselyte in Europe, 397 in Pacific-Asia, 43 in Latin America, and 15 in South Africa during this era. Although these Mormon missionary numbers are impressive as stand-alone figures, when compared with world population statistics, they shrink in significance. On annual average, not even sixty Latter-day Saint missionaries were evangelizing in the United States and Canada between 1830 and 1890. In other words, the burden of evangelizing tens of millions of North Americans was shouldered by a few dozen Mormon men and women each year.[12]

---

9. Gary Shepherd and Gordon Shepherd, *Mormon Passage: A Missionary Chronicle* (Urbana: University of Illinois Press, 1998), 9.

10. Shipps, "From Satyr to Saint," 56–57.

11. Eileen Lindner, ed., *Yearbook of American and Canadian Churches 2009* (Nashville, Tenn.: Abingdon Press, 2009), based on 2007 LDS membership figures; and *2009 Deseret News Church Almanac* (Salt Lake City: Deseret News, 2008), 198.

12. Gordon Irving, "A Preliminary Compilation of Data Relating to Numerical Strength and Geographical Distribution of the LDS Missionary Force, 1830–1974," *Task Papers in LDS History*, no. 1 (Salt Lake City: Historical Department of The Church of Jesus Christ of Latter-day Saints, 1975), 8–15.

This is not to suggest, however, that Latter-day Saint missionary endeavors were fruitless. The church experienced rapid growth, especially in Europe, during these early decades. Joseph Smith organized the Church of Christ, to which he would later add the title "of Latter-day Saints," in April 1830, in Fayette, New York, with six male members to meet legal guidelines for the establishment of a new ecclesiastical organization in that state. Over the next decade, the Latter-day Saints would be pushed by mobs and pulled by revelations to and from communities in Ohio, Missouri, and Illinois. By 1840, they were gathered as a people in Nauvoo, Illinois, a growing city built on drained Mississippi River swamplands. Nearly seventeen thousand American and British converts, thanks to an expanding evangelization operation, joined with the Latter-day Saints during this first decade. Then a mob assassinated Joseph Smith in 1844, leading to the Pioneer Exodus of 1846–1847, which landed the Saints in the Great Salt Lake Valley. So in addition to a relatively small missionary force laboring east of the Rocky Mountains, the Mormon move to Utah would almost completely isolate the Latter-day Saints from their fellow Americans.[13]

Mormon growth in America continued into the second half of the nineteenth century. By 1850, just three years after the Latter-day Saints began the colonization of the Intermountain West, there were almost 52,000 church members in America, Europe, and the Pacific Islands. During the 1850s and 1860s, church membership swelled as a growing number of missionaries fanned out across the United States and across the Atlantic, Pacific, and Indian oceans to European, Pacific Islander, Asian, and even African nations. Joseph Smith's successor, President Brigham Young and his leadership corps encouraged all converts to gather from "Babylon" to the safety of "Zion" nestled in the mountain valleys of America's Great Basin. When the transcontinental railroad finally banded America together by steel rails in 1869, there were about 90,000 Latter-day Saints, all but 5,000 of whom were living in Utah. A decade later, by the 1890 Manifesto, 188,000 members were listed on the church's rolls, most of whom were concentrated in Great Basin communities in Utah, Idaho, Wyoming, Colorado, Arizona, and Nevada. American religious historians Edwin Scott Gaustad and Philip L. Barlow underscore the

---

13. Edwin Scott Gaustad and Philip L. Barlow, *New Historical Atlas of Religion in America* (New York: Oxford University Press, 2001), 236–241; *2009 Deseret News Church Almanac*, 199–202; and Richard D. Poll, ed., *Utah's History* (Provo, Utah: Brigham Young University Press, 1978), 692–693, see "Table H: Membership of Religious Denominations in Utah, 1870–1975."

subsequent Mormon gathering and scattering in their historical atlas by way
of three maps that chart the geographic distribution of Latter-day Saints in
the United States. The first map (1890) describes the time when "the Saints
inhabit a narrow north–south swath from eastern Idaho to Arizona." The second map (1950) shows how "this swath has broadened in the West and become
supplemented by a light presence east of the Rocky Mountains." And the
third map (1990) shows "where the church enjoys a moderate but significant
presence in many parts of the country and considerable and often dominating
occupancy in all the western states, including Alaska and Hawaii." Gaustad
and Barlow point out that it took three generations, or about a century, before
the church truly spread beyond its Utah roots.[14] As a result, few nineteenth-
century Americans ever saw, heard, smelled, or touched a Mormon with their
own eyes, ears, noses, or hands.

Mormon Self-Representation in American Print Culture, 1830–1846

In the absence of extensive interpersonal contacts, it is not surprising that
the printed word, in the form of scriptures, periodicals, doctrinal treatises,
and historical works, was the most common means by which the Latter-day
Saints exhibited their religion.[15] In her illuminating study of the evolving
image of Mormonism in the United States—from the Civil War to the civil
rights movement—Jan Shipps points to the power of the printing press in
popular culture, prior to the advent of other mass-media mediums like radio
(1930s), television (1950s), and I would add the Internet (1990s). She reminds
twenty-first-century readers that "printed sources were vitally important in
the formation of perceptions and attitudes, especially perceptions and attitudes about people and things with which the public had little or no direct
contact." Shipps further documents that plenty has been published over the
past two centuries on the church and its relationship with traditional
Christian America. Consequently, modern scholars can excavate important
parts of the Mormon past through a study of what the Mormons have written about themselves and what non-Mormons have written about the
Mormons. Not surprisingly, most Americans formed their opinions and

14. Gaustad and Barlow, *New Historical Atlas of Religion in America*, 236–241; *2009 Deseret
News Church Almanac*, 199–202; and Poll, *Utah's History*, 692–693.

15. Larry W. Draper, "Publications," in *Encyclopedia of Mormonism*, ed. Daniel H. Ludlow, 4
vols. (New York: Macmillan, 1992), 3:1174–1175.

prejudices about the Latter-day Saints and their religion principally through the printed page. Of course many Protestant ministers, whose life's work was to minister to the Mormons in the Intermountain West as home missionaries in the late nineteenth century, shared their own experiences with their affiliated congregations back East, but such secondhand lectures were equivalent to printed sources the parishioners might pick up and read off a shelf.[16]

Like many Americans living in the Protestant milieu of antebellum New England, Latter-day Saints were devoted readers of the King James Version of the Bible. But their Restoration was marked by a new scriptural tome, the Book of Mormon (1830), and it would eventually claim additional sacred texts to a widening canon of scriptures.[17] It is important to note that neither Joseph Smith nor his followers ever anticipated that the Book of Mormon would supplant the Hebrew Old Testament and the Christian New Testament as the word of God. But they did believe that both books could stand side by side in proclaiming the divinity of Jesus of Nazareth and his gospel. (In the late twentieth century, Mormon leaders eventually subtitled the Book of Mormon "Another Testament of Jesus Christ.") This scriptural text is largely the account of two Hebrew families who migrate from Jerusalem to the New World during the prophetic ministry of Jeremiah and the secular reign of Zedekiah. Over the next millennium, their posterity fluctuates between righteous living and wickedness, eventually leading to their spiritual and temporal destruction.[18] As in the present day, the book's content was typically lost on outsiders because few ever took the time to read its pages before condemning its very existence, as historian Nathan O. Hatch points out.[19] Yet for early Mormon converts, its latter-day appearance was perhaps even more important than the doctrines it propounds. As literary scholar Terryl L. Givens argues, the Book of Mormon acted most importantly as a sign of Joseph Smith's prophetic calling; it signaled that the heavens were again open and that men and women could commune with a God endowed with parts and

---

16. Shipps, "From Satyr to Saint," 55–57.

17. *The Book of Mormon: An Account Written by the Hand of Mormon, upon Plates taken from the Plates of Nephi* (Palmyra, N.Y.: E. B. Grandin, 1830).

18. Peter Crawley, *A Descriptive Bibliography of the Mormon Church*, 2 vols. (Provo, Utah: Religious Studies Center at Brigham Young University, 1997), 1:29–32.

19. Nathan O. Hatch, *The Democratization of American Christianity* (New Haven, Conn.: Yale University Press, 1989), 115–122. See also Jan Shipps, *Mormonism: The Story of a New Religious Tradition* (Urbana: University of Illinois Press, 1985), 25–39.

passions.[20] Not surprisingly, the Latter-day Saints were quickly tagged with the then pejorative name "the Mormons" because of their insistence on the validity of this extra-biblical text.

Having already transgressed the sacrosanct Protestant boundary of *sola scriptura* with their Book of Mormon, Latter-day Saints did not find it difficult to accept two additional scriptural texts. The Doctrine and Covenants and the Pearl of Great Price contain revelations and texts revealed to Joseph Smith during the 1830s and 1840s. Even before the church existed as a legal entity in New York, supporters of Joseph Smith accepted his prophetic pronouncements as scripture, carrying the same weight as the words of Moses or Paul. Soon church members were commanded by revelation to gather and publish these revelations, many of which were initially printed in the church's periodicals like *The Evening and the Morning Star* and the *Messenger and Advocate*. However, the church's first attempt to print a compilation of these inspired utterances as the Book of Commandments (1833) in Missouri was thwarted by an anti-Mormon mob that trashed the press and destroyed most of the printed signatures. Two years later, Smith oversaw the publication of an expanded edition of latter-day revelations titled the Doctrine and Covenants (1835) in Kirtland, Ohio.[21] These new sacred texts helped differentiate the Latter-day Saints in the crowded spiritual marketplace of antebellum America.

The Latter-day Saints also published a number of church-sponsored periodicals to represent themselves during the Founding period. Church leaders were eager to tell their faith tradition's own story through newsprint to their fellow believers and to their neighbors of other faiths. To reach both audiences, Mormon editors often published two papers—one spiritual and the other secular—in their early gathering places in Missouri, Ohio, and Illinois. The church's original pair of newspapers, *The Evening and the Morning Star* (1832–1833) and the *Upper Missouri Advertiser* (1832–1833), was published during the same period in Independence, Missouri, America's most western newspapers in their day. The monthly *Star*, under the editorship of William

20. Terryl L. Givens, *By the Hand of Mormon: The American Scripture That Launched a New World Religion* (New York: Oxford University Press, 2002), 43–88.

21. *A Book of Commandments, for the Government of the Church of Christ, Organized according to Law, on the 6th of April, 1830* (Zion [Independence], Mo.: W. W. Phelps and Company, 1833); *Doctrine and Covenants of the Church of the Latter Day Saints: Carefully Selected from the Revelations of God, and Compiled by Joseph Smith Junior, Oliver Cowdery, Sidney Rigdon, Frederick G. Williams* (Kirtland, Ohio: F. G. Williams and Company, 1835). Crawley, *Descriptive Bibliography*, 1:37–42, 54–57.

W. Phelps, focused on the religious life of the Latter-day Saints. Its pages were filled with Joseph Smith's revelations, doctrinal treatises, minutes of church conferences, and news from the church's missionaries scattered throughout the United States. The weekly *Advertiser*, in contrast, was printed with the entire Missourian community in mind, offering local and national news. Both papers lasted just over a year before an anti-Mormon mob tossed the printing press from a second story window in July 1833, as they drove the Latter-day Saints from Jackson County, Missouri.[22]

Months later, in Kirtland, Ohio, nine hundred miles away from the Missourian violence, a group of church members determined to resume Mormon newspaper publishing. Continuing in the spiritual tradition of the *Star*, the editors of the new *Latter-day Saints' Messenger and Advocate* (1834–1837), which over the next three years would include Oliver Cowdery, Frederick G. Williams, Warren A. Cowdery, and William A. Cowdery, printed their first monthly issue in October 1834. Beginning in 1837, this leading Mormon paper was discontinued and replaced with the *Elders' Journal of the Church of Latter Day Saints* (1837–1838). When the Latter-day Saints were forced to leave Ohio the following year, they packed up their printing press and reassembled it in Far West, Missouri, where they resumed its print run, under the editorial guidance of Joseph Smith, Thomas B. Marsh, and Don Carlos Smith. Within months, however, anti-Mormon mobs again forced church members to shutter their publication activities. Mormon representatives secreted their press type in a yard for safekeeping. In Kirtland, Ohio, the *Northern Times* (c. 1835–1836) was the Mormon newspaper which focused on political issues. Church leaders including Oliver Cowdery, Frederick G. Williams, and William W. Phelps used it to advance their Democratic views, but local Whig newspapers, including the *Cleveland Whig* and the *Painesville Telegraph*, limited its effectiveness in the surrounding communities.[23]

After being driven by mobs beyond the borders of Missouri in early 1839, the Latter-day Saints found refuge in Quincy, Illinois, for a season and then moved north to the Mississippi River village of Commerce, which they renamed Nauvoo. As in Ohio and Missouri, church members were eager to

---

22. Andrew Jenson, *Encyclopedic History of The Church of Jesus Christ of Latter-day Saints* (Salt Lake City: Deseret News Publishing Company, 1941), 239–240; Draper, "Publications," 3:1174–1175; and Crawley, *Descriptive Bibliography*, 1:34–35.

23. Jenson, *Encyclopedic History*, 218, 492–493; and Crawley, *Descriptive Bibliography*, 1:51–53.

begin printing several newspapers in their new home. A few Mormons slipped back into Far West, Missouri, where they recovered the buried type used to print the *Elders Journal*. Issues of the new monthly, but then semi-monthly, *Times and Seasons* (1839–1846) first rolled off the church's press in November 1839 and continued in circulation for the next six years. Ebenezer Robinson, Don Carlos Smith, Robert B. Thompson, Gustavus Hill, John Taylor, Wilford Woodruff, and even Joseph Smith helped publish the church's paper. The *Times and Seasons* was produced with the Saints in mind: its columns were filled with ecclesiastical announcements, church conference proceedings, public teachings of Joseph Smith, and news from the church's mission fields in North America and Great Britain. Published in the same building, the *Wasp* (1842–1843), later renamed the *Nauvoo Neighbor* (1843–1846), was Nauvoo's civic newspaper produced weekly under the guidance of church leaders William Smith and later John Taylor. All of these newspapers came to an end when mobs again forced the Mormon faithful from their Illinois homes, this time into the safety of the Iowa Territory.[24]

Printed doctrinal treatises were the third medium by which the Latter-day Saints broadcasted their spiritual beliefs and religious practices to their fellow Americans. Evangelism became the lifeblood of Mormonism during the antebellum era, following the 1830 organization of the church. Nevertheless, six years would pass before the first Mormon missionary tract was printed, in imitation of the publications of Protestant tract organizations on both shores of the Atlantic. But once the printing floodgates opened, Latter-day Saint missionaries received a stream of missionary tracts. Given the large number of such theological publications, one must focus on several representative works to gain an appreciation of their contents. Apostle Orson Hyde's *A Prophetic Warning to All the Churches, of Every Sect and Denomination* (1836) is widely considered to be the original Mormon evangelistic tract.[25] Hyde produced the religious pamphlet while serving as a missionary with fellow Apostle Parley P. Pratt in Toronto, Canada. As many of Joseph Smith's revelations instructed church members to lift up their warning voices to their non-Mormon neighbors, it is not surprising that Hyde stressed humankind's necessary preparations for Jesus Christ's pending Second Coming. He claimed that contemporary Christianity has strayed from the primitive Christian church,

---

24. Jenson, *Encyclopedic History*, 875–876, 928–929; and Crawley, *Descriptive Bibliography*, 1:88–89, 91–96, 192–193, and 218–219.

25. Orson Hyde, *A Prophetic Warning to all the Churches, of every Sect and Denomination, and to every Individual into whose Hands it may Fall* (Toronto, Canada: Privately printed, 1836).

an apostasy anticipated by several New Testament writers. Modern Protestantism and Catholicism thus lacked God's approbation. Therefore, Hyde called upon his readers to seek baptism by authorized ministers; such authority, he and his fellow Latter-day Saints believed, rested only with Mormon priesthood holders.[26]

The following year Hyde's former missionary companion Parley P. Pratt produced *A Voice of Warning* (1837) while serving a mission in New York.[27] Considered by many historians to be the preeminent nonscriptural Mormon publication of the nineteenth century, Pratt's systematic explication of Latter-day Saint doctrine would be echoed in dozens of tracts and treatises in later years. *Voice of Warning* demarcates the theological chasm between the Latter-day Saints and their historical Christian counterparts, based on scriptural texts and prophetic revelations. Pratt's influential missionary text "opens with a series of biblical examples of the fulfillment of ancient prophecy, and then moves to a discussion of those prophecies which it asserts deal with the establishment of a new covenant, the gathering of Israel, the rebuilding of Jerusalem, and the events surrounding the Second Advent."[28] Pratt proceeded to argue for the necessity of baptism by those vested with priesthood authority, highlighted the theological contributions of the Book of Mormon including the future destiny of the Lehite remnant (Native Americans) in the last days, argued for a pending Second Advent of Jesus Christ and the ultimate resurrection of all humankind, and concluded with a detailed comparison between "The Doctrine of Christ" and "The Doctrines of Men." Pratt's *Voice of Warning* captured the hearts of his fellow missionaries and many potential converts alike. With its wide distribution, ultimately in over thirty editions and in a number of foreign languages, Mormon evangelization was never the same. The Latter-day Saints had asserted their break from traditional Christianity, in no uncertain terms, in an attempt to declare their own orthodoxy.[29]

Parley Pratt enjoyed grand evangelistic success in the Northeastern United States following the publication of his *Voice of Warning*. In fact, Pratt grew so influential that in early 1838 an infuriated Methodist clergyman and editor,

26. David J. Whittaker, "Early Mormon Pamphleteering" (PhD diss., Brigham Young University, 1982); Draper, "Publications," 3:1175.

27. Parley Parker Pratt, *A Voice of Warning and Instruction to all People, Containing a Declaration of the Faith and Doctrine of the Church of the Latter Day Saints, commonly called Mormons* (New York: W. Sandford, 1837).

28. Crawley, *Descriptive Bibliography*, 1:63–64.

29. Crawley, *Descriptive Bibliography*, 1:69–71.

La Roy Sunderland, devoted eight articles in his church's periodical *Zion's Watchman* to expose what he discerned as a growing Christian heresy. Sunderland's essays condemned the Latter-day Saints' extra-biblical scriptures, the Book of Mormon and Doctrine and Covenants, as well as Pratt's *Voice of Warning*, relying on E. D. Howe's *Mormonism Unvailed* [*sic*] (1834),[30] an anti-Mormon treatise, for much of his attack. Under theological fire, Pratt retaliated with a sharply worded rebuttal, *Mormonism Unveiled* (1838), the first direct rebuttal to an anti-Mormon publication.[31] Pratt's printed response "established a formula which would be followed by Mormon pamphleteers for another century, balancing a defense of the Church's claims with an assault on the religion of the attacker."[32] The apostle lambasted Sunderland's use of the Spaulding-Rigdon theory by sharing his own experiences of coming into contact with the church and then personally introducing Sidney Rigdon, a Campbellite associate of his, to Latter-day Saint doctrine. The Mormon apologist further asserted that the Latter-day Saints worship a corporal God complete with body, parts, and passions who continued to speak to humans, including Joseph Smith, through His (God's) own mouth and lips, in contrast to the rest of Christendom. Pratt also chastised the Methodists for performing infant baptisms, a practice condemned in the Book of Mormon.

Based on the success of Orson Hyde's and Parley Pratt's missionary publications, a number of other Latter-day Saints produced their own tracts and apologetic texts both at home and increasingly abroad. Pratt's younger brother and fellow apostle, Orson (figure 2), published his first landmark doctrinal treatise titled *A[n] Interesting Account of Several Remarkable Visions* (1840), while evangelizing in the British Isles.[33] Although the church's founding prophet Joseph Smith experienced his initial theophany in the spring of 1820, privately related the spiritual encounter to select family members and friends thereafter, and described it in his own personal writings in 1832, Smith had

---

30. E. D. Howe, *Mormonism Unvailed* (Painesville, Ohio: Printed and published by the author, 1834).

31. Parley Parker Pratt, *Mormonism Unveiled: Zion's Watchman Unmasked, and its editor, Mr. L. R. Sunderland, exposed: Truth Vindicated: the Devil Mad, and Priestcraft in Danger!* (New York: Privately printed, 1838).

32. Crawley, *Descriptive Bibliography*, 1:76–79.

33. Orson Pratt, *A[n] Interesting Account of Several Remarkable Visions, and of the Late Discovery of Ancient American Records* (Edinburgh: Ballantyne and Hughes, 1840).

FIGURE 2 Apostle Orson Pratt with Mormon missionaries in New York, 1869, courtesy of the Church History Library, The Church of Jesus Christ of Latter-day Saints, Salt Lake City, Utah.

never printed an account of his First Vision for public consumption. Orson Pratt, with the apparent blessing of Joseph Smith, determined to broadcast the opening moment of the Restoration twenty years later through the printing press at his disposal. (Smith would not follow suit until 1842, when he printed his narrative in the *Times and Seasons*.) Orson Pratt's *Remarkable Visions* can be divided into five sections. It opens with a recital of Joseph Smith's First Vision and then rehearses the angelic visitation of Moroni to Joseph Smith in 1823 and the subsequent coming forth of the Book of Mormon. The tract's middle part is devoted to Smith's translation of the ancient American record as a modern American seer and includes a description of the gold plates. A summary of the plot and teachings of the Book of Mormon, including the testimonies of the three witnesses who were given a vision and heard a voice from heaven, and the eight witnesses, who were allowed to handle and physically examine the plates, respectively, is the fourth section. Pratt devoted the final segment to a doctrinal and historical overview of the church, especially those teachings and practices that separate it from Protestantism and Catholicism. His tract was reprinted many times and was translated into Danish, Dutch, and Swedish, making it one of the church's most successful nineteenth-century missionary tools.[34]

A final doctrinal treatise of the early church that deserves mention is Apostle Lorenzo Snow's *The Only Way to be Saved* (1841), which eclipsed all other nineteenth-century Mormon tracts in the number of copies distributed.[35] While presiding over the London Conference of the British Mission, Snow determined to produce a pamphlet that explained the church at its most basic level. He described the first principles and ordinances of the gospel—faith, repentance, baptism, and the gift of the Holy Ghost—through familiar passages from the Bible, resulting in a more apologetic and less polemic text. As a testament to its effectiveness, it was reprinted nearly two dozen times in English and also translated into Armenian, Bengali, Danish, Dutch, French, German, Greek, Italian, and Swedish, demonstrating the emerging internationalization of the church in Europe and Asia.[36]

A fourth major genre of Mormon publishing during these early years was historical works. Not surprisingly, many of these writings were focused on the persecutions endured by the Latter-day Saints at the hands of their fellow Americans, as the Saints were driven from New York to Ohio, Ohio to Missouri, Missouri to Illinois, and then Illinois to what would become Utah. And most of these historical works emerged in the aftermath of the Mormon expulsion from Missouri during the winter of 1838–1839. At least four publications are representative of this Mormon historiographical trend. To begin with, John P. Greene, the brother-in-law of then-Apostle Brigham Young, experienced firsthand the wrath of the anti-Mormon mobs in Missouri and later Illinois. Church leaders assigned Greene in May 1839 to manage their affairs in New York City and to fundraise in the East for the poverty-stricken Saints. While fulfilling these responsibilities, Greene drafted and published *Facts Relative to the Expulsion of the Mormons or Latter-day Saints from the State of Missouri, Under the "Extermination Order"* (1839).[37] Months earlier, Joseph Smith had written to the destitute Saints from confinement in Liberty Jail that they must gather all evidence concerning their removal from Missouri to prepare legal redress

34. Crawley, *Descriptive Bibliography*, 1:127–129.

35. Lorenzo Snow, *The Only Way to be Saved: An Explanation of the First Principles of the Doctrine of the Church of Jesus Christ of Latter-day Saints* (London: D. Chalmers, 1841).

36. Crawley, *Descriptive Bibliography*, 1:174.

37. John Portineus Greene, *Facts Relative to the Expulsion of the Mormons or Latter Day Saints, from the State of Missouri, under the "Exterminating Order"* (Cincinnati: R. P. Brooks, 1839).

petitions. Greene's book drew heavily from the "Memorial to the Legislature of Missouri," a report drafted by a number of leading Latter-day Saints who aired their grievances before the Missouri House of Representatives in December 1838. Greene also appended the narration of Brigham Young's brother Joseph of the Haun's Mill massacre, the text of Governor Lilburn W. Boggs's infamous extermination order against the Mormons, as well as letters from Joseph Smith and several leading brethren who were then incarcerated.[38]

Writing in this same vein, pamphleteer Parley P. Pratt drafted his own account of the horrors endured by the Mormons during the Missouri period. After the Latter-day Saints surrendered to Missouri militiamen in Far West in 1838, Pratt was incarcerated in jails in Richmond and Columbia, Missouri, for eight months. He spent much of his imprisonment writing hymns and essays, including a historical account of his own experiences, which he was able to smuggle out of the jail with the help of his wife and child during a visit. Two months after his July 1839 escape, Pratt visited family members in Detroit, Michigan, en route to the British Isles to evangelize. During his stopover, Pratt published his *History of the Late Persecution Inflicted by the State of Missouri upon the Mormons* (1839).[39] Largely autobiographical, Pratt's writing focuses on the unlawful destruction of the Mormon printing press in Independence, Missouri, and the subsequent forced Mormon migration from Jackson County in 1833. Moreover, he offered details on the 1838 Independence Day celebration of the Latter-day Saints at Far West, the difficulties in Caldwell and Davies counties, and the eventual removal of the Latter-day Saints from Missouri. Pratt also detailed the court proceedings against the Mormon prisoners in Missouri jails, including his own incarceration.[40]

A year after Greene and Pratt published their memoirs of the Missouri persecutions, First Presidency member Sidney Rigdon prepared his own reminiscence for the press. His *Appeal to the American People* (1840) was a cry for help for the beleaguered Mormons.[41] It too was the result of Joseph Smith's

38. Crawley, *Descriptive Bibliography*, 1:86–88.

39. Parley Parker Pratt, *History of the Late Persecution Inflicted by the State of Missouri upon the Mormons, in which Ten Thousand American Citizens were robbed, Plundered, and Driven from the State, and many others Imprisoned, Martyred, &c. for their Religion, and all this by Military Force, by order of the Executive* (Detroit: Dawson and Bates, 1839).

40. Crawley, *Descriptive Bibliography*, 1:89–90.

41. Sidney Rigdon, *An Appeal to the American People: Being an Account of the Persecutions of the Church of Latter Day Saints; and of the Barbarities Inflicted on them by the inhabitants of the State of Missouri* (Cincinnati: Glezen and Shepard, 1840).

plea for Latter-day Saints to document their grievances against the Missourians in hope of redress. After being rebuffed by Missouri lawmen and legislatures, Smith, Rigdon, and Elias Higbee traveled to Washington, D.C., to plead their case before national leaders, including the president of the United States. About this same time Latter-day Saints in Nauvoo, Illinois, listened to a reading of Rigdon's manuscript during a church conference and consented as a body to publish the work with the imprimatur of the church. In Rigdon's absence, Orson Hyde and George W. Robinson raised funds for and secured its publication in Cincinnati, Ohio. Rigdon's work tells largely the same story that John Greene and Parley Pratt did but with more flamboyance and even exaggeration; it was clearly written to stir up American sympathy for the Mormons and condemnation against the mobs.[42]

As trying as it was to Latter-day Saints to be expelled from their homes, shops, and farms in Missouri, nothing matched the devastating impact on their psyche created by the martyrdom of their prophet Joseph Smith and his brother, Hyrum, in the summer of 1844. *A Correct Account of the Murder of Generals Joseph and Hyrum Smith, at Carthage* (1845) was William M. Daniels's purported eyewitness account of the assassination.[43] When it was used by the prosecution to implicate various anti-Mormons in the murders, however, it was revealed that Lyman O. Littlefield, a worker at the *Times and Seasons*, actually wrote the account based on Daniels's recounting of the story on several occasions. Littlefield used Daniel's name to promote his own writing beyond the Mormon market so that it would have greater cachet and readership, and Daniels was baptized a Latter-day Saint thereafter. The volume is seemingly important because it offers firsthand witness statements of what transpired in Carthage that June evening. But its overall accuracy is questionable as the narrators include sensational details, including shafts of heavenly light that supposedly scattered the mob following the murders. Still, its dubious construction suggests how desperate many Mormons were to bring the judgments of man and God upon their oppressors and how they envisioned divine intervention in the midst of their tragedies.[44]

By way of summary, during the first decade and a half of the Latter-day Saint movement, from the 1830 organization of the church until the 1846 forced

42. Crawley, *Descriptive Bibliography*, 1:103–104.

43. William M. Daniels, *A Correct Account of the Murder of Generals Joseph and Hyrum Smith, at Carthage, on the 27th day of June, 1844; by Wm. M. Daniels, an Eye Witness* (Nauvoo, Ill.: John Taylor, 1845).

44. Crawley, *Descriptive Bibliography*, 1:298–301.

exodus of Latter-day Saints from the United States into Mexican territory, the Mormons were eager to promote their often-misrepresented faith throughout America and eventually the British Isles. Following the example of their Christian contemporaries, antebellum Latter-day Saints shared their religious message and contested their public image through the printed word. During the Second Great Awakening, church members published new books of scriptures, doctrinal expositions, newspapers, personal and ecclesiastical histories, hymnals, and even poetry. "On the one hand, the Church sought to establish a favorable image through missionary work and the preparation and distribution of tracts and other literature," historian Leonard J. Arrington describes. "On the other hand, those opposed to the Church, its doctrines and practices, also prepared and distributed tracts, pamphlets, and other literature conveying an unfavorable image." This war of podiums and presses pitted two competing image-making campaigns, each side claiming to be the legitimate Christian offering. Latter-day Saints "were not hesitant about taking the initiative in creating a positive image of the Restored Church. We published the Book of Mormon and took it to the people as our numbers would permit; this was a period when, literally, every member was a missionary," Arrington continues. "Ever aware of the importance of literary symbols, Joseph Smith worked on a revision of the Bible, published the Book of Abraham, published works of his own with poetic qualities, and encouraged our finest literary people, Parley Pratt and Orson Pratt, to publish tracts and pamphlets, some of which had distinct literary merit."[45]

Mormon Self-Representation in American Print Culture, 1847–1890

The highly publicized 1844 mob assassination of the church's founder Joseph Smith, coupled with the subsequent expulsion of the Latter-day Saints from the warmth and safety of their homes in Nauvoo, Illinois, during the winter of 1846, generated newfound sympathy in the hearts of some American observers. As the beleaguered religious minority slogged its way across the mudflats of Iowa to the safety of primitive camps in Winter Quarters on the banks of the Missouri River, non-Mormons looked on with genuine concern and sadness. The Latter-day Saints went from being pilloried to pitied in the court of American public opinion. In the spring of 1847 the vanguard pioneer company of the Latter-day

---

45. Draper, "Publications," 3:1173; and Arrington, "Mormonism: Views from Without and Within," 140–143.

Saints set out for the mountain valleys of the Great Basin, anticipating settling near the Great Salt Lake. They were leaving America for the refuge of Mexico. Not only did they survive, but they soon thrived within years of forming their religious kingdom in the West. While the Latter-day Saints themselves rejoiced in the theocratic kingdom they were finally left alone to create in the tops of the mountains, Americans became worried that they were losing control, especially now that the Mexican War had made Salt Lake City part of the Union with its strategic position between the developed Eastern states and the gold and other riches of California to the West. But in 1852, when the Mormons proclaimed to the entire world that they were practicing polygamy most Americans were mortified and determined to eliminate this abomination.[46]

Between their 1847 arrival in the Salt Lake Valley and the 1890 announcement of the end of plural marriage by their leaders (the Pioneer period), the Latter-day Saints continued their quest of self-representation through the publication of new scripture and periodicals, as well as doctrinal and historical works. The Mormon printed word rolled off presses in a number of American states, including California, Maryland, Missouri, New York, and Utah, and far-off nations like Australia, Denmark, England, France, Germany, and Wales. The publication of the Book of Mormon (1830), the Book of Commandments (1833) and the Doctrine and Covenants (1835) assaulted conventional Protestant understandings regarding closed scriptural cannon. But to Latter-day Saints, these books of additional scripture were prime evidence of Joseph Smith's prophetic calling and the reality of a restoration of Christ's primitive church with living prophets and apostles. So when Apostle Franklin D. Richards compiled an assortment of the late Joseph Smith's revelations, translations, and history, together with other doctrinal writings, and published it as the Pearl of Great Price (1851), his fellow Latter-day Saints celebrated.[47] This new volume contained recovered accounts from the lives of the biblical patriarchs, including Adam, Enoch, and Abraham, together with a new prologue by Moses to the Genesis account of creation. In 1880 church members voted to canonize this collection as the church's fourth standard work, or official scripture.[48]

---

46. Shipps, "From Satyr to Saint," 52.

47. *The Pearl of Great Price: Being a Choice Selection from the Revelations, Translations, and Narrations of Joseph Smith, first Prophet, Seer, and Revelator to the Church of Jesus Christ of Latter-day Saints* (Liverpool: F. D. Richards, 1851).

48. Crawley, *Descriptive Bibliography*, 2:234–238; and Rodney Turner, "Franklin D. Richards and the Pearl of Great Price," in *Regional Studies in Latter-day Saint Church History: British Isles*, ed. Donald Q. Cannon (Provo, Utah: Department of Church History and Doctrine, Brigham Young University, 1990), 177–191.

In addition to the publication of new sacred texts, Latter-day Saints also continued to represent themselves through church periodicals. Joseph Smith relied on Mormon leaders and laity alike to produce the church's periodicals, including much of the content. But following Smith's 1844 martyrdom, his apostolic successor Brigham Young and his fellow members of the Quorum of the Twelve Apostles consolidated the church's official publishing efforts. Moreover, the exodus of the Mormon pioneers from America's Midwest to its isolated Great Basin between 1846 and 1852, occurred at the same time that much of Latter-day Saint publishing was relocated to Great Britain, where paper and presses were cheaper and more accessible. In fact, the longest-running and most influential internal periodical was the *Latter Day Saints' Millennial Star* (1840–1970), which was published in a number of English cities. For decades it served both the British and American church membership, especially in the pre-*Deseret News* (1850–present) era in Utah. The British-based *Journal of Discourses* (1854–1886), a voluminous set of stenographic reports of the public remarks of Mormon officials, was another influential periodical that connected European and American Latter-day Saints during this era.[49]

Despite the shift of Mormon publishing from North America to Europe during much of this time, the American Latter-day Saints enjoyed several church-sanctioned periodicals in their midst. The *Frontier Guardian*, a weekly newspaper published by Apostle Orson Hyde between February 1849 and February 1852, is another example of a notable church periodical in the early post-exodus years from Nauvoo, Illinois. Hyde was assigned by Brigham Young to produce this important source of news for the Latter-day Saint pioneers passing through Kanesville (modern-day Council Bluffs), Iowa, on their way to Zion in the West. In fact the *Frontier Guardian* was the only periodical for American church members for over a year, which magnified its importance as a clearinghouse for all newsworthy events, including doctrinal and historical offerings that might impact the church during this time. Much of its focus was on the preparation of the Mormon immigrants for their trek to Utah. Hyde continued his editorship

49. Draper, "Publications," 3:1173–1177. Sources on these British periodicals include Alan K. Parrish, "Beginnings of the *Millennial Star*: Journal of the Mission to Great Britain," in *Regional Studies in Latter-day Saint Church History: British Isles*, ed. Donald Q. Cannon (Provo, Utah: Department of Church History and Doctrine, Brigham Young University, 1990), 133–149; and Ronald G. Watt, "The Beginnings of 'The Journal of Discourses': A Confrontation between George D. Watt and Willard Richards," *Utah Historical Quarterly* 75, no. 2 (Spring 2007): 134–148.

until he too left the plains of Iowa for the mountains of Utah. Jacob Dawson rebranded the paper as the *Frontier Guardian and Iowa Sentinel* thereafter, but the Latter-day Saints were basically gone from the area by the spring of 1853.[50]

Periodicals like the *Millennial Star* and the *Frontier Guardian* were forerunners for the church's most prolific era of newspaper publishing beyond the borders of Utah. During the first two decades of the church, its publishing program was largely defensive and reactive in nature. Mormon leaders and members used the printing press to defend their church against the charges made by outsiders, which were many during this era. As previously noted, the Latter-day Saint claim to extra-biblical revelation and the assertion that all other churches were theologically flawed and thereby rejected by God made certain that the critics and enemies of the church would constantly target it and its membership for derision and persecution. Months after Orson Hyde departed from Kanesville, Iowa, and resigned his editorial post at the *Frontier Guardian*, Brigham Young determined to move from a defensive to an offensive posture. Young convened a special general conference in August 1852, two months earlier than usual to assure that missionaries could get through the mountain passes on their way to the Pacific and Atlantic coasts of America and begin their evangelization. In the opinion of historian David J. Whittaker, this missionary conference was a watershed moment in the pioneer period, as it centered on the public announcement of plural marriage, the message that over one hundred missionaries were about to broadcast to the world, in North American, Europe, the Pacific, Asia, and even Africa.[51]

Joseph Smith pondered about the ancient practice of plural marriage as early as 1831, while working on his inspired "translation" of Genesis in the Hebrew Bible. In subsequent years he took dozens of plural wives and later encouraged members of his Nauvoo, Illinois, inner circle to likewise "do the works of Abraham." Although few outsiders were aware of Smith's

50. Jenson, *Encyclopedic History*, 270; Jean Trumbo, "Orson Hyde's *Frontier Guardian*," *Iowa Heritage Illustrated* 77 (Summer 1996): 74–85; and Myrtle Stevens Hyde, "Orson Hyde and the *Frontier Guardian*," *Nauvoo Journal* 8 (Fall 1996): 62–70.

51. David J. Whittaker, "Early Mormon Polygamy Defenses," *Journal of Mormon History* 11 (1984): 43–44. Standard sources on Mormon plural marriage include Lawrence Foster, *Religion and Sexuality: The Shakers, the Mormons, and the Oneida Community* (Urbana: University of Illinois Press, 1984); Jessie L. Embry, *Mormon Polygamous Families: Life in the Principle* (Salt Lake City: University of Utah Press, 1987); B. Carmon Hardy, *Solemn Covenant: The Mormon Polygamous Passage* (Urbana: University of Illinois Press, 1992); Kathryn M. Daynes, *More Wives Than One: Transformation of the Mormon Marriage System, 1840–1910* (Urbana: University of Illinois Press, 2001); and B. Carmon Hardy, ed., *Doing the Works of Abraham: Mormon Polygamy: Its Origin, Practice, and Thought* (Norman, Okla.: Arthur H. Clark Company, 2007).

unconventional marriage arrangements, some insiders were deeply offended by his teachings and broadcasted his actions in the Nauvoo *Expositor* (1844). Within a month of this exposé of Mormon polygamy, Joseph Smith and his brother Hyrum were murdered by a mob in Carthage, Illinois. Nevertheless, between 1844 and 1852, a growing number of Latter-day Saints practiced plural marriage in relative secrecy. Not surprisingly, the 1852 public announcement by the Mormons that they were openly practicing polygamy in the relative isolation of America's Great Basin ignited a firestorm of Christian opposition against the Latter-day Saints that would not burn out for the rest of the nineteenth century. To try to influence public opinion and contest the prevailing image of the church, Brigham Young called a number of his trusted lieutenants to begin printing newspapers in major American cities. Within the next three years, he assigned Apostle Orson Pratt to oversee *The Seer* in Washington, D.C., Apostle Erastus Snow to edit the *St. Louis Luminary*, Apostle John Taylor to manage *The Mormon* in New York, and future Apostle George Q. Cannon to edit the *Western Standard* in San Francisco. This was the beginning of the Mormon offensive push to represent themselves, rather than merely reacting. Although originally published in newspaper format, many of these journalism writings were later published as books or missionary tracts. But the editors of these periodicals shut them down when the U.S. Army began marching to Utah in 1857.[52]

Orson Pratt edited and published the *Seer*, in Washington, D.C. During the same 1852 general conference when he was asked by Brigham Young to proclaim the Mormon practice of plural marriage publicly, it was announced that he would be overseeing Mormon evangelization in the eastern United States and the British Canada for the next several years. Pratt was also called to publish a monthly periodical in defense of the church, especially plural marriage, while back East. The first issue of the *Seer* came off the press in January 1853 and regular issues were published through June 1854, when its publication was moved from the nation's capital to the center of Mormon publishing in Liverpool, England, under the direction of Apostle Franklin D. Richards. Only two new editions were published there but all previous material was reprinted for the benefit of the English-speaking European Saints. A total of twenty numbers or editions of the *Seer* were published during this time. Pratt's most important work on his defense of plural marriage was later translated into Danish in 1855 and used throughout the fledgling

---

52. Draper, "Publications," 3:1174–1175.

Scandinavian Mission thereafter. A book was later published as well in English.[53]

Just months after Orson Pratt relocated the *Seer* to the British Isles, Erastus Snow began editing the St. Louis *Luminary* (1854–1855) in Missouri. This weekly newspaper was published specifically to advance the cause of the church, including the promulgation and defense of plural marriage, its target audience being both Mormons and non-Mormons on America's frontier. Its first issue complete with masthead declaring the New Testament sentiment that "Light Shineth in Darkness, and the Darkness Comprehendeth it not," came off the press in November 1854; its last, in December 1855. By the mid-1850s, Mormon immigration from the British Isles and Scandinavia was in full swing; and tens of thousands of European converts passed through St. Louis, Missouri, on riverboats plying the Mississippi River before they began their westward trek by wagon and by foot across the Great Plains of North America, beginning at Atchison, Kansas.[54] The *Luminary* provided these converts with crucial information as they prepared to cross the American desert.

An overlapping church periodical hundreds of miles to the east was John Taylor's newspaper *The Mormon* based in New York City (1855–1857). Like Erastus Snow's St. Louis *Luminary*, Taylor's weekly was written for both Latter-day Saints and those of other faiths, and it came off the press between February 1855 and September 1857. The paper's anticipated mission was broadcasted on its masthead: "It is better to represent ourselves than to be misrepresented by others." Through its pages, Taylor communicated regularly and effectively with many Latter-day Saints scattered along America's eastern seaboard as they prepared to gather with the main body of the Saints in Utah. Moreover, his paper helped prepare large number of European converts who passed through the immigration ports ringing the isle of Manhattan for the arduous journey that lay ahead to the west. But when John Taylor received word that armed forces were marching to Utah to replace Brigham Young as territorial governor, he hurried back to

53. David J. Whittaker, "The Bone in the Throat: Orson Pratt and the Public Announcement of Plural Marriage," *Western Historical Quarterly* 18 (July 1987): 293–314; Whittaker, "Early Mormon Polygamy Defenses," 43–63; Breck England, *The Life and Thought of Orson Pratt* (Salt Lake City: University of Utah Press, 1985), 159–186; and Jenson, *Encyclopedic History*, 783–784.

54. Andrew Karl Larson, *Erastus Snow: The Life of a Missionary and Pioneer for the Early Mormon Church* (Salt Lake City: University of Utah Press, 1971); Val G. Hemming, "A Voice from the Land of Zion: Elder Erastus Snow in Denmark, 1850 to 1852," *Dialogue: A Journal of Mormon Thought* 35, no. 1 (Spring 2002): 131–143; and Jenson, *Encyclopedic History*, 735–736.

Utah, his departure marking the end of Mormon periodicals on the East Coast for many decades.[55]

But this Latter-day Saint periodical offensive was not limited to America's Midwest or its East Coast. John Taylor's nephew, George Q. Cannon, published a fourth newspaper in San Francisco, California, the *Western Standard* (1856–1857).[56] First appearing in February 1856 and continuing until October 1857, Cannon's weekly rag "took a brave stand in refuting the slander and misrepresentations which at the time of its publication were being circulated by the enemies of the Church, in consequence of which quite an anti-Mormon agitation was aroused against the editor and the other Elders and local Saints who resided in California at the time." But like his uncle Cannon was forced to silence his press and evacuate to the safety of Utah, as Johnston's Army continued its ominous march to the Salt Lake Valley.[57]

Taken together, Orson Pratt's *Seer*, Erastus Snow's *Luminary*, John Taylor's *Mormon*, and George Q. Cannon's *Western Standard* mark an important moment in Mormon self-image making. The editorial contributions of three of these men were summed up in a toast offered by a Latter-day Saint in their honor in the summer of 1857: "Editors John Taylor, Erastus Snow and George Q. Cannon—may the Snow storm blow, the Cannon roar, and the Taylor cut until the gainsayers of Zion are silenced."[58] The quartet's domestic publishing efforts were echoed by international Mormon newspapers, including Dan Jones's *Trump of Zion* in Wales, John Van Cott's *Scandinavian Star* in Denmark, and Augustus Farnham's *Zion's Watchman* in Australia. And additional church periodicals would be published in Germany and Sweden later in the century. Moreover, the leadership of various auxiliaries of the church in Salt Lake City later issued their own organization's periodicals, including the

55. B. H. Roberts, *The Life of John Taylor*, reprint ed. (Salt Lake City: Bookcraft, 1989), 242–270; Samuel W. Taylor, *The Kingdom or Nothing: The Life of John Taylor, Militant Mormon* (New York: Macmillan, 1976), 175–191; Francis M. Gibbons, *John Taylor: Mormon Philosopher, Prophet of God* (Salt Lake City: Deseret Book, 1985), 137–149; and Jenson, *Encyclopedic History*, 535–536.

56. George Q. Cannon, *Writings from the* Western Standard (Liverpool: George Q. Cannon, 1864).

57. Joseph A. Cannon, "George Q. Cannon and the *Western Standard*: Defending Utah's Pioneers in Print from the California Coast," *Pioneer* (Summer 1998): 22–25; Bitton, *George Q. Cannon*, 69–106; Roger Robin Ekins, ed., *Defending Zion: George Q. Cannon and the California Mormon Newspaper Wars of 1856–1857* (Spokane: Arthur H. Clark Company, 2002); Jenson, *Encyclopedic History*, 945.

58. Quoted in Bitton, *George Q. Cannon*, 86–87.

Juvenile Instructor, the *Contributor*, the *Woman's Exponent*, and the *Young Woman's Journal*.[59]

In addition to representing themselves through in-house newspapers, the Latter-day Saints also took advantage of opportunities to shape public opinion through non-Mormon national periodicals. Yet such promising occasions were few and far between during the nineteenth century. Marginalized religious and social groups, like the Mormons, generally struggled to gain access to nationwide media outlets, where the news was packaged for mass consumption. "When controversy over the 'Mormon Question'—the label given to the national debate over Mormonism's polygamy, theocracy, and general relationship to the nation—swirled daily across the pages of America's newspapers and magazines, defenders of Mormonism confronted a fundamentally uneven playing field," historian Matthew J. Grow writes of the nineteenth century. "Anti-Mormon crusaders often had access to mainstream periodicals, publishers, and pulpits, while the Saints could generally respond only through their own newspapers and pamphlets, which had much smaller circulations and were indelibly tainted because of their Mormon association."[60] Both the Latter-day Saints and their critics were well aware of this lopsided reality; nevertheless, both sides continued to promulgate their side of the story as they contested the image of the church in the United States.

The Latter-day Saints did find a listening ear in the editorial board of the *North American Review*, one of the most popular and well-respected magazines in the United States. Whether its editors were interested in driving up sales by publishing articles on the church or whether they were advocates of journalistic fair play is difficult to deduce. What is clear is that they allowed the Mormons in a meaningful way and through a most reputable source to challenge the image and identity that non-Mormons had imposed upon the Latter-day Saints. Beginning in the 1880s and continuing for nearly the next three decades, the *Review* published over a dozen articles on the Latter-day Saint movement. Five of these essays were written by leading Mormon apologists: First Presidency counselor George Q. Cannon wrote on the politics of the Latter-day Saints in the Intermountain West,

---

59. Subsequent church auxiliary periodicals include *Improvement Era* (1897–1970); *The Elders' Journal* (1903–1907), which became *Liahona the Elders' Journal* (1907–45); *Children's Friend* (1902–1970); *Utah Genealogical and Historical Magazine* (1910–1940); and *Relief Society Magazine* (1915–1970). Draper, "Publications," 3:1175.

60. Matthew J. Grow, "Contesting the LDS Image: The *North American Review* and the Mormons, 1881–1907," *Journal of Mormon History* 32, no. 2 (Summer 2006): 111–112.

Church President John Taylor described church–state relations in Utah, Mormon politico Joseph A. West contextualized the controversial church doctrine of blood atonement, church feminist Susa Young Gates challenged conventional wisdom on plural marriage and its effects on Mormon women and children, and Apostle Reed Smoot held forth on post-Manifesto plural marriage. Another eight articles that appeared in the *Review* were drafted by critics of the church, including pieces by *Salt Lake Tribune* editor Charles C. Goodwin, Utah Governor Eli H. Murray (twice), journalist Kate Field, church antagonist Eugene Young, and Republican Senator Shelby M. Cullom (twice). Non-Mormon political scientist James W. Garner contributed perhaps the most even-handed academic assessment of the issues surrounding the Latter-day Saints. "While the *Review* did not allow absolute parity between the two sides, it did foster an open debate with sustained Latter-day Saint participation," Grow concludes.[61] And the Mormons clearly welcomed the chance to represent themselves rather than be represented by their enemies.

In addition to a plethora of church-sponsored periodicals, Latter-day Saints also published a growing number of doctrinal works during the Pioneer period. Not surprisingly, a number of these offered theological arguments for the practice of polygamy. From Orson Pratt's August 1852 public relations offensive until 1884, when a final justification was published, a variety of Mormon apologists authored nearly two dozen additional pamphlets and tracts in defense of polygamy. All of these printed apologetics, however, were derivatives of Pratt's work during the early 1850s to explicate the Latter-day Saint understanding of this theology and religious practice. Men like Richard Ballantyne and Jesse Haven, for example, who were both called as missionaries at this time to India and South Africa, respectively, drew upon the arguments made by Orson Pratt at the conference and thereafter in print in their own missionary publications. Between them they wrote several defenses of plural marriage. Both men and their fellow missionaries struggled mightily in the mission field because of the surge in anti-Mormonism resulting from the public announcement of plural marriage. Benjamin F. Johnson, a missionary called at this time to the Sandwich (Hawaiian) Islands, likewise produced his own defense of plural marriage titled *Why the "Latter-day Saints" Practice a Plurality of Wives* (1854), largely modeled after Orson Pratt's later editorials in the *Seer*. In Utah, Belinda

61. Grow, "Contesting the LDS Image," 113, 115–136.

Marden Pratt, one of Parley P. Pratt's plural wives, offered the first female defense of Mormon plural marriage in print called *Defence of Polygamy* (1854). And Orson Spencer, while in Liverpool, England, published *Patriarchal Order, or Plurality of Wives!* (1853).[62]

Also, Latter-day Saints wrote on a number of other theological topics during this era, in addition to polygamy. Printed doctrinal treatises grew in popularity and production both in Utah and Great Britain as Mormon theology became more systemized and codified by thinkers like the Pratt brothers and put forth in their missionary tracts. "These ephemeral pamphlets fundamentally changed Mormonism. For as they multiplied, the tenets of the Church, bit by bit, were identified in print," bibliographer Peter Crawley writes. "In the absence of an official statement of doctrine, the ideas printed in these missionary tracts came to serve as the Church's confession of faith. And thus was Mormonism transformed from an anticreedal religion to one identified with a number of distinguishing doctrines."[63]

Although most of the church's distinguishing doctrines, beliefs, and practices had been put in ink for the public, including plural marriage, no apologist or Mormon theologian had yet assembled and systematized all of these pieces. Parley Pratt, author of earlier church classics, including *A Voice of Warning* (1837) and *Mormonism Unveiled* (1838), would take it upon himself to write such a volume, beginning in August 1851, before his departure to South America as president of the Pacific Mission. First serialized as chapters in the *Deseret News*, it came off the printed press as a book in the spring of 1855.[64] "*Key to Theology* is Mormonism's earliest comprehensive synthetical work," Crawley explains. "Its scope is complete: beginning with a definition of theology, it traces the loss of the true gospel among the Jews and the gentiles; then in linking chapters it discusses the nature of the Godhead, the origin of the universe, the restoration of the gospel, the means by which man regains the presence of God, the resurrection, the three degrees of glory, and the ultimate position of exalted men and women as

62. Whittaker, "Early Mormon Polygamy Defenses," 45–59. See also Davis Bitton, "Polygamy Defended: One Side of a Nineteenth-Century Polemic," in *The Ritualization of Mormon History and Other Essays* (Urbana: University of Illinois Press, 1994), 34–53.

63. Peter Crawley, "Parley P. Pratt: Father of Mormon Pamphleteering," *Dialogue: A Journal of Mormon Thought* 15, no. 3 (Autumn 1982): 17.

64. Parley Parker Pratt, *Key to the Science of Theology: Designed as an Introduction to the First Principles of Spiritual Philosophy; Religion; Law and Government; as Delivered by the Ancients, and as Restored in this Age for the Final Development of Universal Peace, Truth and Knowledge* (Liverpool: F. D. Richards, 1855).

procreative beings."[65] This groundbreaking volume would be Parley Pratt's final major work as he would be murdered two years later in 1857.

Parley's brother Apostle Orson Pratt also wrote a number of important doctrinal works during this same era. Orson Pratt's *A Series of Pamphlets* (1851) was a collection of sixteen missionary tracts, focusing on various doctrines and historical moments of the church.[66] He compiled them together just before his return from the British Isles to the United States. His bound tracts included his most important theological works, including *Divine Authority, Kingdom of God, Remarkable Visions, New Jerusalem, Divine Authenticity of the Book of Mormon, Reply to a Pamphlet Printed in Glasgow, Absurdities of Immaterialism,* and *Great First Cause.* This volume became popularly known as *O. Pratt's Works* and helped shape the rhetoric of missionaries for decades to come. It was from his writings that a great number of Mormon converts gained knowledge of the church and its theology and history.[67] Of Pratt's contribution, historian David J. Whittaker writes: "Orson Pratt's greatest impact upon Mormonism came through his clearly and precisely written theological studies. Within each work he moved carefully from one point to another, gradually developing his position with the same exactness he would have used in solving a mathematical equation. More than anything else, his concern for definiteness gave his works a finality early Mormons found reassuring in an unstable world, and his ability to simplify— to reduce things to their lowest common denominator—was especially appreciated by elders defending the faith in mission fields all over the world."[68]

Besides the Pratt brothers, a number of Latter-day Saint apologists offered their own doctrinal contributions as the Mormons pioneered in the Great Basin. Orson Spencer, a long-time Baptist minister who accepted the Mormon faith in 1841, for example, published a series of a dozen letters that he exchanged with Baptist periodical editor William Crowell, letters that lay out

---

65. Crawley, "Parley P. Pratt: Father of Mormon Pamphleteering," 17.

66. Orson Pratt, *A series of pamphlets, by Orson Pratt, one of the twelve apostles of the Church of Jesus Christ of Latter-Day Saints, with portrait. To which is appended a discussion held in Bolton, between Elder William Gibson, President of the saints in the Manchester Conference, and the Rev. Mr. Woodman. Also a discussion held in France, between Elder John Taylor, one of the twelve apostles, and three reverend gentlemen of different orders containing a facsimile of writings engraved on six metallic plates, taken out of an ancient mound in the state of Illinois, in the year 1843* (Liverpool: R. James, 1851).

67. Crawley, *Descriptive Bibliography,* 2:195–199.

68. David J. Whittaker, "Orson Pratt: Prolific Pamphleteer," *Dialogue: A Journal of Mormon Thought* 15, no. 3 (Autumn 1982): 32.

specific Latter-day Saint beliefs. These letters were initially printed in Nauvoo's *Times and Seasons* and in Liverpool's *Millennial Star* in 1843. Four years later, while serving as president of the British Mission, Spencer determined to continue his correspondence with Crowell for the anticipated benefit of Mormon observers. His letters back to America were first printed as tracts and then gathered and printed as a collection titled *Letters Exhibiting the Most Prominent Doctrines of the Church of Jesus Christ of Latter-day Saints* (1848).[69] The dozen or so letters focus on theological matters, including the coming forth of the Book of Mormon, the spirit of revelation, modern-day miracles, baptism by immersion, gift of the Holy Ghost, Christian apostasy, restoration of apostolic church, corporality of God, priesthood, judgments in the last days, and the restitution of all things. Peter Crawley suggests that this is "the first of the major synthetic works and one of Mormonism's most important books. Six more editions, with additional letters, would be issued during the nineteenth century."[70]

While serving as a mission president in Great Britain Apostle Franklin D. Richards published *A Compendium of the Faith and Doctrines of the Church of Jesus Christ of Latter-day Saints* (1857), a decade after Orson Spencer's book.[71] Originally begun as a series of notes on gospel themes, Richards's compilation begins each chapter with a summary of the particular doctrine and then draws upon what scriptural references can be found in the Old and New Testaments, along with scriptural passages from Latter-day Saint texts including the Book of Mormon, Doctrine and Covenants, and Pearl of Great Price. Moreover, he listed any relevant statements by Joseph Smith on the subject. Section headings include the fall of Adam, the atonement, faith, repentance, baptism, laying on of hands, the resurrection, the holy priesthood, Christ's first coming, Christ's second coming, scattering of Israel, the gathering of Israel, the Book of Mormon, and Joseph Smith, for starters. Franklin Richards's *Compendium*, not surprisingly, became a favorite of fledging missionaries in the field who were anxious to present church doctrines in a more systematic

---

69. Orson Spencer, *Letters Exhibiting the Most Prominent Doctrines of the Church of Jesus Christ of Latter-day Saints* (Liverpool: Orson Spencer, 1848).

70. Crawley, *Descriptive Bibliography*, 1:364–367; 2:30–33; Richard Wallace Sadler, "The Life of Orson Spencer" (MA thesis, University of Utah, 1965), 50–58; and Seymour H. Spencer, *Life Summary of Orson Spencer* (Salt Lake City: Mercury Publishing, 1956), 43–59.

71. Franklin D. Richards, *A Compendium of the Faith and Doctrines of the Church of Jesus Christ of Latter-day Saints: Compiled from the Bible; and also from the Book of Mormon, Doctrine and Covenants, and Other Publications of the Church* (Liverpool: L.D.S. Book Depot, 1857).

way, with supporting scriptural evidence to their listeners. Many editions were subsequently printed, demonstrating the volume's importance in this process of systemization of Mormon thought.[72]

In the aftermath of the martyrdom of Joseph Smith and the exodus west, a good deal of attention was placed on documenting the experiences and leaders of the early church. As Mormonism's first generation began to pass away, by bullet or disease or natural causes, their lives were commemorated in print. Perhaps the most important of these was the work of the Restoration's matriarch Lucy Mack Smith on her son, titled *Biographical Sketches of Joseph Smith the Prophet* (1853).[73] Another important Pioneer period historical work is the *Autobiography of Parley Parker Pratt* (1874).[74] Before his murder in Arkansas in 1857, Pratt wrote about his life with the help of his plural wife Keziah Downes, especially his conversion to and experiences within the church, an account which was later edited and published by his namesake son. It was published nearly seventeen years after Pratt's murder and covered the five decades of his life.[75] One critic suggests that the book offers "a different perspective on Mormon history: a revealing and often moving picture of the early eastern and mid-western mission of the church, at the end of which the exodus to the Rockies seems more anticlimactic than epic compared to the tragic failure of community relations and democratic process during the Missouri period and the euphoria of Nauvoo, Illinois."[76]

In conclusion, throughout the Founding (1830–46) and Pioneer (1847–90) periods of the church, Latter-day Saints excelled as missionaries both at home

---

72. Franklin D. West, *Life of Franklin D. Richards* (Salt Lake City: Deseret News Press, 1924), 182–183.

73. Lucy Smith, *Biographical Sketches of Joseph Smith the Prophet, and his Progenitors for many Generations* (Liverpool: S. W. Richards, 1853); Richard Lloyd Anderson, "The Reliability of the Early History of Lucy and Joseph Smith," *Dialogue: A Journal of Mormon Thought* 4, no. 2 (Summer 1969): 12–28; and Lavina Fielding Anderson, ed., *Lucy's Book: A Critical Edition of Lucy Mack Smith's Family Memoir* (Salt Lake City: Signature Books, 2001).

74. Parley P. Pratt, *The Autobiography of Parley Parker Pratt, one of the Twelve Apostles of the Church of Jesus Christ of Latter-day Saints, Embracing his Life, Ministry and Travels, with Extracts, in Prose and Verse, from his Miscellaneous Writings*, ed. Parley P. Pratt Jr. (New York: Russell Brothers, 1874).

75. Reva Stanley, *A Biography of Parley P. Pratt: The Archer of Paradise* (Caldwell, Idaho: Caxton Printers, 1937), 296.

76. R. A. Christmas, "The Autobiography of Parley P. Pratt: Some Literary, Historical, and Critical Reflections," in *Tending the Garden: Essays on Mormon Literature*, ed. Lavina Fielding Anderson and Eugene England (Salt Lake City: Signature Books, 1996), 109, 105–116.

and abroad, despite their small numbers and limited financial resources, in large measure because of their aggressive use of the printed word. Given the fact that tens of thousands of American, European, Asian, Pacific Islander, and African Protestants (and a sprinkling of Catholics) converted to the church in this era indicates that many found the message of a Restoration, rather than merely a Reformation, of historical Christianity compelling enough to endure the high social costs of casting their lot with the besieged Mormons. Nineteenth-century Latter-day Saints were well aware that much of their missionary success could be attributed to their polarizing publishing program. "The press is a powerful lever or agency through which the Lord can reach the minds of the people," Brigham Young reminded George Q. Cannon in 1856.[77] As millenarian Christians, the Latter-day Saints were quick to emphasize their separating spiritual beliefs and practices rather than showcasing their cultural contributions to their fellow Americans. This allowed them to highlight the distinctive teachings of the church, for if the Restoration offered nothing new to potential converts from traditional Christianity, why would anyone join and pay the high costs of discipleship?

Evangelistic Success, Public Relations Struggle

But there was a real downside to emphasizing their theological differences rather than building upon their doctrinal similarities with traditional Christianity, a legacy that the Latter-day Saints would have to deal with well into the twenty-first century. The very Christian body that the Mormons would revile and reject would paint them beyond the pale of Christianity, as a result. The Latter-day Saints would be forever considered outsiders by their Protestant, Catholic, and Orthodox Christian brothers and sisters. In other words, the evangelistic and publishing strategy employed by Latter-day Saints during the nineteenth century yielded considerable converts but very few friends. It was a public relations disaster. As a result, the Latter-day Saints allowed themselves to be sidelined from America's cultural mainstream because of their *religious differences* (like plural marriages, theological exclusivism, and theocratic government), in spite of their *nonreligious achievements* (like frontier city building, desert irrigation, and artistic prowess). It was not until the September 1890 Manifesto that the church sought (or was forced) to

---

77. Quoted in Bitton, *George Q. Cannon*, 75.

be somewhat assimilated into American culture in spite of, *not because of,* its religious contributions to America.

In 1890 the U.S. Congress and President William Henry Harrison announced that America would host the next world's fair in Chicago. And just two months before President Wilford Woodruff proclaimed the end of additional church–sanctioned plural marriages that September, the World's Fair National Commission accepted the site of Chicago's Jackson Park for the 1893 Columbian Exposition. Desirous of showcasing the best of the United States to the rest of the world, national and state leaders invited their fellow citizens to imagine ways of exhibiting the best of Americana, including its cultural contributions, agricultural achievements, social successes, and religious realizations. Like other Americans who heard this clarion call, many Latter-day Saints in Utah sensed that upcoming events in Chicago offered new ways for self-representation and a chance to contest their public image in ways previously not available. The Columbian Exposition would mark the beginnings of formal church public relations. Public education, not private evangelization, was a new emerging strategy. For the first time Mormons sought to be understood, not necessarily joined, by outsiders. Limited in the past to mainly the printed word, they would embrace this opportunity to increase interpersonal contacts and tell their own story in person to the outside world in Chicago.[78]

Over seven thousand Latter-day Saints from Utah traveled to the Chicago World's Fair to showcase their own contributions and become part of America. While many traveled as tourists, oblivious to the opportunities to "exhibit" Mormonism, other church members actively participated to reshape their church's public image. Hundreds of congregants helped create, manage, and staff their territory's impressive Utah Building; most believed their besieged religion would benefit from Utah's increased national profile. Moreover, many Latter-day Saint women represented the female interests and achievements of both Utah and its dominant religion. These women hoped to use the Columbian Exposition as a platform to improve the social status of their gender and their religion. That summer 250 of the Mormon Tabernacle Choir's best singers competed in a Welsh Eisteddfod, a musical competition held in conjunction with the Chicago World's Fair. Mormon apologist Brigham H. Roberts sought to gain Latter-

78. Norman Bolotin and Christine Laing, *The World's Columbian Exposition: The Chicago World's Fair of 1893* (Urbana: University of Illinois Press, 1992), 2–3.

day Saint representation at the affiliated Parliament of Religions.[79] Territorial representative Edwin A. McDaniel summed up the motivation of these various groups of Latter-day Saints from Utah: "The benefit we hope Utah will derive from her representation at the exposition is, that she may be lifted above the cloud which has heretofore hung over her—that she will be presented to the public in such a manner as to receive the recognition due her which has long been withheld, owing to a wrong impression conveyed through a lack of knowledge of her people."[80]

79. Andrew Jenson, *Church Chronology: A Record of Important Events Pertaining to the History of the Church of Jesus Christ of Latter-day Saints* (Salt Lake City: Deseret News, 1899), 201.

80. Edwin A. McDaniel, "Utah at Chicago," *Utah Monthly Magazine* 9 (March 1893): 219–220.

2

The Utah World's Fair Commission

THE UTAH TERRITORY AT THE COLUMBIAN EXPOSITION

> Utah's exhibit at the World's Fair is doing a great deal towards people knowing that there is wealth, productiveness, and advanced civilization in "the tops of the mountains."*
>
> —*Deseret News*, 1893

> During the past six months this Territory has been better advertised than ever before. The entire contingent from Utah have talked themselves hoarse and distributed much literature, and the value to the Territory has been double the amount expended.**
>
> —GEORGE D. PYPER, 1893

BETWEEN MAY AND October 1893, members of the Utah World's Fair Commission endeavored to showcase the cultural contributions of their Territory at the Columbian Exposition. Days after the Jackson Park fairgrounds opened to the world, Utah poetess Josephine Spencer traveled to Chicago by train as a reporter for The Church of Jesus Christ of Latter-day Saints-owned *Deseret News*. Of particular interest to Spencer and her Mormon readers back west was how well the Utah Building and a number of related exhibits represented their beloved Territory. In her mind, the quality of the American state and territorial buildings and the accompanying displays served as a public yardstick of local philanthropy, as well as a barometer of community patriotism. So Spencer was delighted to discover that the Utah Building (figure 3) and the Territory's showcases were on par with those of other

---

* "From the Fair Grounds," *Deseret Evening News*, September 14, 1893.

** "Closing of the Utah Exhibit," *Millennial Star* 55, no. 50 (December 11, 1893): 801.

FIGURE 3 Mormon and non-Mormon Utah dignitaries in front of the Utah Building and Brigham Young Monument at the Chicago World's Fair, 1893, courtesy of the Church History Library, The Church of Jesus Christ of Latter-day Saints, Salt Lake City, Utah.

American states, and in several cases surpassed their neighbors. The Territory's classical structure stood two stories tall and its foundational footprint measured forty-eight feet by eighty-four feet, giving it an imposing façade. "The front of the building which faces south on one of the principal avenues is made attractive by its wide windows, spacious doorway and porch," she wrote of Utah's fair headquarters. "The latter supported by graceful ionic columns, and reached by a broad flight of steps leading from the pavement, and the grounds outside by the green turf, which makes the handsome lawn, and the full-foliaged trees which proved a pleasant shade for the grounds and building." The head offices of Montana, Idaho, North Dakota, and Colorado encircled the Utah Building. "It is a great deal for Utah to be represented even in a small way at the Exposition, for no such opportunity has ever been or ever will be again offered for advertising the resources of our Territory and the talents and industry of her people," Josephine Spencer concluded with territorial pride.[1]

1. Josephine Spencer, "Some of the State Buildings at the Exposition," *Juvenile Instructor* 28, no. 21 (November 1, 1893): 657–661.

The 1893 Chicago World's Fair, which celebrated the discovery of America by Columbus four centuries earlier, provided Latter-day Saints their first post-Manifesto (1890) opportunity to exhibit the best of Utah and Mormonism to a domestic and global audience. Although the management and membership of cultural, social, political, legal, and ecclesiastical organizations from around the world were eager to participate in the upcoming global exposition, Mormon leaders and laity in Utah were at first ambivalent about the prospects of formal church participation in the Columbian Exposition. After decades of being pilloried in both the national and international presses as well as made to feel unwelcome by their fellow Americans whenever they ventured beyond the borders of their Great Basin Kingdom, some Latter-day Saints were wary of institutional involvement in the cosmopolitan gathering. Granted, a few church members had attended earlier expositions. Between 1851 and 1893 there were nearly thirty world's fairs in North America, Europe, and Australia. These nineteenth-century cultural extravaganzas were held every few years, except when thwarted by major wars. Church leadership in Europe, for instance, held a special missionary conference in conjunction with the 1851 Great Exhibition of the Works of Industry of all Nations in London; yet Mormons did not seek formal representation at the event. Moreover, Utah had been organized as a U.S. territory only since 1850 and sent no territorial representatives to the Great Exposition in London. Neither the Utah-headquartered church nor the secular Utah Territory participated in a world's fair or international exposition for another two decades.[2]

Utah Territory was inextricably linked to the church during the era. The fortunes of both organizations rose and (more often) fell with the same tides of American public opinion. Utah and Mormonism were virtually synonymous in terms of reputation and demographic statistics in the second half of the nineteenth century, although the ratio of Mormons to non-Mormons in Utah would decrease over time. About 85,000 Latter-day Saints were living in the Utah Territory by 1870. They accounted for 98 percent of the total territorial population of 86,786 and represented 99 percent of the total

2. Gerald Joseph Peterson, "History of Mormon Exhibits in World Expositions" (Master's thesis, Brigham Young University, 1974), 7–15; Peter J. Vousden, "London Missionaries and the Great Exhibition of 1851," *BYU Studies* 44, no. 3 (2005): 123–135; and T. Edgar Lyon, Jr., "In Praise of Babylon: Church Leadership at the 1851 Great Exhibition in London," *Journal of Mormon History* 14 (1988): 49–61.

territorial religionist populace.[3] Utah representatives, nearly all of them Latter-day Saints, finally seized upon the 1873 Vienna World's Fair as an opportunity to showcase their Territory's achievements to the world, in an attempt to fast-track their statehood petition back in the United States. Utah's involvement in this European fair helped the outside world better appreciate the Territory's natural resources and grasp that there was more to Utah than Mormonism and polygamy. A smattering of Latter-day Saints attended the American expositions in Philadelphia (1876), Atlanta (1881), Boston (1883–1884), Louisville (1883–1884), and New Orleans (1884–1885), but they were not official representatives of either the political or ecclesiastical institution. By way of explanation, these domestic expositions were convened during the height of the anti-polygamy persecution, and Mormon leaders and laity were battening down the hatches in hiding, not going out among the peoples and nations of the world. The Woodruff Manifesto, however, opened the door to future Mormon participation in these types of gatherings. The heretofore evangelistic Latter-day Saints were beginning to look for much-needed public relations opportunities in America.[4]

By the early 1890s, the leaders and citizens of Utah—the majority being Latter-day Saints—became convinced of the image-shaping utility of such a cosmopolitan exposition in Chicago. Both Mormon and non-Mormon Utahns were eager to be seen as progressive Victorian Americans at this important moment in U.S. history, when the peoples of the world would be coming to America for the Chicago World's Fair. Moreover, they hoped to sway still unsympathetic policy makers in Washington, D.C., that their Territory deserved the much-sought-after federal approbation of statehood. "The people of Utah took an active interest in the Exposition from the first, and rejoiced heartily with Chicago when Congress decided that the World's Fair should be located on the shores of Lake Michigan," Edwin A. McDaniel

---

3. By 1884, church membership in Utah had jumped to about 106,000, against a total of 168,000. This dropped the Mormons to only 63 percent of the total Utah population, but still 96 percent of the total Utah religious denomination/church membership for the year. According to the 1890 U.S. census there were 118,201 Latter-day Saints in Utah, out of a total of 210,779, about 56 percent of the total population, but still accounted for 92 percent of the total number of religionists in Utah. (See Richard D. Poll, Thomas G. Alexander, Eugene E. Campbell, and David E. Miller, eds., "Table H: Membership of Religious Denominations in Utah, 1870–1975," in *Utah's History* [Provo, Utah: Brigham Young University Press, 1978], 692–693. For more on the number of religionists in Utah, see also Lee L. Bean, "Religious Membership in Utah: Growth without Change," in *Utah at the Beginning of the New Millennium: A Demographic Perspective*, ed. Cathleen D. Zick and Ken R. Smith [Salt Lake City: University of Utah Press, 2006], 127–134.)

4. Peterson, "Mormon Exhibits in World Expositions," 13.

recalled of Utahns' interest in the Columbian spectacle. "The efforts of the citizens of Chicago to secure the Exposition were seconded by the citizens of Utah."[5] Local exposition clubs were formed up and down pioneer Utah to produce agricultural, literary, manufacturing, and mining exhibits, by which the Territory and its citizens could showcase the best they had to offer. Funded through the territorial legislature and philanthropic citizens, the Utah World's Fair Commission was created and sustained for the express purpose of removing the prejudice that existed against Deseret, the original Mormon name for the Territory. Utah Latter-day Saints especially hoped to show to the world that they were not a backward people, as suggested in the popular press, but Americans who were making a difference and adding strength to the expanding Union.

The Utah World's Fair Commission

"The idea to create a world's fair commemorating the 400th anniversary of Columbus' voyage to American was conceived not by a single inspiration but by a great many enterprising minds throughout the world," historians Norman Bolotin and Christine Laing explain.[6] A number of prominent Americans sought to celebrate the arrival of Europeans in the New World, especially in light of the successes of France's international fairs in 1878 and 1889, as well as the Centennial Exposition, the first American world's fair, which was held in Philadelphia in 1876. Almost ten million people had converged on the city of brotherly love and enjoyed over thirty-thousand exhibits. While the success of the Pennsylvanian fair was a source of pride for many Americans, others felt that their relatively new country still had more to showcase to the world. Some U.S. newspapers promoted a Columbian fair as early as 1882, but it was not until 1888 that a Washington, D.C., consortium proposed to Congress an official plan, along with a plea for several million dollars to facilitate the event. At this point, a number of other American cities and their representatives put forth their own formal prospectuses to compete with the District of Columbia. New York City, St. Louis, Washington, D.C., and Chicago quickly became the front-runners to host the Columbian Exposition on U.S. soil.[7]

---

5. Edwin A. McDaniel, *Utah at the World's Columbian Exposition* (Salt Lake City: Salt Lake Lithographing, 1894), 9.

6. Norman Bolotin and Christine Laing, *The World's Columbian Exposition: The Chicago World's Fair of 1893* (Urbana: University of Illinois Press, 1992), 1.

7. Bolotin and Laing, *World's Columbian Exposition*, 1–3.

Each of these major American cities staked their claims and flaunted their qualifications; eventually their backers appeared before both houses of Congress to lobby for their respective site plans. New York City, despite its massive population and funding resources, struggled to come up with a suitable location, since many citizens were against using Central Park for such a prolonged event. Washington, D.C., despite its early entry into the race and its status as the nation's capital city, had plenty of sites but few monetary resources. Chicago, on the other hand, had two thousand acres of parks, including several recreational areas with waterfront approaches on Lake Michigan. Jackson and Washington parks were ideal for such a gathering. Moreover, visitors' transportation needs could be accommodated by the twenty-four railroads that already provided service to Chicago from all corners of the United States. The city also had steamship lines and passenger excursion boats that could carry over two million people a day. In fact, Chicago had one of the best transportation systems in America, both in terms of quantity and quality. Congress designated Chicago—because of its central location, financial resources, and ideal sites—as the host of the Columbian fair in February 1890, and U.S. President William Henry Harrison blessed the decision that April. On July 2, 1890, the World's Fair National Commission finally accepted the site of Jackson Park for the Columbian Exposition. That September in Salt Lake City, Utah, President Wilford Woodruff proclaimed the end of additional church–sanctioned plural marriages.[8]

By 1890 there were forty-four states in America; Utah would remain a territory until 1896, due to church–state issues, primarily the continued Latter-day Saint practice of plural marriage. Nearly all of the Union's states and territories, including Mormon-dominated Utah, sought to advertise their achievements on the international stage through the erection of local government-sponsored buildings and exhibits in the northern section of Jackson Park. These structures were exempt from the exacting architectural guidelines that united the fairgrounds' other buildings together in a modern renaissance style. The citizens of California, for example, constructed a building modeled after a Spanish mission. Virginians styled their base of operations on Mount Vernon. And the representatives of Florida recreated Fort Marion to the delight of fairgoers. The western territories of Arizona, New Mexico, and Oklahoma banded together to construct a shared headquarters. Organizers anticipated that these costly edifices would become popular meeting places

---

8. "The Site Selected," *Ogden Standard Examiner*, July 3, 1890; Bolotin and Laing, *World's Columbian Exposition*, 2–3.

for residents of the various states and territories, serve as headquarters for government and civic officials, and help showcase their home state' contributions to the greatness of America. Exhibition officials hoped that homesick American tourists would visit their state's building to relax and meet up with friends and family members from home. There they could "swell with pride" at what their state or territory had built and displayed for the rest of the world to see about their homelands. At the same time, most of the states' exhibits were displayed in the nearby Columbian Exposition halls.[9]

When the Utah Territorial Legislature assembled in the spring of 1890, its members passed a bill that empowered Governor Arthur L. Thomas to select a trio of World's Fair Commissioners. These appointed officials were responsible to lobby for the Territory's interests at the upcoming Columbian Exposition. But Governor Thomas declined to select anyone to these positions in a timely manner. Months later, President Harrison preempted Governor Thomas and picked Salt Lake City's P. H. Lannan and Ogden's Fred J. Kiesel as Utah's two federal delegates to the World Columbian Commission headquartered in Chicago, and he named Kanosh's Charles Krane and Park City's William M. Ferry as Utah's alternate commissioners. Over the next three years, Lannan and Kiesel oversaw their Territory's growing involvement in the Chicago World's Fair. Lannan lobbied for Utah's best interests in Illinois, while Kiesel looked after the Territory's needs back home in the America West. Based on their initial performance as federal delegates, both men were appointed to prominent positions on the committees within the National Commission. Lannan, for instance, was named an alternate on the Board of Control or Executive Committee of the Commission, made up of eight men who governed on behalf of the whole National Commission on a regular basis.[10]

Once the National Commission was formed and its responsibilities assigned to its delegates, it was time to allocate sites for the nation's state and territorial buildings in the northern region of Chicago's Jackson Park. Not surprisingly, this competitive process and its results were contested from beginning to end as members of the Union vied for the best possible location

---

9. David J. Bertuca, comp., *The World's Columbian Exposition: A Centennial Bibliographic Guide* (Westport, Conn.: Greenwood Press, 1996), 167; Bolotin and Laing, *World's Columbian Exposition*, 111–112; and John J. Flinn, comp., *Official Guide to the World's Columbian Exposition* (Chicago: Columbian Guide Company, 1893), 160–161.

10. "Worthily Done," *Deseret News*, December 2, 1893; and McDaniel, *Utah at the World's Columbian Exposition*, 9–11.

for their visitor's center. In the days leading up to the allocation of lots, all of the delegates to the National Commission toured Jackson Park, armed with blueprints displaying the potential sites. It quickly became clear that lot thirty-eight, with its exposure to main pedestrian thoroughfares, would be fought over by a number of states, especially those from the East Coast. The allocation process devolved into a free-for-all, each state and territory contesting for the premier spots. Utah representative Lannan determined to fight for his territory's preferred site. A westerner who believed that possession was key when it came to property rights, Lannan came up with an ingenious plan. It rained on the day the lots were assigned; still Utah's delegate squatted on the site during the downpour, his head covered by an umbrella, his mouth puffing on a cigar. Lannan's strategy and theatrics had their desired effect: the National Commission awarded Utah lot thirty-eight, despite its territorial status.[11]

About this same time, Utah Commissioner Kiesel attended the January 1892 meetings of the Utah legislature to lobby for the financial interests of the Territory at the Columbian Exposition. He mobilized a number of Utah residents sympathetic to his cause, who too were convinced of the importance of Utah's being nobly represented in Chicago. The chambers of commerce of both Salt Lake and Ogden, Utah's two major cities, gathered thousands of resident signatures on a special petition that encouraged their elected representatives to allocate $100,000 to the Utah World's Fair cause. During the legislative session, however, a major debate arose over the proposed amount. Eventually the House passed a bill offering $25,000, only a quarter of the needed funding, and appointed a commission of five men to oversee the spending and construction of the Utah Territory building. In response, the Council members canceled the five appointments and instead suggested that the governor should select fifteen commissioners for the same task and raised the proposed allocation to $50,000, still only half of the needed amount. After more wrangling and negotiating between the two legislative bodies, they agreed to the $50,000 amount and fifteen-commissioner plan. Both houses passed the revised plan and then forwarded it the Governor Thomas for his signature. But Thomas vetoed the proposed bill, citing the Organic Act of the Territory, which ensured that the governor not the legislature had the power to appoint all officers. Kiesel and his supporters did all they could to resolve the stalemate between the governor and the legislature, but the legislative session came to a close before the compromise was reached.

---

11. McDaniel, *Utah at the World's Columbian Exposition*, 11–13.

A growing number of Utah citizens grew concerned that their Territory might lack representation at the Exposition, as funding remained uncertain.[12]

To complicate matters, when representatives of other American states and territories learned from Utah newspapers of the funding deadlock, they attempted to confiscate Utah's acquired lot in Jackson Park. Their maneuverings put additional financial pressure on the Utah committee, especially Commissioners Kiesel and Lannan and Governor Thomas. In late March 1892, Governor Thomas finally picked Robert Craig Chambers, Richard Mackintosh, and Nelson A. Empey as Utah's World Fair Commissioners. Days later the three men gathered with a number of colleagues at Salt Lake City's exclusive Alta Club. There they discussed the tasks that needed to be accomplished to exhibit Utah in a credible manner. The group elected Chambers as their president and Edwin A. McDaniel as their secretary. To the new commissioners, Lannan rehearsed his efforts on behalf of Utah in Chicago as a member of the National Commission, including how he secured the coveted site for the territorial building. With only $3,000 earmarked for personal expenses at their disposal, the commissioners determined they would need at least $50,000 to construct a territorial building and exhibit worthy of Utah. But they could not proceed with their plans until they had money to bankroll their exhibition ambitions. Although somewhat discouraged by the task ahead of them, the commissioners and their staff pledged to ensure that Utah received the national and international attention that it deserved.[13]

Days later, the Utah World's Fair Commissioners met again to finalize their administrative organization. They elected Mackintosh as vice president, Empey as executive commissioner, and Heber M. Wells as treasurer. They spent the balance of the meeting debating how to most effectively fundraise to meet the financial demands of constructing a territorial building together with attention-gathering exhibits in Chicago. The commissioners decided to apply for a substantial financial advance: they would contact a number of Utah banks and request loans up to $3,000. These "World's Fair Loans" would then be securitized by a certificate of indebtedness by leading territorial residents who pledged to pay back the amount plus 8 percent interest if the legislature failed to fund the enterprise. Over the next several weeks, the commissioners advanced their plan and laid out its specifics. Moreover, after consulting with several prominent lawyers the commissioners were convinced

---

12. McDaniel, *Utah at the World's Columbian Exposition*, 13–14.

13. McDaniel, *Utah at the World's Columbian Exposition*, 14–15, 69.

that it was legal for the legislature to allocate funds to such an undertaking. The plan was a success as Utah bankers and citizens agreed to the proposed terms. The $50,000 was now available, whether through the legislature or private citizens of Utah.[14]

The Utah World's Fair Commissioners were now ready to contract formal plans for its territorial building in Jackson Park. Commissioners Empey and McDaniel traveled by train to Chicago, where they formally accepted lot thirty-eight from the Columbian Exposition's lead architect Daniel Burnham on behalf of the citizens of Utah. Burnham and his colleagues counseled the Utah delegation to not erect a costly building, but rather to invest their financial resources in their Territory's exhibits. They stressed to the Utah representatives that what they displayed in their territorial headquarters and across the fairgrounds was more important than the main edifice itself. Not only was this sound advice—it was the financial constraint that bound the Utah Commission. Over the next year, Utah spent about $60,000 on its exhibits and building. But other western states expended double or triple that amount. Colorado, for example, paid out $177,000 and Montana used up $119,200. Notwithstanding the tremendous variance in spending, many Utahns felt that their Territory was able to stretch its dollars in impressive ways. "I think all who visited the Exposition and saw the exhibits made by the States above referred to, and compared the exhibits and buildings with the buildings and exhibits of Utah, will be convinced that, for the amount expended, Utah accomplished as much as any other State," one Salt Laker claimed once the Chicago World's Fair was over.[15]

The commissioners next invited the Territory's leading architects to propose plans for the Utah Building. Although a number of architectural firms submitted impressive plans, most of these plans called for an expensive edifice that outstripped available funds. The commission awarded the coveted contract to the firm of Dallas and Hedges, with the stipulation that the building must be completed on time and under budget. By July 1892, the preliminary schematics were completed and McDaniel carried them to Ogden for display to drum up interest in Utah's involvement in the Columbian Exposition. "The blue prints of the Utah building are out and show an extremely handsome and imposing structure," one reporter noted.[16] He also shared that because of financial constraints the Utah Commission had come

---

14. McDaniel, *Utah at the World's Columbian Exposition*, 16, 69–70.

15. McDaniel, *Utah at the World's Columbian Exposition*, 17 and 83.

16. "Utah at the Exposition," *Ogden Standard Examiner*, July 10, 1892.

up with an innovative way to gather the materials: they would ask for donations of building supplies from wood, iron, glass, and stone dealers across the Territory. Later that month, Dallas and McDaniel traveled to Chicago and presented their Territory's final architectural plans to Burnham for official approval. But Burnham was skeptical that the proposed structure could be built for $12,000, the cap set by the commission. By now, time was running out: Dallas spent the next three days in Chicago modifying his original plans so that they would fall in line with the imposed financial limitations. He again submitted his plans to Burnham, who accepted the revisions. More detailed drawings were drafted once the men were back in Utah, and by the end of August they had work-ready blueprints and cost estimates. They bid out the project to Chicago construction firms and awarded it to William Harley and Son for $10,500, hundreds of dollars below the price ceiling. On September 1, 1892, the Utah commissioners broke ground in Jackson Park and workmen started construction.[17]

Other Utah Exhibits at the Jackson Park Fairgrounds

Although the Utah Building promised to be the Territory's showcase at the Chicago World's Fair, Utahns also oversaw the creation and administration of a number of crowd-pleasing exhibits, as urged by the fair organizers. Their displays were required to follow official exposition guidelines. In 1891, the World's Columbian Commission issued a book-sized report, detailing the preliminary classifications of exhibits. The major departments were organized as follows: (1) Agriculture (food and its accessories, forestry and forest products, agricultural machinery and appliances); (2) Horticulture; (3) Livestock (domestic and wild animals); (4) Fish, Fisheries, Fish Products, and Apparatus of Fishing; (5) Mines, Mining, and Metallurgy; (6) Machinery; (7) Transportation (railways, vessels, vehicles); (8) Manufactures; (9) Electricity and Electrical Appliances; (10) Fine Arts (painting, sculpture, architecture, decoration); (11) Liberal Arts (education, engineering, public works, constructive architecture, music, drama); and (12) Ethnology and Archaeology (progress of labor and invention, isolated and collective exhibits). The Chicago commissioners then subdivided these departments into smaller classifications called groups and then split these groups into classes. They separated the department of agriculture, for example, into nineteen groups and

17. McDaniel, *Utah at the World's Columbian Exposition*, 17–19.

then further into 118 classes. All together, there were 176 groups and classes. Nearly everything imaginable would be exhibited on the Jackson Park fairgrounds.[18]

In keeping with these guidelines, members of the Utah World's Fair Commission recommended that a number of departments be organized to best advertise the Territory in Chicago. They were confident that Utah could contribute to the overarching fields of agriculture, mines and mining, manufactures, fine arts, ethnology and archaeology, education, and woman's work. But they determined to focus their limited resources on a few specific categories rather than spreading their Territory's treasures too thin. So the commissioners invited the following Utahns to head the corresponding departments: J. W. Sanborn of Logan over agricultural; Dominick "Don" Maguire of Ogden over mining, ethnology, and archaeology; F. W. Jennings of Salt Lake City over manufactures; George M. Ottinger of Salt Lake City over fine arts; and J. F. Millspaugh of Salt Lake City over education. The all-male commission also handpicked a number of Mormon and non-Mormon Utah women to serve as officers of the Territory's Board of Lady Managers. Over the next year, these appointed officials and their departmental members worked hard to prepare appropriate showcases for Chicago.[19]

To begin with, the Utah World's Fair Commissioners believed that their Territory would sparkle through an exhibition of its celebrated and varied minerals specimens. In August 1892 they selected Don Maguire, an Irish Catholic mining engineer and entrepreneur, as chief of the Territory's Department of Mines and Mining. The commissioners instructed Maguire to collect a comprehensive sample of Utah mineral deposits for display in Chicago to advertise the spectacular mining past, present, and future of the Territory. Maguire spent the next eight months visiting Utah's scattered mining camps to locate and procure the finest samples available. He eventually collected museum-quality examples of Utah agate, albertite, antimony, asbestos, bauxite, bismuth, coal, copper, elaterite, garnet, gilsonite, gold, granite, jasper, kaolin, lava, lead, lignite, lime, limestone, manganese, mica, molybdanite, nitrate of potash, onyx, opal, ozocerite, plumbago, pottery clay, quicksilver, realgar, salt, selenite, shale, silver-bearing sandstone, silver, slate, soda, sulphur, topaz, tripoli, wurlzite, and zinc. In early April 1893, just weeks before the Columbian Exposition was scheduled to open, Maguire boarded a

---

18. *Classification of the World's Columbian Exposition, Chicago, U.S.A., 1893* (Chicago: Donohue and Henneberry, 1891).

19. McDaniel, *Utah at the World's Columbian Exposition,* 19–20.

train for Chicago, accompanied by Sandy resident James Cushing, to stage the displays for the minerals in the massive Mines and Mining Building just south of the Utah Building.[20]

Agricultural was the second area in which Utah's commission had high expectations for the Territory to meet at Jackson Park. They appointed well-known Mormon George D. Pyper as superintendent of the Utah Agricultural Pavilion. Pyper was to work under the direction of Professor J. W. Sanborn, at the Utah State Agricultural College (known today as Utah State University) in Logan. Like Maguire, Pyper spent the next several months scouring Utah Territory for the finest agriculture specimens he could locate and then freighting them to Chicago by train. Pyper arrived in Chicago on May 1, 1893, the exposition's opening day, only to discover that Utah's exhibition area in the Agricultural Building was still under construction. Still, he was pleased to note that in time Utah's twenty-six foot by eighty foot agricultural pavilion enjoyed a prominent position, encircled by the state pavilions of Illinois, Kentucky, New Jersey, Ohio, Pennsylvania, and Washington. Unlike these surrounding states, however, Utah did not have the financial resources to make an elaborate farming display, so Pyper, Sanborn, and Salt Lake City farmer Heber Bennion would work together to produce a "neat, plain, farmer-show" that highlighted the produce itself and not the decorative garnish.[21]

A third department in which Utah promised to exhibit well was ethnology, a mix of anthropology and archaeology, because of the Territory's plentiful Native American artifacts. The Utah World's Fair Commissioners again tapped Don Maguire to prepare a credible ethnological exhibit for the Columbian fairgrounds. From summer 1892 until spring 1893, Maguire hunted throughout the Territory in search of ancient American remains and relics. He first traveled to the shoreline of the Great Salt Lake near Willard, Utah, where forty-three prehistoric burial mounds awaited his excavation: these were the sacred resting places of Native Americans who inhabited the region before the coming of Euro-American mountain men and Mormon settlers. With the aid of two assistants, a team of horses and a plow blade, Maguire oversaw the roughshod extraction of pottery, ashes, bones, stone mills, rolling stones, awls, arrowheads, bricks, and a human skeleton. Trained

---

20. Don Maguire, "Report of the Chief of the Department of Mines and Mining, Utah World's Fair Commission," in McDaniel, *Utah at the World's Columbian Exposition*, 91–97.

21. George D. Pyper, "Report of Superintendent of Utah Agricultural Pavilion at the World's Fair," in McDaniel, *Utah at the World's Columbian Exposition*, 99–104.

as a miner, not as an archeologist, Maguire and his team cherry-picked the most interesting items for Utah's exhibit. Maguire's team next traveled to known Native American burial grounds near Plain City, where they ripped the graves open and added two human skulls to their collection. They repeated the process in South Ogden, Paragoonah, Provo, and Payson. Aided by Professor Montgomery of the University of Utah and photographer James H. Crockwell, Maguire's band catalogued and photographed their most significant finds. They also visited St. George and Nine Mile Canyon. While in San Juan County, Bluff City's Platt D. Lyman loaned Maguire's men four well-preserved "cliff dweller" mummies for display in Chicago. Although Maguire's acquisition methods stun and upset modern readers, his belief that Utah's ancient human treasures would fascinate visitors in Chicago would prove correct.[22]

The final territorial department organized for the Chicago World's Fair was the Utah Board of Lady Managers. Comprised of both Mormon and non-Mormon women, the board was led by Margaret Blaine Salisbury, Emily F. Richards, C. W. Lyman, Electa Bullock, and Eunice C. Thatcher. In 1892, these officers helped establish auxiliary women's organizations throughout the Territory. Generally founded on a county basis, two of the first Utah female World's Fair Associations (or Clubs, as they were more commonly called) were formed in Utah County and Salt Lake County, complete with a local executive board, directors, and bylaws. Any Utah woman could join, if she was willing to pay the one dollar membership fee and sign her name to the respective organization's bylaws. Women were also encouraged to meet with their groups on a weekly basis in the months leading up to the Columbian Exposition. These scattered auxiliary organizations were responsible for gathering and manufacturing the finest samples of Utah home industries and women's interests, to be exhibited in the White City.[23] "As many people coming to Chicago will have little idea of the far West, each woman should feel she was a Columbian Exposition apostle, be drawn out of ourselves and make it our part to co-operate," leaders charged the women of Utah County during their inaugural meeting. "Time will prove whether the women of Utah excel in any of the arts or professions," one newspaper editor noted. "We feel safe however in anticipating a strong phalanx of bright intelligent

22. Don Maguire, "Report of the Department of Ethnology, Utah World's Fair Commission," in McDaniel, *Utah at the World's Columbian Exposition*, 105–110.

23. "Utah at the World's Fair," *Ogden Standard Examiner*, June 26, 1892.

and able representatives."[24] The Columbian Exposition encouraged and necessitated the building of bridges between women of every spiritual creed in Mormon-dominated Utah. Hundreds of women throughout the Territory crossed religious lines and became respected colleagues through the experience. By March 1893, the women of Utah were ready to head to Chicago and exhibit their Territory and its majority religion.[25]

The Utah Territory at the Chicago World's Fair

On May 1, 1893, the organizers of the Chicago World's Fair unlocked its doors to the general public. The festivities of Opening Day included invocations and dedications, but the most exciting event occurred when U.S. President Grover Cleveland activated the White City's electricity, setting in motion a massive generator in Machinery Hall. Suddenly water jets shot from the lagoons and the flags of the world's nations were unfurled to the pleasure of fairgoers. Over the next five months the sights, sounds, and smells of the Columbian Exposition lured nearly twenty-eight million Americans and foreigners to Jackson Park. The Chicago World's Fair became the site of a number of firsts in history. It was here that Aunt Jemima of maple syrup fame got her start and where Americans were first introduced to chili con carne, Crackerjacks, the Ferris wheel, long-distance phone calls, zippers, and night sporting events under floodlights. The White City also provided inspiration for Frank Baum's Emerald City in the *Wizard of Oz* and Katherine Bates's lyrics to "America the Beautiful." And a young boy named Walt Disney, whose father worked as a plasterer in the White City, was inspired later in life to create an enchanting theme park known worldwide as Disneyland, after touring the Jackson Park fairgrounds. The masses delighted in the multitude of exhibits scattered throughout the Columbian Exposition.[26]

As hoped by the Utah commissioners, their territorial building was a crowd pleaser in Jackson Park. As *Deseret News* reporter Josephine Spencer

24. "The Ladies of Utah County," *Salt Lake Tribune*, September 24, 1892; and "World's Fair Salt Lake County Association of Women," *Deseret News*, October 22, 1892.

25. "World's Fair Work: S. L. County Ladies Organized," *Woman's Exponent* 21, no. 7 (October 1, 1892): 52; "By Laws of the Salt Lake County World's Fair Association," *Woman's Exponent* 21, no. 9 (November 1, 1892): 69; "Editorial Notes," *Woman's Exponent* 21, no. 17 (March 15, 1893): 141; Jill Mulvay Derr, Janath Russell Cannon, and Maureen Ursenbach Beecher, eds., *Women of Covenant: The Story of Relief Society* (Salt Lake City: Deseret Book, 1992), 140.

26. Bolotin and Laing, *World's Columbian Exposition*, 27–31; and Bertuca, *World's Columbian Exposition: A Centennial Bibliographic Guide*, 364–365.

described to readers back west, the Utah Building's exterior façade was framed by a scaled-down replica of the Eagle Gate bronze that loomed sentinel-like over State Street in Utah's capital city. To the right of the building stood a full-body statute of Mormon leader Brigham Young by celebrated sculptor Cyrus E. Dallin, and to the left was a garden gazebo. After passing under the Eagle Gate and climbing a short flight of steps, visitors entered the edifice through large doors and immediately found themselves in the main central hall filled with display cases. To the entry's right was a set of doors that opened into two tucked-away reception rooms, and to the left was a matching set of doors leading to the Utah Commission's suite of offices. The reception hall offered guests a respite from the hustle and bustle of the crowds, a place where visitors could retire in plush chairs for a good rest off their feet. A circular flight of stairs transported guests from the ground floor to a second-story interior balcony area from which they could take in the exhibits and crowds from above. Also on the elevated story, directly above the reception rooms and commissioner offices below on the ground floor were the private residences of the appointed Utah commissioners who lived in the building the duration of the Columbian Exposition. As such, the excitement and action were generally limited to the main level of the Utah Building.[27]

The center of the Utah Building's main room was dominated by a massive circular divan, a popular piece of furniture in its day, which provided seating for footsore visitors, together with ornate wooden chairs scattered throughout the hall. The matching beige carpets, walls, and woodwork gave the room an airy feeling that encouraged visitors to focus their attention on the myriad of small and large display cases lining the walls of the exhibit hall. Homespun handicrafts of women working under the auspices of the Utah Board of Lady Managers were featured prominently in the room, including noteworthy lacework, knitting, crocheting, embroidery, leatherwork, silk, linens, and leather goods gathered from all over the Territory. Where not covered by display cases, the room's walls were adorned with the paintings of well-regarded Utah artists such as James Taylor Harwood, Henry Adolphus Culmer, Marie Gorlinski Hughes, and Kate Wells. Framed prints of Utah landscapes by photographer James H. Crockwell also decorated the walls. Seventeen-year-old Utahn LeRoi C. Snow wrote of the room: "All of the furniture is home-made, and the pictures have been made and drawn in Utah. Hanging about eighteen feet from the floor is a flag made from the wool of sheep, and the stars and

---

27. Spencer, "Some of the State Buildings at the Exposition," 658.

stripes have been dyed. This flag is about sixteen feet in length, and about four feet wide."[28] The banner was a not-so-subtle reminder of Utah's patriotism. For visitor browsing, a sample of Utah home literature, including the writings of Orson F. Whitney and Alfred Lambourne and other local poets and songwriters, was housed in a large bookcase of the late President Brigham Young. Bound copies of Mormon periodicals like the *Contributor, Juvenile Instructor, Young Woman's Journal,* and *Woman's Exponent* also lined its shelves.[29]

The Utah Board of Lady Managers tapped Emmeline B. Wells to edit an anthology of poetry written by many of Utah's leading female writers and poetesses specifically for display at the Columbian Exposition. The thirty-four poems making up *Songs and Flowers of the Wasatch* (1893) are largely secular in nature, notable exceptions being Latter-day Saint Eliza R. Snow's "Invocation" ("Oh, My Father"), a popular poem turned LDS hymn on the existence of both a Heavenly Father and a Heavenly Mother, as well as Roman Catholic Ruby Lamont's "Sonnets on the Virgin Mary." The anthology's final poem "Utah," by Latter-day Saint Ruth M. Fox, summarizes all that both the women (and men) of Utah were trying to advertise to outsiders at the fair. "Thy mountains are pregnant with minerals rare;/Thine orchards and meadows are fruitful and fair,/With scepter of peace which thou hold'st in thine hand/Thou sittest a queen in the midst of the land," Fox concluded by extolling the natural resources and hidden treasures of the Utah Territory.[30] "It is certainly a very beautiful book, and Utah may well be proud of the work, both poetical and artistic," a reviewer noted of this poetry collection.[31] Utah women hoped that visitors to the Utah Building, after perusing their poems, might reevaluate the refinement and sophistication of not only Utah, but also its fair daughters, heretofore viewed as subjected women and sexual slaves in a polygamous society. Emmeline B. Wells also edited and made available *Charities and Philanthropies: Woman's Work in Utah* (1893) at the Utah Building.[32]

---

28. LeRoi C. Snow, "My Visit to the World's Columbian Exposition," *Young Woman's Journal* 5, no. 2 (November 1893): 66–67.

29. Spencer, "Some of the State Buildings at the Exposition," 659; and "Editorial Notes," *Woman's Exponent* 21, no. 21 (April 15 and May 1, 1893): 156.

30. Emmeline B. Wells, ed., *Songs and Flowers of the Wasatch* (Salt Lake City: George Q. Cannon and Sons, 1893).

31. "Editorial Notes," *Woman's Exponent* 21, no. 23 (June 1, 1893): 175.

32. Emmeline B. Wells, ed., *Charities and Philanthropies: Woman's Work in Utah* (Salt Lake City: George Q. Cannon and Sons, 1893).

This same women's organization also determined to write a religious history of Utah for fairgoers in Chicago and as a commemorative keepsake from the exposition for Utahns. Latter-day Saint suffrage activist Sarah M. G. Kimball chaired the publication committee and was aided by Roman Catholic W. S. McCornick, Methodist W. D. Mabry, Presbyterian J. McVicker, Baptist H. B. Steelman, Evangelical Sunday School Association and Christian Endeavor Association member C. H. Parsons, Unitarian R. P. Utter, and A. C. Ewing, who served as committee secretary. "It is the earnest desire of members of the committee that a closer feeling of unity, and a broader desire for general helpfulness may result from the study of this little volume which we dedicate with love and prayers to the World's Columbian Exposition," the volume's preface declares (vi–vii). The book reads like a typical compilation of turn-of-the-century denominational histories with chapters on Mormons, Catholics, Episcopalians, Presbyterians, Methodists, Baptists, the Central Christian Church, Unitarians, the Utah Sunday School Association, the Utah Christian Endeavor Work, and Judaism. But the volume also reveals the power structure of religion in Utah: half of the book's pages are devoted to Mormon historian Andrew Jenson's overview of the church in Utah. The balance of the contents is filled with the histories of ten other Christian and Jewish denominations and associations. That these female representatives from these various faiths were willing to engage in such an interfaith project illustrates the importance they viewed this singular historic moment in Chicago. Their resulting *World's Fair Ecclesiastical History of Utah* (1893) was featured prominently in the Utah Building.[33]

But the most celebrated display in the Utah Building, and perhaps in all of the state and territory buildings, was that of a fifteen-hundred-year-old Native American mummy, excavated years earlier from a cliff dweller tomb in San Juan County, Utah. Recall how Don Maguire, on behalf of the Territory's department of archaeology and ethnology, gathered artifacts from the southeastern Utah archaeological digs of Charles McCloyd, Charles Graham, and the Wetherill brothers, including this mummy, for display in Chicago. His staff exhibited the petrified corpse, still wrapped in linens, in a glass museum case surrounded by the artifacts discovered in the same ancient grave, including clothing, a corn pot, and a woven basket, in various states of decay. The ancient American artifacts and artworks, relics, pottery, braiding, carving, and embroidery, captured the imagination of visitors from all over the fair. These were the major exhibit but there were other displays scattered throughout the main hall and in the hallways leading to the reception room and commissioner offices.[34]

The exhibits and public relations efforts of Utah Territory also spilled beyond the physical footprint of the Utah Building and into many of the fairground's buildings dedicated to the exhibition of specific industries. In the liberal arts department, for instance, Utah staged an impressive exhibit that judges later awarded nine medals. The Territory's display on education was well received and caught the attention of potential immigrants to the Great Basin. "The Utah educational exhibit was not intended to be in competition with other States as to results attained, but was made for the purpose of showing visitors our system in embryo," one official noted. "The groundwork of what is to be the educational system of the State was well illustrated by the exhibition made in this department, and, among people who were versed in the science of public educational systems, was highly commended."[35] The Territory also staged a handful of exhibits in the Transportation Building, including that of a home-manufactured buggy that received one of the judges' medals and generated publicity for Utah. But these minor displays were overshadowed by Utah's major exhibitions—mining and agriculture—together with the ethnographical and the Board of Lady Managers' displays inside the Utah Building.[36]

Utah's mining exhibit was not ready until May 15, 1893, two weeks after the public opening of the Chicago World's Fair, due to construction delays of the attractive oak display cases. When finished, the Utah mining pavilion measured twenty-seven feet by sixty feet and was surrounded by the displays of Montana, Idaho, Mexico, and New Mexico. All of the minerals were clearly labeled, to the relief of observers unfamiliar with many of the specimens. Utahn Don Maguire lived in Chicago during the duration of the fair and personally staffed the exhibit pavilion as hundreds of thousands of fairgoers from all over the world admired Utah's mineral resources, along with those of other American states and territories. He and James Cushing distributed brochures advertising the diverse and plentiful mining opportunities in Utah. "It is a source of pride and gratification to state that in variety of specimens shown, the entire collection of the exhibits of our immediate neighbors could not

34. Spencer, "Some of the State Buildings at the Exposition," 659–660; and Maguire, "Report of the Department of Ethnology," 105–110.

35. McDaniel, *Utah at the World's Columbian Exposition*, 38.

36. McDaniel, "Secretary's Report," 79–81.

equal Utah," the commission's secretary would later note. "It was this wonderful variety that secured for Utah the distinction of having the best mineral
exhibit of the Exposition."[37]

Maguire and Cushing were overwhelmed by domestic and international
fairgoers and foreign government officials who took interest in their territory's natural resources. Still, the two men did all they could to promote Utah's
mineral exhibits in the Mines and Mining Building (figure 4). "In the great
Exposition our mineral exhibit stood in the first rank of States and nations.
Our minerals outnumbered in variety and beauty those of any other country.
And from other States and nations every mark of favor and courtesy was
shown to us," Maguire described.[38] That summer the World's Fair judges would
award the Utah Mines and Mining Exhibits thirty medals for their specimens
at the exposition. And when the fairgrounds were closed that October,

FIGURE 4 Entrance to the Utah mineral pavilion in the Mines and Mining Building at the
Chicago World's Fair, September 1893, courtesy of the Church History Library, The Church
of Jesus Christ of Latter-day Saints, Salt Lake City, Utah.

37. Maguire, "Report of the Chief of the Department of Mines and Mining," 95–96; and
McDaniel, "Secretary's Report," 77–78.

38. Maguire, "Report of the Chief of the Department of Mines and Mining," 95.

Maguire and his staffers were in a strong position to make mineral sample exchanges with a number of entities, including British Columbia, Canada, Chile, Japan, Mexico, New South Wales, Nova Scotia, and South Africa, as well as exchanges with fellow U.S. states and territories like Arkansas, Arizona, California, Colorado, Montana, New Mexico, Washington, Wisconsin, and Wyoming. Utah's specimens, together with those acquired from these nations and states, were anticipated to become part of the University of Utah's school of mining collection or Utah's Exposition Building, to help the citizens of Utah better appreciate all that they had to offer.[39]

Likewise, the Utah agricultural pavilion received hundreds of thousands of visitors during the Columbian Exposition. George Pyper, Heber Bennion, and J. W. Sanborn's no-frills farmer show drew large crowds day after day. "Our oats, wheat and barley were unrivaled; our grasses stood every test applied, and showed a marked superiority over those from any other State. It was clearly demonstrated that Utah yields more wealth from the soil per capita, than any other State," Pyper exclaimed. The Territory's agricultural exhibits included over three dozen varieties of wheat, over two dozen types of wheat shown in straw, over two dozen varieties of oats, over one dozen types of oats shown in straw, nearly a dozen types of barley, six types of barley shown in straw, seventeen types of grasses, and a variety of corns. Utah's miscellaneous displays featured hay and haymaking, sugarcane, sugar beets, wool production, spring water, farm photographs, irrigation, farming statistics, soil statistics, and a variety of plows. Curious visitors also paid rapt attention to Utah's irrigation maps and innovative irrigation diagrams, which described how the Mormon pioneers had made the Territory's desert "blossom as the rose." Fair commissioners eventually decorated Utah with thirteen awards for its agricultural exhibit, including the world's grand prize for its barley. Pyper was convinced that Utah's exhibit would have been even more successful had they been able to provide more specific agricultural statistics. Nevertheless, Pyper was thrilled with their pavilion's showing in Chicago: "I will say that this one booth alone has been of inestimable value to the Territory. It opened the eyes of the East to our wonderful agricultural resources and possibilities, and no doubt will bring to the Territory many desirable citizens interested in agricultural pursuits."[40]

---

39. Maguire, "Report of the Chief of the Department of Mines and Mining," 95–96.

40. Pyper, "Report of Superintendent of Utah Agricultural Pavilion," 99–104.

Mormon writer Josephine Spencer was similarly pleased with the Territory's building and major exhibits on the fairgrounds, yet she felt that Utah had even more to offer than was being showcased in Chicago. "In regard to the display in the Utah Building it may be said that though not as satisfactory and complete as it might have been had more money been devoted to the enterprise and more interest taken by the people in general in the matter of Utah's proper representation at the Fair, yet the exhibit taken altogether is excellent as far as it goes, and no doubt attracts considerable attention," she conceded. Spencer then suggested that more of Utah's craftsmanship, like hand-painted china and skilled embroidery, might have better showcased Utah's talents, especially that of its ladies. She reasoned that perhaps many of the artists were afraid that their works would be damaged in transport from Utah to Chicago and lamented that the displays in the Utah Building in Chicago could not hold a candle to the quality and quantity showcased at home fairs throughout Utah. Notwithstanding these weaknesses, Spencer reminded her Utah readers with pride that people "from every country and clime on the face of the globe" visited the Columbian Exposition and were there exposed to the many offerings of Utah and her citizens. Utahns had seized upon this unprecedented opportunity and would certainly be rewarded in the future with an improved image and greater public awareness of the Territory's many contributions to the greatness of America.[41]

The Utah Building received positive reviews in the promotional literature created for the Chicago cultural celebration. The authors of the *Handbook of the World's Columbian Exposition* described the renaissance-style Utah Building as "quite attractive" and noted that its lead architect had also drawn up plans for a number of the most attractive edifices in Idaho, Nevada, and Wyoming. "The entrance is reached by a spacious approach and broad steps leading to a semicircular portico, which forms the principal feature of the south front," they depicted and then detailed the buildings interior layout and exhibits.[42] Similarly, the compiler of *The Best Things to be Seen at the World's Fair* highlighted the Utah Building and featured a woodcut image of the building, an advertisement not afforded to all of the American states and territories. He was impressed by the imposing Eagle Gate statue, a miniature copy of the original standing in downtown Salt Lake City, but could not resist the opportunity to criticize the notorious Mormon practice of plural marriage.

---

41. Spencer, "Some of the State Buildings at the Exposition," 660–661.

42. *Rand, McNally and Company's Handbook of the World's Columbian Exposition* (Chicago: Rand, McNally and Company, 1893), 198–199.

"The gilded eagle, with outstretched wings, symbolizing hospitable protection to all who may seek it, rests on four flaring supports, which slope from the center to the sustaining columns. Apart from its association with polygamy, it is simple, tasteful and pleasing in appearance."[43] The specter of plural marriage would continue to haunt the Latter-day Saints in their quest for respectability during and after the exposition. Finally, the pocket-sized *Official Guide to the World's Columbian Exposition* praised Utah Territory for having the vision to erect its own building, unlike some other territories and states. It also featured a hand-drawn sketch of the building for its readers.[44]

During the summer of 1893, the Utah Building also housed the Territory's official bureau of information. Commission Secretary Edwin McDaniel and his team, including a number of staffers from the Utah Board of Lady Managers, were besieged by the interest expressed by domestic and foreign visitors seeking official information on Utah Territory. Unlike many other state and territorial contingents, the Utahns did not prepare a formal brochure for the masses of fairgoers. To complicate matters, foreign government representatives eschewed any printed promotional literature featuring Utah unless it was stamped with the commission's sanctioned seal. So the information bureau's staff had to mark every piece of paper related to Utah with the Territory's endorsed hallmark. But they still ran out of literature on a regular basis, including copies of the Salt Lake Chamber of Commerce's recent annual report. In fact, it was the Rio Grande Western and the Union Pacific railroads that had vested interests in promoting the scenic territory, which provided the best literature on Utah during the Columbian Exposition. J. H. Bennett of the Rio Grande Western, for example, gave out copies of the picture book *Utah*, which was deemed by many to be the most attractive book distributed at the fair on any of the states and territories. And Edward L. Lomax of the Union Pacific Railroad also distributed his company's own marketing literature on Utah. Both promotional railroad pieces were also stamped with Utah's official seal, thereby legitimizing it in the minds of the curious. Taken altogether, Utah staffers handed out about 21,500 promotional brochures on their territory, in addition to miscellaneous newspapers and brochures.[45]

---

43. John J. Flinn, comp., *The Best Things to be Seen at the World's Fair* (Chicago: Columbian Guide Company, 1893), 161–162.

44. John J. Flinn, comp., *Official Guide to the World's Columbian Exposition*, 160–161.

45. "Utah at the World's Fair," *Ogden Standard Examiner*, June 26, 1892; and McDaniel, "Secretary's Report," 84–85.

Territorial officials and staffers tracked the number of daily visitors to the Utah Building during the duration of the Columbian Exposition. These representatives understood the importance of being able to justify and account for the large investment of territorial funds in this unprecedented spectacle. They were delighted by the high traffic generated by both their territorial edifice and exhibits in Jackson Park. According to the commission's best estimates, an average of ten thousand guests visited the Utah Building every day for over five consecutive months. This numeric approximation was aided by mechanical turnstiles equipped with counters in the main entrance, as well as human headcounters responsible for computing how many visitors entered the Utah Building during five minute increments at 9:00 A.M., 11:00 A.M., and 3:00 P.M. each day, since auxiliary exits allowed for foot traffic leakage. Each night at 6:00 P.M. when the Utah Building closed down along with the other state and territory structures, staff members reconciled these two sets of numbers, which resulted in trustworthy attendance figures. Granted, some days were busier than others for the Utah Building staffers. On September 8, for example, nearly sixteen thousand people swarmed the site, many of whom were in town to celebrate Utah Day at the Fair. Ironically, non-Utahns were sometimes more impressed with the Territory's exhibits than were Utah residents. Some Utahns, like Josephine Spencer, felt that the Utah Territory might have done more in Chicago to advance its standing.[46]

As one would expect, Utah visitors used their territory's edifice in Jackson Park as a natural gathering place for family and friends while they toured the World's Fair. Most were eager to document their presence in Chicago for posterity. "Men and women feel a pride in having their names recorded, however humbly, in connection with the great events, and Utah at the World's Columbian Exposition would not be complete did it not contain the names of the Utah citizens who visited the Fair and registered at the Utah building," Edwin McDaniel noted.[47] So the territorial commission provided a registration book for its fellow Utahns to record their personal information, hoping that all guests from Utah, regardless of gender or age, would sign their names and describe their backgrounds in the book. As with some of the best-laid plans, however, many Utahns penned their names in the wrong alphabetical section, did not record where they were staying or where they were from in

46. McDaniel, *Utah at the World's Columbian Exposition*, 41.

47. McDaniel, *Utah at the World's Columbian Exposition*, 173.

Utah Territory, or neglected to register how long they would be in the White City. To complicate matters, a number of non-Utahns, likely Latter-day Saints from other states and territories of the Union, sought to register in the Utah Territory book because of their affinity or personal ties to the Territory, even though the Utah organizers made available a separate book for these friends of the eventual Beehive State. Finally, there were some Utah residents who wrote illegibly and others who registered multiple times or not at all. Taking all of these factors into consideration, however, about seven thousand Utahns converged on the White City, and the vast majority of these were Latter-day Saints.[48]

As American as Our Neighbors

After decades of geographical isolation and theological separation from their non-Mormon brothers and sisters, Latter-day Saints and Utahns sought to be as American as their neighbors. The 1893 Chicago World's Fair offered citizens of the traditionally Mormon Utah Territory the chance to remake their image and refashion their appearance in Jackson Park on the world's largest stage. The Utah World's Fair Commission, a government-sanctioned body, coordinated efforts to remove prejudice against its territory, including bias against its predominant religion, the Mormon faith. All involved in this territorial effort realized that to heighten the profile of one was to improve the reputation of the other. Utahns of both LDS and non-LDS persuasion were eager to remove the dark cloud of misrepresentation and past misunderstandings that had hung for so long over the Territory. They anticipated that their renewed public embrace of Victorian values might grant them membership in the American establishment from which they had been so long estranged. Moreover, Utahns of every stripe hoped that their territory might finally be granted its long sought after statehood in the near future. Through a careful orchestration of displays showcasing Utah's natural resources, agricultural successes, archaeological treasures, and refined women, the peoples of Utah made tremendous strides in beginning to convince outsiders that they were as American as their Union neighbors. "Utah certainly has lost nothing by participating in the World's Columbian Exposition," a reporter for the Ogden *Standard Examiner* exclaimed. Even the wealthy and populous state of

---

48. Andrew Jenson, *Church Chronology: A Record of Important Events Pertaining to the History of the Church of Jesus Christ of Latter-day Saints* (Salt Lake City: Deseret News, 1899), 201; and McDaniel, *Utah at the World's Columbian Exposition*, 173–175.

California had only three thousand of its sons and daughters attend the Chicago World's Fair. "To her credit it may be said that no State or Territory of the Union can boast of a greater percentage of population attending the great Fair that she, and certainly no citizens from any other section appreciated the wonders of the memorable Exposition more than did the Utonians," the same newspaperman noted.[49] The over-representation of Latter-day Saints from Utah indicates their deep-seated desire to finally be recognized and well regarded.

Over two million non-Mormon visitors toured the Utah Building during the summer of 1893. This number does not even account for those fairgoers who were exposed to other major and minor Utah exhibits scattered throughout Jackson Park. "It is safe to say, therefore, that no better opportunity could have been afforded in the way of advertising than by taking part in the Exposition," one Utahn exulted. "Utah is better known to-day than ever before."[50] In fact, when the Utah commissioners returned to Utah, they presented a formal report to their newly elected governor Caleb W. West. "For years past there has been a widespread prejudice [i.e., anti-Mormonism] against Utah and her citizens. We know that the exhibit we made at Chicago has served, in a great measure, to obliterate that feeling among the masses of the people, and the good seed sown will continue to bear fruit for years to come." The commissioners then highlighted the celebrated contributions of the Territory of Utah to the Fair, including its mining resources, agricultural achievements, and irrigation displays. Even more important, however, was the Territory's displayed human capital: "Our citizens are as intelligent and enterprising as those of any other country. Our men and women challenged the admiration of the world."[51] The Territory of Utah, the commissioners believed, would be the recipient of great "blessings" in the years to come because of its financial investments in the Columbian Exposition. Another Utah resident said: "During the past six months this Territory has been better advertised than ever before. The entire contingent from Utah have talked themselves hoarse and distributed much literature, and the value to the Territory has been double the amount expended."[52]

49. "World's Fair Report," *Ogden Standard Examiner*, January 18, 1894.

50. McDaniel, *Utah at the World's Columbian Exposition*, 41.

51. McDaniel, *Utah at the World's Columbian Exposition*, 43.

52. "World's Fair Report," *Ogden Standard Examiner*, January 18, 1894.

3

Mormon Matriarchs

LDS LADIES AT THE WORLD'S CONGRESS OF REPRESENTATIVE WOMEN

We, the [Mormon] women of Utah, have been considered
slaves and fools, have been looked upon as without mind
or intelligence. That we are true to our husbands and
families has been accounted to us as a sure mark of vile
inferiority of intellect. And now we are met by these
wide-minded, deep-thoughted women in Chicago as
equals, as women with at least mind enough to speak for
ourselves. What a glorious opportunity to preach some
of the most important truths of our religion!*
— *Young Woman's Journal*, 1893

We wish the sisters to comprehend the fact that though
[Mormon participation] may seem a small affair in itself,
yet it will go into the history of the great Congress, and
be on record and circulated all over the world. It was an
unprecedented opportunity and there never was before
in the history of the world such a gathering of women, as
the World's Congress of Representative Women
assembled on that wonderful occasion.**
— *Woman's Exponent*, 1893

ON MAY 20, 1893, just weeks after the Utah World's Fair Commissioners
opened their Territory's building at the Chicago World's Fair, a member of
The Church of Jesus Christ of Latter-day Saints penned a letter to her fellow Latter-day Saints back West. She excitedly described what had just tran-

---

* "Editor's Department," *Young Woman's Journal* 4, no. 7 (April 1893): 326.

** "Editorial Notes," *Woman's Exponent* 21, no. 24 (June 15, 1893): 181.

spired at the World's Congress of Representative Women. "It goes without question that you are interested in the sisters who came to this great congress of women as representatives from our own loved Utah," she exclaimed. "Well, the day upon which our meetings were held was the 19th of this month. It dawned clear and warm, for which we were thankful, as it has been very cold nearly all the time since our arrival." The unidentified woman then offered her fellow Latter-day Saints a blow-by-blow account of the participation of their church representatives in two special Mormon sessions at the women's congress. Eventually published in the *Young Woman's Journal*, her account chronicled details such as what music was played, who offered the prayers, where the participants sat, how the delivered remarks were received, when impromptu comments were offered, and even why Zina Young Card's homemade silk dress created a stir of admiration among the non-Mormon women during the gathering. The correspondent concluded her recital with a summary of the tributes that non-Mormon luminaries Elizabeth Sele Saxon, Isabella Beecher Hooker, and Mrs. Solomon Thatcher paid to Latter-day Saint women in the White City. She further pointed out that Apostle John Henry Smith, and his male ecclesiastical companions in attendance, "gave us their approval at its close, and all were cognizant of the fact that God was with us" in Chicago.[1]

Ironically, the First Presidency's male representative Brigham H. Roberts would be denied a similar opportunity to speak on behalf of the church in the same Art Palace during the subsequent World's Parliament of Religions that September. Why were Mormon women like Zina Young Card and Emmeline B. Wells welcomed with open arms in Chicago while their male counterparts like Roberts were excluded? It seems that most Americans viewed Latter-day Saint women as hapless victims of polygamy, while they believed Mormon men to be the lascivious perpetrators of the alternative marriage system. These women needed to be lifted up while the Mormon patriarchy deserved to be put down, many thought. Moreover, professional relationships and personal friendships between Mormon and non-Mormon women seem to have made a major difference in the varied receptions. Female leaders of the Latter-day Saint auxiliaries were charter members of the National Council of Women (NCW) and affiliated feminist organizations. Representatives of the Relief Society (figure 5), YLMIA (Young Ladies Mutual Improvement Association), and the Primary Association not only attended the 1888 and 1891 meetings in Washington, D.C., they also helped plan the gatherings. "From the first the Utah women have enjoyed an excellent reputation in the Council for their

---

1. "Miscellaneous," *Young Woman's Journal* 4, no. 9 (June 1893): 427–429.

C.R.Savage,   Salt Lake City.

FIGURE 5 General President of the female Relief Society Zina D. Young of The Church of Jesus Christ of Latter-day Saints, courtesy of the Church History Library, The Church of Jesus Christ of Latter-day Saints, Salt Lake City, Utah.

thorough business methods. The Relief Society and the Young Ladies' Mutual Improvement Associations have not only promptly paid their dues, and other solicited contributions, but they have also sent to the various sessions each year two or more representatives," Susa Young Gates explained. Although some women initially objected to the inclusion of Latter-day Saints in American feminist organizations in the late 1880s, they were overruled by inclusive voices, like that of Susan B. Anthony.[2]

2. Susa Young Gates, *History of the Young Ladies' Mutual Improvement Association of The Church of Jesus Christ of Latter-day Saints, from November 1869 to June 1910* (Salt Lake City: Deseret News, 1911), 204.

The female leadership of the World's Congress of Representative Women likewise privileged feminist values over religious beliefs.[3] Theirs was a women's organization—not a Christian association—although nearly all of their members were Protestants. The goal of the 1893 female congress was gender equality not religious aggrandizement. Moreover, many conservative women's church groups, for whatever reason, declined to participate in the National Council of Women (NCW) and the 1893 conference, freeing up room for the Mormons. Although many of the affiliated female organizations, including the Latter-day Saint Relief Society and Young Ladies' National Mutual Improvement Association (YLMIA), were associated with religious bodies, they were there to showcase their religion's contributions to the improvement of women's circumstances rather than debate theology. Of the Mormon involvement in such groups, Susa Young Gates wrote: "Certainly this has not been done with idle or sinister motives. An honest desire to meet and dispel the prejudices of women of the world has been one of the motives of the Mormon women. There has been no effort made to proselyte in the Council for that is contrary to the Council's idea; but a frank opportunity to know what manner of women the Mormon women are has been offered during these congresses."[4] For Latter-day Saint women in Utah, the 1893 Exposition offered unique opportunities to work with other women's groups. "The ideals and concerns of the Relief Society, however, meshed comfortably with many of the objectives of the councils, and its highly effective network and long experience in fund raising relieved it of many of the financial impediments faced by some of the newer women's groups," historian Carol Cornwall Madsen explains.[5]

The 1893 World's Congress of Representative Women was a watershed moment in the American feminist movement. "This Congress was, without doubt, the largest and most representative gathering of women ever convened in this or any other country," General Secretary Clarence E. Young claimed of

3. Sources on the World's Congress of Representative Women include Mary Kavanaugh Oldham Eagle, ed., *The Congress of Women Held in the Woman's Building, World's Columbian Exposition, Chicago, U S.A., 1893; With Portraits, Biographies, and Addresses* (Chicago: International Publishing, 1895); and Jeanne Madeline Weimann, *The Fair Women: The Story of the Woman's Building, World's Columbian Exposition, Chicago, 1893* (Chicago: Academy Chicago, 1981).

4. Gates, *History of the YLMIA*, 204.

5. Carol Cornwall Madsen, "'The Power of Combination': Emmeline B. Wells and the National and International Councils of Women," *BYU Studies* 33, no. 4 (1993): 651–652.

the gathering.[6] Feminist May Wright Sewall declared: "The proceedings of a group of meetings [which are] probably among the most remarkable ever convened. This is not said in forgetfulness of the councils of Nicea and Trent, of the pregnant interview between King John and his Barons, and of the first Continental Congress; but in the belief that with these, and with similar creed-making, epoch-making assemblies, the World's Congress of Representative Women must be counted."[7]

For Mormon women, the feminist gathering marked a turning point in the way that they viewed themselves and how they were perceived by outsiders. The international female congress provided Latter-day Saint women another stage upon which to represent their gender, religion, and Territory, all of which needed promotion and celebration. A number of Utah women proudly and ably wore all three of these "hats" in Chicago: they were committed to the promotion of the equality of their gender in social, economic, and political spheres and hoped to convince their fellow citizens that they too were patriotic Americans and that their Territory of Utah deserved its long-sought-after statehood. As Latter-day Saints, they were determined to debunk the demeaning stereotypes of their religious tradition and clarify their standing within the church to the outside world while at the Columbian Exposition. As such, they focused their lobbying efforts at the World's Congress of Representative Women on the rehabilitation of their reviled religion and the place of women therein.

Building Bridges through Women's Organizations

Throughout the first decade or so of the formally established church (1830–1840), Mormon leaders organized a number of male priesthood quorums or groups to help administer its ecclesiastical programs. But it was not until 1842 that Mormon women had a complementary organization of their own. That year a number of female church members in Nauvoo, Illinois, informally banded together to create a benevolent society, much like their counterparts across America. Moved by their initiative and encouraged by their charity, Joseph Smith set out to officially create a women's ecclesiastical organization that same year. The resulting Latter-day Saint women's Relief Society

---

6. May Wright Sewall, ed., *The World's Congress of Representative Women: A Historical Resume for Popular Circulation of the World's Congress of Representative Women, Convened in Chicago on May 15, and Adjourned on May 22, 1893, Under the Auspices of the Woman's Branch of the World's Congress Auxiliary* (Chicago and New York: Rand, McNally and Company, 1894), v.

7. Sewall, *World's Congress of Representative Women*, 1.

has since served as the corresponding female auxiliary to the male priesthood quorums, at all general and local levels of church administration. Another female-led auxiliary organization emerged in 1869, to encourage the development of young Latter-day Saint women. By 1877 its earlier names had been abandoned for the YLMIA. Like the Relief Society before it, the YLMIA soon had active groups throughout church congregations. One year later, in August 1878, one more female-led auxiliary organization emerged to look after the needs of Mormon children: the Primary Association.[8] These Latter-day Saint auxiliary organizations and their female members produced and promoted their own journals and magazines, in order to showcase their own home literature and progressive thinking. The *Woman's Exponent*, for instance, founded in 1872 by Louisa Lula Greene, has the honor of being "the first 'permanent' woman's magazine west of the Mississippi and second in the nation after the Boston *Woman's Journal*," according to historian Leonard J. Arrington. In time it was recognized as the Relief Society's authoritative public voice in print, and spoke volumes of Mormon women's desire and ability to be heard within their religious and social communities.[9]

During the summer of 1887, the Elizabeth Cady Stanton-led National Woman Suffrage Association (NWSA) formally invited nearly one hundred American women's organizations to participate in their upcoming 1888 conference. The leadership of the NWSA planned to organize the International Council of Women (ICW) and the National Council of Women of the United States (NCW) when its members gathered in Washington, D.C. To their chagrin, two dozen solicited associations, including the Baptist Women's Missionary Society, Methodist Women's Missionary Society, Congregational Women's Missionary Society, and Protestant Episcopal Women's Missionary Society, rejected their call for participation. Nevertheless, fifty-three American organizations accepted the summons and sought for representation on the pending council. The trio of church–sponsored and female-led auxiliaries—the Relief Society, presided over by Emily S. Richards; the YLMIA, led by Luella C. Young; and the

8. Jill Mulvay Derr, "Relief Society," in *Encyclopedia of Latter-day Saint History*, ed. Arnold K. Garr, et al. (Salt Lake City: Deseret Book, 2000), 992. For histories of these three Mormon auxiliaries, see Jill Mulvay Derr, Janath Russell Cannon, and Maureen Ursenbach Beecher, *Women of Covenant: The Story of the Relief Society* (Salt Lake City: Deseret Book, 1992); Gates, *History of the YLMIA*; and Carol Cornwall Madsen and Susan Staker Oman, *Sisters and Little Saints: One Hundred Years of Primary* (Salt Lake City: Deseret Book, 1979).

9. Leonard J. Arrington, "Blessed Damozels: Women in Mormon History," *Dialogue: A Journal of Mormon Thought* 6, no. 2 (Summer 1971): 26.

Primary Association, headed by Nettie Y. Snell—were eager to be involved. Mormon women, believed by outsiders to be among the most oppressed class of Americans, demonstrated their progressive nature. "There is a happy significance in the fact that, in common with other organized bodies of women in the country, the three organizations of women in the Mormon Church were invited to send representatives, and all three accepted the invitation," Susan Young Gates recalled.[10] Eventually, Presidents Richards, Young, and newly appointed Janet Young Easton of the Primary would represent the church in the nation's capital in 1888.[11]

Despite the anti-Mormonism still running at fevered pitch in 1888, church authorities anticipated that this type of high-profile involvement might improve the image of the church both at home and abroad. They wanted to exhibit their own religious tradition rather than relying on the misrepresentations of outsiders. Moreover, they were justifiably concerned that if they did not send delegates that the Industrial Home Society, a Protestant anti-polygamy organization in Utah, would defame the church in Chicago, with no counter voices. For the previous seventeen years, Utah women, the majority being Latter-day Saints, had been enfranchised, but they had lost their right to vote in 1887, with the passage of the Edmunds-Tucker Act. The Industrial Home Society and like-minded women's groups across America helped stir up the anti-polygamy sentiment that led to the legislation's passage. It would not be until 1890 that church President Wilford Woodruff would issue his Manifesto banning additional plural marriages in the United States. So it is not surprising that there were many American women who had little interest in welcoming their Mormon sisters into this feminist organization at this particular moment. In fact, the lingering effects of Mormon polygamy continued to cause friction between Latter-day Saint and non Latter-day Saint women into the early twentieth century.[12]

How negatively did most Americans imagine Mormon women during the late nineteenth century? According to historians Gary L. Bunker and Davis Bitton, there were ten dominant graphic representations of Latter-day

10. Gates, *History of the YLMIA*, 200.

11. Robbins, *History and Minutes of the National Council of Women of the United States* (Boston, E. B. Stillings, 1898) 4–7; and Madsen, "Power of Combination," 649.

12. Gates, *History of the YLMIA*, 201; Madsen, "Power of Combination," 649–650; and Rebekah J. Ryan, "In the World: Latter-day Saints in the National Council of Women, 1888–1987," in *Latter-day Saint Women in the Twentieth-Century: Summer Fellows' Papers* 2003, ed. Claudia L. Bushman (Provo, Utah: Joseph Fielding Smith Institute for Latter-day Saint History, 2004), 132.

Saint women in the popular press, some of which were also leveled at American women in general. To begin with, Mormon women were often stereotyped as commodities: they were viewed as cleaners, mothers, cooks, nurses, or some other occupation, rather than females with identities of their own. Americans also expected Mormon women to be embattled or constantly embroiled in domestic disputes with their sister-wives and extended families. The introduction of a new plural wife often precipitated such confrontations. The impoverished Mormon woman was another stock image that filled the minds of many Americans. Latter-day Saint women were often graphically portrayed as poor and destitute, with no hope of economic or social advancement. As Republican leaders before the Civil War linked Mormon polygamy with African American slavery as the twin barbarisms of the United States, it is not surprising that Mormon women were seen as subjugated to their taskmaster husbands. Females in Utah were perhaps the only group in the United States that black slaves could pity. Mormon women were also depicted as worldly creatures who occasionally reveled in the supposed debauchery in Utah. "Anything that suggested orgies or sex would have been titillating to the mass audience," Bunker and Bitton point out. "For this purpose baptism and temple ceremonies were occasionally portrayed pictorially and of course distorted in order to show attractive, semi-nude female figures."[13] But these semi-pornographic caricatures tell us more about the erotic fantasies of American men than the realities of life for Mormon women in Utah.

The five remaining generalizations of Mormon women were equally unflattering and offensive to Latter-day Saints of both genders. Females in Utah were described as stupid and slow, unable to think and reason for themselves. As many nineteenth-century Latter-day Saints were immigrants from Europe, the conventional wisdom suggested that they must have been deluded or deceived into joining up with the Mormons and gathering from their homelands to Utah. Who else but the dregs of society would make such a choice? The unsightly Mormon woman was yet another mainstay image for many Americans. Not only were Latter-day Saint women ugly, but they produced hideous offspring that populated the American West; some even believed Mormon offspring to be subhuman. Occasionally Mormon women were represented as fickle and flirtatious with non-Mormon men, as they were allegedly eager to escape polygamy and Mormon theocracy. They could also

13. Gary L. Bunker and Davis Bitton, *The Mormon Graphic Image, 1834–1914: Cartoons, Caricatures, and Illustrations* (Salt Lake City: University of Utah Press, 1983), 123–128.

be acquisitive or covetous of worldly goods and the latest fashions: they were consumers and the patriarchs of their plural households were expected to foot the bill. The final prevalent image of Latter-day Saint women was that they were domineering and rode roughshod over their husbands. While this stereotype was used to characterize all American women at times, the circumstances of plural marriage magnified the representation of Utah. Bunker and Bitton conclude: "Mormon women were misrepresented in about the same way as women in general, but with a difference: polygamy made it possible to give an added fillip to the unkind portrayals." In fact, most of these images were more anti-Mormon than they were anti-female, which put Mormon women in double jeopardy. Latter-day Saint sisters were eager to exhibit themselves and their religion through participation in women's gatherings, rather than be misrepresented by hostile authors and artists, who helped sell books and newspapers at their expense.[14]

By expressing her strong views on the need for inclusivism, celebrated feminist Susan B. Anthony helped pave the way for Mormon representation in the 1888 global women's gathering. In her mind, the tent of feminism needed to be expansive enough to house even the Latter-day Saints. "The National always has allowed the utmost liberty. Anything and everything which stood in the way of progress was likely to get knocked off our platform.... We have come now to another turning-point and, if it is necessary, I will fight forty years more to make our platform free for the Christian to stand upon whether she be a Catholic and counts her beads, or a Protestant of the straitest orthodox creed," Anthony argued. "These are the principles I want you to maintain, that our platform may be kept as broad as the universe, that upon it may stand the representatives of all creeds and no creeds—Jew or Christian, Protestant or Catholic, Gentile or Mormon, pagan or atheist."[15] Her comments to the National Council of Women reveal the uneasy tension that the question of Mormon inclusion raised in this nascent association. Even though Anthony welcomed Mormon women into the feminist movement, she despised Latter-day Saint polygamy and patriarchy. Years later she clarified her position to an Mormon woman who hoped to garner a book endorsement. "I do not consider that I endorsed Mormonism, or the beliefs

---

14. Bunker and Bitton, *Mormon Graphic Image*, 128–136; and Leonard J. Arrington, "Mormonism: Views from Without and Within," *BYU Studies* 14, no. 2 (Winter 1974): 143–148.

15. Ida Husted Harper, *The Life and Work of Susan B. Anthony*, 3 vols. (Indianapolis: Bowen-Merrill Company, 1898), 2:631.

or actions of Mormons, by protesting against the exclusion from the Council of associations of women who were doing a large humane work, because they belonged to the Mormon Church. I cannot let you use my name in any way in your book. You fail to comprehend that I am among those who hate polygamy and all the subjection of women in the Mormon faith."[16] Eight decades later Mormon women were still appreciative of Anthony's inclusivist attitude, nevertheless.[17]

The inaugural convention of the ICW, led by the NWSA, convened at Albaugh's Grand Opera House in Washington, D.C., between March 25 and April 1, 1888. Almost one hundred women speakers addressed the crowd of women coming from seven different nations and from the ranks of fifty-three national societies. Promoters claimed that it was the first international attempt to organize women around the world. Female education, philanthropy, temperance, industries, professions, legal conditions, political conditions, moral education, and organizations were unifying themes of the congress sessions. That week they also established the NCW in the United States, under the leadership of Frances E. Willard, president, and Susan B. Anthony, vice president. One officer of the newly formed NCW described the meetings as much-anticipated reaping after four decades of planting the seeds of women's rights by like-minded women across the United States. Before the 1888 meetings concluded, the leadership of the NCW determined to henceforth host a countrywide convention every three years in Washington, D.C. Between these triennial meetings, they planned to hold executive sessions in other major U.S. cities. Moreover, they hoped to convene similar meetings on an international basis as well, the ICW being comprised of various national councils from around the world. Representatives of the church's Relief Society and YLMIA (but not the Primary) determined to attend the 1891 meeting in the nation's capital three years later.[18]

The inaugural session of the NCW convened at the Albaugh's Grand Opera House during late February 1891. Female church leaders again converged on the District of Columbia on behalf of their auxiliary organizations,

---

16. Harper, *Life and Work of Susan B. Anthony*, 3:1151–1153.

17. Belle S. Spafford, "After Eighty Years," *Relief Society Magazine* 55, no. 7 (July 1968): 488; and Ryan, "In the World," 131.

18. Robbins, *History and Minutes of the NCW*, 18–22. One historian suggests that "it seems likely that the Relief Society and MIA were considered more focused on women's issues and thus more in line with the council's motives," as a possible reason why the Primary Association did not participate in 1891, although it did in 1888 (Ryan, "In the World," 144–145, n. 15).

all at their own expense. President Zina D. Young and Jane S. Richards represented the Relief Society, while President Elmina S. Taylor and Caroline S. Thomas attended on behalf of the YLMIA. Seeking to keep her Mormon sisters back in Utah informed of the historic gathering, Thomas drafted a report on their journey, which was then published in the *Young Woman's Journal*. After four days of travel by train, Thomas and her companions arrived in D.C. and took lodging at the Riggs House, where the other NCW delegates were staying. She reported that May Wright Sewall, chairman of the credentials committee, welcomed the Mormon delegation warmly, but asked for a detailed description of their organizations' constitution. According to the feminist organization's bylaws, each pledging group needed to provide a formal statement of application. Thomas and her Latter-day Saint colleagues were befuddled by Sewall's request: they had never had to draft, much less provide, a constitution or written statement about their organizations and goals to a non-Mormon audience in the past. In Mormon-dominated Utah, the purpose and structure of both organizations were taken for granted. Fortunately, the Mormon delegation had brought with them an internal report on the Relief Society and the YLMIA, prepared by the organization's presidencies in Utah. From these two documents, the Latter-day Saint women were able to glean the information required by Sewall's committee and draft the necessary reports.[19]

The Mormon representatives were then left to wait anxiously to learn the fate of their proposed membership. Had they traveled all the way to the East Coast to be denied participation? Was there a place for them to stand side-by-side socially with their American sisters? Finally, Susan B. Anthony shared the good news that the Relief Society and the YLMIA had been formally accepted into NCW membership. "We afterwards learned that only one lady present objected to us, and she on the ground that our associations were used for propagating polygamy; but being confronted with the manifesto, yielded to the inevitable and we were admitted," Thomas described.[20] After paying a $100 initiation fee, the Mormon delegates were delighted to receive highly sought after crimson badges, which granted them seating on the main platform. Both Mormon women's associations were honored as two of only ten national female organizations to be selected as members of the meeting's arrangements committee. In

---

19. Robbins, *History and Minutes of the NCW*, 25–32; and Gates, *History of the YLMIA*, 201.

20. Carrie S. Thomas, "Report of the Y.L.M.I. Delegate to the Woman's National Council at Washington, D.C.," *Young Woman's Journal* 8, no. 2 (1891): 381–382.

addition, the Latter-day Saint women were invited to participate in the NCW's closed-door executive sessions and cast votes on issues.[21]

The National Council of Women meetings began on Sunday, February 22, with Protestant-style church services. Over the next three days, the Mormon women attended plenary and concurrent sessions on a variety of topics, including female charities and philanthropies, women in the churches, temperance, education, political status, organized work, and life of women. On Wednesday, the final day of the NCW conference, several Latter-day Saint delegates contributed to a "miscellaneous" session that lasted for several hours. Caroline S. Thomas addressed the gathered women on the mission and activities of the YLMIA, while Sarah M. Kimball and Emmeline B. Wells jointly spoke on the work of the Relief Society. "The Y.L.M.I. Associations have great reason to be proud of the knowledge that they belong to that magnificent body, the Woman's National Council, comprising, as it does, the brightest, most intelligent and learned women of the period, who extend to them the hand of friendship, seemingly pleased and willing to help new comers," Thomas concluded her letter-report.[22] The Mormon women's delegation was gratified by the treatment of their non-Mormon sisters and convinced that their participation in such gatherings in the future would ultimately bear positive fruit on their behalf. It would be the means of rehabilitating the image of the church, especially among American women in positions of power and influence.[23]

While in the nation's capital, these Latter-day Saint delegates learned of another upcoming women's congress. Bertha Palmer and Ellen Henrotin, leaders of the Woman's Branch of the World's Congress Auxiliary, formally requested that the National Council of Women hold its 1893 annual meeting in Chicago as part of the Columbian Exposition. Palmer and her feminist colleagues were determined to have their own conference to celebrate their achievements beyond the shadow of men, where they had been hidden and blocked from view for so long. "Hence it was that a congress in which women should meet to present their position and work in every field of labor which they have entered; a memorial congress in which women might read their own interpretation of their natures, their

---

21. Madsen, "Power of Combination," 649–650; and Robbins, *History and Minutes of the NCW*, 25–26.

22. Thomas, "Report of the Y.L.M.I. Delegate," 382.

23. Gates, *History of the YLMIA*, 201; Robbins, *History and Minutes of the NCW*, 28–32.

own version of their rights, responsibilities, duties, and destiny, seemed an indispensable feature of the Congress Auxiliary scheme."[24] They later sent invitations to the leadership of the General Federation of Women's Clubs, the Woman's Christian Temperance Union, and many other female organizations including those of the church, likewise encouraging them to hold their annual gatherings during the Chicago World's Fair, all under the umbrella organization of the World's Congress of Representative Women. Leaders of the Relief Society and YWMIA determined to represent the church in Chicago.

In the years leading up to the 1893 Chicago World's Fair, many Mormon women in America kept informed about the upcoming Woman's Congress through Latter-day Saint periodicals, especially the *Woman's Exponent* and the *Young Woman's Journal*, and by local and national newspapers. In September 1891, for example, many followed the European travels of Bertha Palmer, president of the Ladies Commission, as she garnered worldwide female support and participation for the 1893 meetings. They also read about the activities of Margaret B. Salisbury and her committee of the Utah Commission for women and learned about Utahns' related responsibilities at the Columbian Exposition, in the *Woman's Exponent*. Moreover, the *Young Woman's Journal*, in October 1892, reprinted a lengthy article on the "Woman's Branch of the Auxiliary," written by Bertha Palmer and Ellen Henrotin of the Department of Woman's Progress. The piece detailed the history of the NCW within the larger context of the American suffrage movement and provided an overview of the 1888 and 1891 woman's congresses in Washington, D.C.[25] "Many ladies are energetic and giving freely of their time and means; others are more backward and need constant persuading and even urging," one 1893 *Woman's Exponent* article noted. "From time to time we have published in regard to what women are doing, and it is desirable, that the women of the Territory should make themselves familiar with the general arrangements, so that they may not fall far behind in intelligence, methods or positive information."[26] These

---

24. Sewall, *World's Congress of Representative Women*, 4–5. Sewall provides abstracts of many of the Mormon presentations and photographs of Mormon luminaries Zina D. H. Young (237), Emily S. Richards (861), and Emmeline B. Wells (876).

25. "Women in the World's Fair," *Woman's Exponent* 20, no. 5 (September 1, 1891): 36; "The World's Congress Auxiliary of the World's Columbian Exposition," *Young Woman's Journal* 4, no. 1 (October 18, 1892): 43–46; "This and That," *Woman's Exponent* 20, no. 6 (September 15, 1891): 44; "World's Fair Notes," *Woman's Exponent* 20, no. 19 (April 15, 1892): 151; and "Editorial Notes," *Woman's Exponent* 21, no. 1 (July 1, 1892): 4.

26. "Woman's Part in the Exposition," *Woman's Exponent* 21, no. 14 (January 15, 1893): 168.

and many other articles suggest how important the upcoming feminist gathering was to women across America and especially in Utah, where women were finding their voices as they struggled for a hearing in the national and international arena of public opinion.

As the opening day of the Chicago World's Fair grew near, Latter-day Saint women became increasingly interested in the Columbian Exposition itself. What did the White City look like? How were the fairgrounds organized? What could they expect to find in Jackson Park? Beginning in early 1893, the *Young Woman's Journal* featured a series of front-page articles that addressed such questions. The February edition featured descriptive text and detailed line engravings of the Administration Building, the Government Building, the Woman's Building (figure 6), the Art Palace (where the Woman's Congress was to be held), and the Electrical Building.[27] The Columbian

FIGURE 6 The Women's Building at the Chicago World's Fair, 1893, taken from *Columbian Gallery*.

---

27. "World's Fair Buildings," *Young Woman's Journal* 4, no. 5 (February 1893): 193–201.

Exposition's Forestry Building, the Horticultural Building, the Dairy Building, the Manufactures and Liberal Arts Building, and the Fisheries Building were all highlighted in the March issue.[28] That May, the very month the paying public swarmed the fairgrounds, the *Young Woman's Journal* featured the Agricultural Building, the Hall of Mines and Mining, the Transportation Building, the Machinery Hall, and the U.S. Naval Exhibit.[29] In all three cases, the texts and graphics were copied from the widely popular guidebook by Horace H. Morgan, *The Historical World's Columbian Exposition and Chicago Guide*, one of the many pre-Columbian Exposition guidebooks that were being sold across the country and world to promote the Chicago Fair. The Mormon editors merely recycled such promotional literature for the benefit of their readers, a common practice in the nineteenth century. These descriptions had their desired effect on Latter-day Saint women and men in Utah: they got them ready to board trains to Chicago with what seemed like the rest of the nation and world.[30]

The feminist sentiments of many Mormon women eager to represent their gender and religion at the Columbian Exposition is captured in Lula Greene Richards's adaptation of a well known Latter-day Saint hymn, "Hope of Israel," retitled "Woman, Rise." It lyrics were printed in the *Woman's Exponent* following the previous descriptions of the World's Fair Buildings.

> Freedom's daughter, rouse from slumber;
> See, the curtains are withdrawn,
> Which so long thy mind hath shrouded,
> Lo! thy day begins to dawn.
>
> Truth and virtue be thy motto,
> Temperance, liberty and peace;
> Light shall shine and darkness vanish,
> Love shall reign, oppression cease.
>
> First to fall 'mid Eden's bowers,
> Through long suffering worthy proved,
> With the foremost claim thy pardon,
> When earth's curse shall be removed.

---

28. "World's Fair Buildings," *Young Woman's Journal* 4, no. 6 (March 1893): 241–247.

29. "World's Fair Buildings," *Young Woman's Journal* 4, no. 8 (May 1893): 337–344.

30. Horace H. Morgan, *The Historical World's Columbian Exposition and Chicago Guide* (St. Louis: Pacific Publishing, 1892), passim.

Chorus:
Woman,' rise! thy penance o'er,
Sit thou in the dust no more;
Seize the scepter, hold the van,
Equal with thy brother, man.[31]

By the spring of 1893, Mormon women from Utah were ready to head to Chicago to exhibit their gender, religion, and Territory. One excited participant shared a preliminary overview of the two Latter-day Saint sessions scheduled for the Woman's Congress, even though the details were still inchoate. "We feel safe however in anticipating a strong phalanx of bright intelligent and able representatives," she wrote optimistically.[32] That March a series of articles was published in the Mormon women's magazines that was seemingly syndicated from the national organizations, sent out almost like press releases giving further details of the upcoming Woman's Congress. Other published articles highlighted the history and contributions of the National Council of Women and encouraged American women from all backgrounds to form local associations to further the feminist organization's goals. Finally in May 1893, just as the world began converging upon the White City, the *Young Woman's Journal* provided Mormon women with the official schedule of the two Latter-day Saint sessions. The same article further described the overarching Woman's Congress, including overviews of the women leaders and organizations, and explained that women would oversee the entire convention. In short, women in Utah were very much aware of the significance and content of the upcoming events in Chicago.[33]

In addition to promoting their gender and Territory in Chicago, Mormon women from Utah were mindful of the unprecedented opportunity to showcase their much-maligned religion at the upcoming World's Congress of Representative Women. An April 1893 editorial in the *Young Woman's Journal* seems to capture the feeling of many Latter-day Saint women working to promote their faith in Chicago. They viewed themselves as both captive women and religionists who needed emancipation from the fetters of negative

---

31. "Woman, Rise," *Young Woman's Journal* 4, no. 5 (February 1893): 201.

32. "Editorial Notes," *Woman's Exponent* 21, no. 17 (March 15, 1893): 141.

33. "World's Congress of Women," *Woman's Exponent* 21, no. 17 (March 15, 1893): 142–143; "National Council of Women," *Young Woman's Journal* 4, no. 6 (March 1893): 279; and "World's Congress of Representative Women," *Young Woman's Journal* 4, no. 8 (May 1893): 380–382. See also "Editorial Notes," *Woman's Exponent* 21, no. 21 (April 15 and May 1, 1893): 156.

publicity and misconstrued image. And Chicago seemed like the ideal city and the Columbian Exposition the perfect venue, to exhibit to the outside world who they really were. "Strange things occur in a perfectly natural way. The importance of the history we are making day by day is not realized by any of us," one Mormon woman editorialized. "I am particularly impressed with the event which is shortly to take place in Chicago, and the part which our sisters are to take in the Congress of Women there to be held. Women are coming from all over the civilized countries of the earth to attend the week's congress in May, in Chicago." The author was nearly beside herself with excitement over the prospect of the leaders of the Relief Society and YLMIA hosting their own two sessions in Chicago, given the opportunity to determine what they wanted to speak on and presenting their own religion to the outside world themselves! "We, the [Latter-day Saint] women of Utah, have been considered slaves and fools, have been looked upon as without mind or intelligence," she continued. "That we are true to our husbands and families has been accounted to us as a sure mark of vile inferiority of intellect. And now we are met by these wide-minded, deep-thoughted women in Chicago as equals, as women with at least mind enough to speak for ourselves. What a glorious opportunity to preach some of the most important truths of our religion!" If nothing else, the Woman's Congress offered them a unique chance to tear down suspicion and lay to rest prejudice among their fellow American and foreign sisters.[34]

The same Mormon writer and her sympathetic readers, moreover, viewed the upcoming Latter-day Saint sessions at the Woman's Congress through the lens of prophetic fulfillment. To these women a new age seemed to be ushering in for both women and Latter-day Saints: "Can you not see the dawning of a better day for us all? Is not this the unlatching of a door that shall soon be flung wide between the women of this gospel and the women of the world?" She recalled hearing Joseph F. Smith, a member of the First Presidency, prophesy five years earlier that "the time was close at hand when the women of this Church would be required to stand in public places and give a reason for the hope within them." In the Latter-day Saint editor's mind, the pending feminist gathering in Chicago was a fulfillment of Smith's prediction. And although not all Mormon sisters would be required, or able, to travel to Chicago, there was something that they could do from their homes and churches in Utah to buoy up their "pioneer sisters" in Chicago.

---

34. "Editor's Department," *Young Woman's Journal* 4, no. 7 (April 1893): 326.

"From this very moment, as members of the Y.L.M.I.A., we should daily remember in our earnest prayers our beloved leader, Sister Elmina S. Taylor, that wisdom and great power may be given her. Together with her are her counselors and aids, and especially those who will go to Chicago to be our mouthpieces. Mighty and strong should these women be, and therefore mighty and strong should be our prayers in their behalf," she pleaded. The Mormon correspondent concluded with the suggestion that the YLMIA leadership and membership who planned to remain in Utah should set aside a day of prayer and fasting on behalf of their Latter-day Saint counterparts in Chicago: "Let us try to realize the importance of this great event, and bend thereto all our faith and prayers." In this sense their involvement in Chicago took on a missionary and spiritual dimension that was not shared with their fellow Utah women.[35]

The 1893 World's Congress of Representative Women

The 1893 World's Congress of Representative Women was a landmark event in the feminist movement in America. Bertha M. Honore Palmer and Ellen Henrotin presided over the Woman's Branch of the Auxiliary, while chairman May Wright Sewall, secretary Rachel Foster Avery, and committee members Sarah Hackett Stevenson, Julia Holmes Smith, Mrs. John C. Coonley, Frances E. Willard, Elizabeth Boynton Harbert, and Mrs. William Thayer Brown led the Department of Woman's Progress—Committee on a World's Congress of Representative Women. Moreover, 528 women from twenty-seven countries were on the congress's advisory council. From this group were culled 209 formal delegates and representatives of 126 women's organizations from around the globe. These female envoys hailed from Belgium (1), Canada (6), Denmark (2), England (30), Finland (2), France (7), Germany (9), Ireland (1), Italy (1), New South Wales (1), Norway (2), Scotland (3), South America (1), Sweden (3), Switzerland (1), and the United States (56). Their geographic backgrounds were matched by the diversity of their organizational focus: charity and philanthropy (17), civil and political reform (34), education (11), industry (6), literature and art (5), miscellaneous (2), moral and social reform (15), orders (2), religion (30), and science (4). Leaders of the World's Congress of Representative Women were quick to point out that if the total membership bases of all 126 female associations represented in

---

35. "Editor's Department," 326–327.

Chicago were combined their numbers would be in the millions. The groundbreaking congress was for women and led by women.[36]

Held at Chicago's Memorial Art Palace between May 15 and 21, 1893, the Woman's Congress featured dozens of sessions daily. Over 150,000 women and men converged on the sessions and auxiliary gatherings, and they quickly familiarized themselves with the daily schedule of the Columbian Exposition. Morning plenary sessions were held in the spacious Washington and Columbus Halls, while afternoon and evening concurrent sessions were hosted in the smaller halls scattered throughout Chicago's Art Palace. That weekend, for example, Hall Three was the site of multiple sessions of the Department Congress of the National Alliance of the Unitarian and Other Liberal Christian Women, Women's Western Unitarian Conference, and Women's Unitarian Conference of the Pacific Coast. Similarly, Hall Four hosted sessions of the Department Congress of the Non-Partisan National Woman's Christian Temperance Union, Hall Eight was the site of morning and afternoon sessions of the Department Congress of the National Society of the Daughters of the American Revolution, and Hall Twenty-Six held the meetings of the Department Congress of the National Columbian Household Economic Association and the Department Congress of Women's Trade Unions. And these were just a few of the women's organizations that held meetings on that day in the Art Palace. All together there were eighty-one official meetings of the congress during that week. Over 325 women offered formal addresses or participated as panelists in the wide-ranging discussions. And hundreds of other meetings were held off-site by female organizations that descended upon Chicago, in addition to the Latter-day Saint sisters who hailed from Utah.[37]

After weeks of cold conditions in Chicago, the morning of Friday, May 19, dawned warm and clear to the delight of the Mormon women boarding at the Palmer House. The improved weather was symbolic of the recent thaw between the Latter-day Saints and their Gentile sisters. The day had arrived when the Mormon women were to hold both their Relief Society (morning) and their YLMIA (evening) sessions in Hall Four of the Art Palace. Congress organizers had offered both Latter-day Saint auxiliary organizations each an entire day (two sessions), but the female Mormon leaders determined to meet together in the same hall and on the same day for one session each or two

36. Sewall, *World's Congress of Representative Women*, 5.

37. Sewall, *World's Congress of Representative Women*, 67–87.

sessions total. President Zina D. Young; vice presidents Jane S. Richards, Bathsheba W. Smith, and Sarah M. Kimball; Secretary Emmeline B. Wells, and Treasurer Mary Isabella Horne presided over Friday morning's Department Congress of the National Woman's Relief Society. These Mormon matriarchs convened the much-anticipated session at 10:00 A.M. with a congregational hymn, "O My Father, Thou That Dwellest," a beloved Latter-day Saint hymn crackling with feminist implications. Not only was there a Father in Heaven to whom the righteous might someday return following their mortal sojourn, there was also a Mother in Heaven, a female counterpart to the traditional male deity of Western monotheism, the opening hymn and Latter-day Saint theology asserted. Sarah M. Kimball, a founding member of the 1842 Female Relief Society of Nauvoo and a president of the Utah Woman Suffrage Association, offered the invocation.[38]

Ironically, and perhaps appropriately, given the outreach nature of the overarching congress, non-Mormon reporter Rosetta "Etta" Luce Gilchrist, a former anti-Mormon and author of polygamy exposé *Apples of Sodom* (1883),[39] provides modern readers with the best firsthand account of the ensuing Relief Society congress. Gilchrist was a newspaper correspondent for the Ashtabula *News Journal*, and she detailed all that transpired in Hall Four that day. "This morning we attended one of the most interesting of the Congresses thus far to me, that of the Utah women, in the National Woman's Relief Society Congress," her recital began. Gilchrist then offered her readers a brief introduction to each Mormon speaker and a synopsis of her remarks.[40]

Relief Society president Zina D. Young offered the opening address of the historic session. "I wish it were possible to express in words the gratitude I feel in associating with you on this happy occasion; yes, with those who have sought to elevate humanity, in the removing of prejudice, in the battle for right, in the great advancement for womankind which has been effected through the efforts and energy of these noble women assembled in this Congress and those they represent throughout the world," the plural wife of the late Brigham Young began with emotion. She then referred to the Latter-day Saints in the Utah Territory, acknowledging that the blessing

---

38. "Miscellaneous," 427–428; Sewall, *World's Congress of Representative Women*, 79–84; and Gates, *History of the YLMIA*, 202.

39. Rosetta Luce Gilchrist, *Apples of Sodom: A Story of Mormon Life* (Cleveland: William W. Williams, 1883).

40. Etta L. Gilchrist, "The World's Fair," *Ashtabula News Journal*, May 23, 1893, reprinted in *Woman's Exponent* 21, no. 24 (June 15, 1893): 177–178; and Derr, et al., *Women of Covenant*, 140.

of God "has been upon our efforts, in the midst of a desert country, in sustaining our poor, gathered from all nations. We acknowledge our Father's care through it all, and give him the honor and praise." Gilchrist described Young as "[a] very bright and comely woman [who] spoke of the children of Utah and told how they are taught lessons of patriotism and purity."[41] Following first vice president Jane S. Richards's report on the Relief Society, M. Isabella Horne spoke on "Pioneer Women of Utah, 1847–48." Gilchrist described Horne's tales of being driven by mobs from Nauvoo during the freezing winter of 1846, the miserable journey across the frozen tundra of Iowa, which took three and a half months to complete, the fact that she give birth along the way, and the mormons interaction with threatening and friendly Native Americans all the way across the American plains to the Salt Lake Valley, where she arrived in October 1847, putting them "1,000 miles east and 700 miles west of any supplies." Horne then related how the Latter-day Saints had to pioneer, deal with snakes, mice, bugs, lack of irrigation, famine, pestilence, rodents, lack of soap, mills to grind their wheat, swarms of crickets, and so on. "To hear Mrs. Horne one could not but think of the Bible story of the Hebrews and their deliverance from the Egyptians. The Mormons are apparently a most religious people and strict in religious observances, and what is more their faith in their religion is marvelous," Gilchrist noted.[42]

Zina Y. Card next spoke on "The Children," specifically about the Primary and Sunday School organizations in Utah, the little ones being the "best crop" of Utah. "As she wore a homemade silk dress, the audience were informed of the fact, and many favorable comments were passed upon this added proof of Utah women's skills," one Latter-day Saint young women noted.[43] Then there was a song led by Cornelia H. Clayton. Nellie Little next delivered an address on "Amusements of the Early Days" in Utah. Gilchrist noted that Little "told of their amusements and referred to the time when they were having a celebration, singing patriotic songs and listening to the reading of the Declaration of Independence, news came to them that U.S. troops were on the way to quell an insurrection" in July 1857, in reference to the Utah War. Gilchrist was also impressed to learn of the prominent place of dance and the theatre in

41. Gilchrist, "World's Fair," 177.

42. Gilchrist, "World's Fair," 177.

43. "Miscellaneous," 428.

Mormon culture, noting that the Mormons begin and end all entertainment with a prayer and that Brigham Young was a lover of the theatre.

Emmeline B. Wells offered papers on two disparate subjects: "Western Women, Authors and Journalists" and "Grain Saving by Women." "I have only told you a few things that have been done by Western women in journalism and authorship. I could tell you much more had I time, but it remains for the future to reveal the magnificent possibilities of song and story of the drama and romance from the gifted pens of the daughters of the valleys of the Rocky mountain fastnesses which lie by the inland sea [Great Salt Lake]," Wells concluded.[44] "A sweet faced mother in Zion, spoke of the authors and journalists in Utah, and the grain saving by women," Gilchrist wrote of Wells's remarks. "She said they had known what it was to be hungry, to hear their children cry for bread, and they felt the grain must not go out of the Territory. They have 55,000 bushels stored now and will have more. Women and children sometimes glean in the fields for this purpose. 'If ever there is a famine,' she said 'come to Zion.'"[45] Dr. Martha Hughes Cannon next spoke on the varieties of women in Utah. "The delegation from Utah represents two classes, the pioneer women of the Territory and the native born daughters of that region. The pioneer women and leaders of the National Woman's Relief Society of Utah are of distinct New England type of character. Some early-day Utah women were of a decided Hebraic type," Cannon explained. "In following out the migrating instinct of their fore-fathers these early-day women of Utah did not forget the principles for which so much had been sacrificed to establish religious toleration on the free soil of America, for when they had reached the end of their journey they proved their patriotism and loyalty by rallying around their husbands and sons while they raised the Stars and Stripes." Emily Shurtliffe then gave an "impromptu" speech and Electa Bullock offered a talk titled "Industrial Women."[46]

As the Relief Society congress session came to a close, Emmeline B. Wells invited Gilchrist to sit with her and her fellow Mormon auxiliary officers on the speaker's platform. In so doing, Wells publicly demonstrated her personal and organizational friendship and forgiveness to the Ashtabula reporter, one

---

44. "Emmeline B. Wells on Women Authors and Journalists," *Chicago Daily Inter-Ocean*, May 20, 1893, reprinted in "Woman's Relief Society," *Woman's Exponent* 21, no. 24 (June 15, 1893): 178. See also the summary of her talk in Sewall, *World's Congress of Representative Women*, 800–802.

45. Gilchrist, "World's Fair," 177–178.

46. "Tell of Their Western Life," *Chicago Daily Tribune*, May 20, 1893, reprinted as "Utah Women in Chicago," *Woman's Exponent* 21, no. 24 (June 15, 1893): 179.

of her religion's former antagonists. Gilchrist was moved by the kind gesture. "I went and sat by Brigham Young's wife [Zina D. Young] and took by the hand each of those women with whom my sympathy has been so long, they knowing (for Wells had told them of me in Utah) that I had written a book against their institution," Gilchrist related to her readers. "Truly their forbearance and kindness is saint-like. This one meeting was to me worth coming to Chicago for."[47]

After the audience sang the Doxology and Elmina S. Taylor offered the benediction, Elizabeth Lisle Saxon, vice president of Tennessee's National Woman Suffrage Association, spontaneously made her way to the podium and feted the Mormon women for their goodness and contribution to the overarching congress. One Latter-day Saint attendee noted that Saxon "paid as high a tribute and told more truth about us than it has ever been my good fortune to hear from any friend. Of course we could not agree that all she said was strictly in accord with our sentiments and belief; but she told of the sweet charities, the true, pure lives led by the sisters of our Church."[48] A Chicago *Daily Tribune* reporter noted of the Mormon contribution in Chicago: "Women who, in the pioneer days, crossed the barren plains and after trials, hardships, and adventures reached America's Dead Sea—the Great Salt Lake—were an important factor yesterday in the Women's Congress. They were all Utah women; they had been Mormons, and in pathetic tones and refined language related their experience of early days in that remarkable territory, which was then populated only by the disciples of Brigham Young." Once again, Mormon women were pioneering for their faith in Illinois—this time in Chicago, nearly three hundred miles northeast of Nauvoo.[49]

That Friday evening, YLMIA president Elmina S. Taylor, vice presidents Maria Y. Dougall and Martha H. Tingey, secretary and treasurer Ann M. Cannon, and corresponding secretary Mae Taylor presided over the Department Congress of the Young Ladies' National Mutual Improvement Association in Hall Four, the same room as the earlier Relief Society session. Women settled into the room to Kate Romney's prelude organ music, including the crowd pleaser, "God is Love," which "created quite a sensation, as it floated through the throng, and breathless attention was the reward,"

47. Gilchrist, "World's Fair," 178. The following year the *Woman's Exponent* published one of Gilchrist's poems, "Dying," (see Etta L. Gilchrist, "Dying," *Woman's Exponent* 23, no. 3–4 [August 1 and 15, 1894]: 171).

48. "Miscellaneous," 428; and Gates, *History of the YLMIA*, 202–203.

49. "Tell of Their Western Life," 179.

according to one Utah woman in attendance.[50] Once the audience was seated, they were led in the singing of the patriotic anthem "My Country, 'Tis of Thee," after which Adella W. Eardley offered the invocation. Following a quartette number by May Talmage, Mary Romney, Minnie J. Snow, and May Preston, the congress session was opened by President Taylor, who welcomed the spectators on behalf of the church. Her associate Maria Y. Dougall then offered a report on the YLMIA. Over the next several hours, Latter-day Saint women addressed the largely non-Mormon audience on a variety of topics, carefully choreographed to advance the cause of their maligned gender, religion, and Territory. In retrospect, their prepared remarks seem designed to showcase the contributions of Mormon women in Utah to the greatness of America.[51]

To begin with, refined speaker May Talmage highlighted the growing sophistication of literature and art in the Utah Territory. She pointed out that although the Mormon pioneers had been driven from American civilization by mobs to the desolation of the Great Basin, they still celebrated the arts and sought after refinement in the tops of the mountains. "She said most of the noted writers in Utah were self-educated, but had become famous in literature. The young women had received their musical training in the Territory, but many of them were vocalists who could no longer be classed as amateurs," a Chicago reporter summarized. "They had gained reputations which were indeed enviable. In painting, designing, and the like they compared favorably with the women of the East, and were real artists. The ideas and sentiments of those Western girls, the speaker said, were lofty and noble, and the young women were encouraged to their best efforts."[52] To buttress Talmage's claim, Annie Laura Hyde recited celebrated Mormon poetess Eliza R. Snow's poem "The Ultimatum of Human Life" and Mary Romney offered an impressive soprano solo. Emily S. Richards next offered an address titled "Legal and Political Status of Utah Women," which celebrated the actual condition of Mormon females. She was followed by Emmeline Wells, whose entire address highlighting the elevated character and contributions of Latter-day Saint women

---

50. "Miscellaneous," 429.

51. "Tell of their Western Life," 179; Gates, *History of the YLMIA*, 203–204.

52. "Young Ladies' National Improvement Association Holds Its First Session," *Chicago Daily Tribune*, May 20, 1893, reprinted as "Utah Women in Chicago," *Woman's Exponent* 21, no. 24 (June 15, 1893): 179. The entire text of her speech was reprinted as May Talmage, "Literature and Art," *Young Woman's Journal* 5, no. 3 (December 1893): 159–161.

was published in the Chicago *Daily Inter-Ocean* newspaper.[53] Martha Horne Tingey then spoke on the special roles of women, especially that of mother and wife. She was one of the only Latter-day Saints to address peculiar theological claims of the Mormons, suggesting that there was a premortal existence during which time individuals demonstrated their faithfulness and that through faithfulness in this life they gain blessings in the life to come. She also talked about humanity's Mother in Heaven. "I say parents, because while we hear a great deal about our Heavenly Father, and very little if anything, about our Heavenly Mother, reason and revelation both teach us that we must also have a Mother there."[54]

The final two talks of the YLMIA session were likewise offered in an attempt to highlight the virtuous nature and uplifting influence of the church in the lives of young Latter-day Saint women as both religionists and Americans. Minnie J. Snow spoke on "Our Girls" and described the ten-thousand-strong membership and activities of the YLMIA up and down Utah Territory. She asserted that the purpose of the YLMIA "is the cultivation and improvement of all the beautiful, noble, virtuous faculties in woman, and where special attention is given to religious and moral training."[55] Julia Farnsworth offered the sessions' closing remarks entitled "Woman in All Ages." After tracing the primacy of mothers and daughters in the glorious civilizations of Egypt, China, Japan, Israel, Greece, Rome, and Europe, she described the female contributions to the greatness of America. Farnsworth then highlighted the legacy of Mormon pioneer women, who helped settle the West, thereby linking the Pacific and Atlantic coasts of the United States. "We love our grand American Government, her colonizers, her sacred institutions, her Constitution, her flag, her Independence! We are taught to support and defend her every legal authority," she asserted in an attempt to refashion the Mormon image from one of treasonous to patriotic. Farnsworth closed with a plea for Utah statehood. "Our star of hope is bright for the future elevation of mind and body. We trust its illumination may add light to the other States and Territories of our Union, until the Congress of her people may see the absolute necessity of admitting Utah as a State. And until that time does come we will work and pray, placing our standard high as the

---

53. "Emmeline B. Wells on Women Authors," 178.

54. Her remarks were reprinted as "Address of Mrs. Mattie Horne Tingey," *Young Woman's Journal* 4, no. 12 (September 1893): 547–549.

55. Snow's remarks were reprinted as "Our Girls," *Young Woman's Journal* 5, no. 3 (December 1893): 161–163.

everlasting hills and as solid as the rock of ages."[56] Kate Romney then offered the benediction.

But before the YLMIA session disbanded, a number of non-Mormon women unexpectedly approached the dais and heaped praise upon their Latter-day Saint sisters, just as others had following the morning Relief Society session. Women's suffrage movement leader Isabella Beecher Hooker—daughter of the Reverend Lyman Beecher and sister of Henry Ward Beecher, Catharine Beecher, and Harriet Beecher Stowe—together with Lady Board of Managers member Clara Thatcher, wife of Solomon Thatcher Jr., one of the Chicago World's Fair commissioners, made impromptu remarks in praise of the Utah women to the audience. "Both expressed their surprise and pleasure over the exalted, refined, and pure sentiments uttered by our young girls," one Latter-day Saint youth described. "But the organizations that existed amongst us were the points of deepest interest, and truly we lead the world in this particular feature." The same young woman noted the approval of Latter-day Saint leaders in attendance, including Apostle John Henry Smith, Brother Romney, Dr. James E. Talmage, and Bishop Taylor. "All were cognizant of the fact that God was with us," she declared.[57] Elder Smith noted in his diary of the event: "I went in the evening to the Chicago Art Palace and heard our sisters deliver themselves in good shape."[58] Like their Relief Society counterparts, the YLMIA representatives helped reshape public opinion about both their oppressed gender and maligned religion while in the White City. And they did so in a manner pleasing to their church's male hierarchy, who thrilled with their success.

By Saturday, May 20, the World's Congress of Representative Women was coming to a conclusion. The previous day's Relief Society and YLMIA sessions marked the end of scheduled Mormon participation in the formal meetings. But there were still plenary and concurrent congress sessions held in the Art Palace's Hall of Washington, Hall of Columbus, and smaller rooms that weekend. Relief Society leader Emmeline B. Wells was flattered when the NCW leadership unexpectedly invited her to act as the honorary American president of the Saturday-morning session in the Hall of Columbus. Dr. Sarah Hackett Stevenson, the first woman admitted to the American Medical Association, was extended the same privilege that evening

56. The entire text of Farnsworth's speech was reprinted as "Woman in All Ages," *Young Woman's Journal* 4, no. 11 (August 1893): 513–517.

57. "Miscellaneous," 429; Gates, *History of the YLMIA*, 204.

58. John Henry Smith, Diary, May 19, 1893, in Jean Bickmore White, ed., *Church, State, and Politics: The Diaries of John Henry Smith* (Salt Lake City: Signature Books, 1990), 292.

in the Hall of Columbus.[59] This was a signal honor for both women. Such a coveted invitation was a major coup for Wells personally and also to the religion that she represented. "An honor never before accorded to a Mormon woman," Wells exclaimed in her diary. "If one of our brethren had such a distinguished honor conferred upon them, it would have been heralded the country over and thought a great achievement."[60] Latter-day Saint women like Wells were able to build bridges of understanding between the Mormon and non-Mormon communities that their male counterparts could only hope of constructing at this time in American history.

The non-Mormon members of the organizing committee and other female delegates welcomed the Latter-day Saint women from Utah during the entire Woman's Congress. The Mormon women in Chicago were especially grateful to be included in several non-conference social gatherings while in the White City. At these events they felt truly accepted and appreciated by their fellow sisters. That week a number of Mormon women accepted the invitation to attend a reception for Chicago's prominent West End Club, held at the upscale Illinois Club House. They also mingled with delegates from other female organizations at receptions hosted by the Illinois Press Association, Chicago Woman's Club, and the World's Congress of Representative Women. Between the Friday morning Relief Society session and Friday evening YLMIA session, the presidencies and members of both female church auxiliaries went to a function at the Woman's Building, a structure built specifically for women at the Columbian Exposition. "It was a charming afternoon and was one of those happy expressions of generous sympathy and interest in the work of the Woman's Congress," one Mormon Utahn noted. While in the Woman's Building, the Mormon sisters were delighted to see their homemade silk curtains and piano scarf adorning the interior. And two colored pictures of Native Americans by Salt Lake City artist Kate Wells hung prominently in the foyer. "The magnificence, the extreme elegance of the entertainments, is beyond language to convey to those who have not seen it for themselves," the same Mormon exclaimed of the Woman's Building. Both their presence and material contributions had been accepted in Chicago.[61]

---

59. Sewall, *World's Congress of Representative Women*, 84.

60. Madsen, "Power of Combination," 652.

61. "World's Congress of Woman," *Woman's Exponent* 21, no. 23 (June 1, 1893): 173; and "Editorial Notes," *Woman's Exponent* 21, no. 23 (June 1, 1893): 175. That October in the McCormick Building, the studio of Kate Wells in Salt Lake City hosted an exhibit that showcased some of the Utah art that was exhibited in Chicago, including J. W. Clawson's "Santa Maria della Salute" (see "Editorial Notes," *Woman's Exponent* 22, no. 7 [October 15 and November 1, 1893]: 53).

For a handful of Latter-day Saint women, however, the social highlight of the Woman's Congress was the Saturday NCW luncheon at the Richelieu, one of Chicago's landmark hotels. It was held in honor of the ICW officers who traveled to the White City. The ornate paper invitation, made official with the seal of the NCW and a list of its officers on its interior, meant more to these Mormon matriarchs than any other complimentary meal offering. In a very real sense the formal summons ratified the growing feelings of kinship and friendship between the heretofore-marginalized Utahns and their domestic and international counterparts. The Latter-day Saints were well aware that it was one thing to be invited to sit as colleagues professionally together on a podium for women's issues; it was quite another to be invited to spend time with one another as friends socially. One Mormon guest described the entire luncheon down to the smallest details—the menus, place settings, decorations, and flowers—to her Latter-day Saint sisters back home. Women from all over the world, wearing the traditional formal dress of their home-lands, were in attendance. "The parlor where the guests assembled was like a garden of lilies and roses, and the beautiful women gathered there were the real gems of luster and loveliness from the various countries whither they had come," she wrote. After dinner the hosts encouraged each guest to take a rose from the table centerpiece as a memento of the occasion. "We feel sure they will never forget the splendor of the rooms, nor the brilliancy of the enter-tainment," the same Latter-day Saint remarked.[62] While in Chicago, Mormon women were delighted to be included in the many private luncheons, dinners, receptions, and gatherings of women. In fact, they made contact with fellow women that would last for many years, developing and deepening friendships, especially as Latter-day Saint women continued to be engaged in the suffrage movement and feminist gatherings.[63]

Breaking down Barriers through Friendship

By 1893 Mormon women had woven themselves into the larger fabric of domestic and international feminism, while Mormon men chose to remain (or were forced to remain) detached from outside organizations and ecumenical associations. Formal church participation in the inaugural World's Congress of Representative Women was set in motion years earlier. During

62. "Luncheon at the Richelieu," *Woman's Exponent* 21, no. 23 (June 1, 1893): 173–174.

63. Madsen, "Power of Combination," 652.

the late 1880s and early 1890s, Mormon women were active participants in a number of national and international women's organizations. The female leadership of the church's female auxiliary organizations petitioned for membership in the feminist National Council of Women during its inaugural meeting. These Mormon sisters were delighted when Susan B. Anthony welcomed them to stand shoulder to shoulder with their fellow American women, despite anti-Mormon opposition to their inclusion. Thereafter, Latter-day Saint women served as energetic delegates at national feminist gatherings.

In 1888, representatives of the Relief Society, the Young Ladies' Mutual Improvement Association, and the Primary Association, all Mormon-female-auxiliaries, attended the National Woman Suffrage Association's conference, as well as the organizational meetings of the International Council of Women and the National Council of Women of the United States, in Washington, D.C. Three years later, in 1891, Relief Society and the YLMIA leaders attended the triennial session of the NCW in the nation's capital, with its members serving in leadership positions. For the next two years, Latter-day Saint women in Utah prepared for the World's Congress of Representative Women. In May 1893, Latter-day Saint women attended the week-long World's Congress of Representative Women and contributed several papers, chaired sessions, and voted on resolutions impacting their gender. "There was no small irony in the fact that some of the same leaders who had so recently patronized and even ridiculed Latter-day Saint women as pawns of a religious hierarchy now gave them a platform from which to represent themselves to an international audience," historian Carol Cornwall Madsen points out.[64]

Through the Women's Congress in Chicago, Mormon women were able to reunite with their national and international female counterparts. They sparkled on the stage of feminism, proving both to themselves and to their fellow American women that they had a voice and that it would be heard beyond the borders of Utah. Welcomed involvement in the World's Congress of Representative Women was a defining moment for Latter-day Saints. Emmeline B. Wells described the Chicago gathering and its utility for her gender and religion in glorious language: "Its value among the nations of mankind in all countries, from which representation came, and the results that will hereafter ensue cannot be estimated in the extent of knowledge and wisdom disseminated, nor in the spirit of love and abundant charity and peace that were diffused throughout its assemblies from its first session until its last."

---

64. Madsen, "Power of Combination," 652.

In fact, Wells was anxious that the remainder of the Columbian Exposition might pale in comparison. "The entire Woman's Congress has been such an unparalleled success, that it is likely to detract from those which immediately follow it," she confided.[65] Another Mormon woman encouraged her fellow sisters to reflect deeply on what had just transpired in the White City. She pointed out that abstracts of the Relief Society and YLMIA proceedings were printed in Chicago's main newspapers for the nation to read about the church: "We wish the sisters to comprehend the fact that though it may seem a small affair in itself, yet it will go into the history of the great Congress, and be on record and circulated all over the world. It was an unprecedented opportunity and there never was before in the history of the world such a gathering of women, as the World's Congress of Representative Women assembled on that wonderful occasion." She further noted that both Latter-day Saint auxiliary sessions were "well attended and as satisfactory and successful as the most sanguine could have anticipated," despite the many competing concurrent sessions in the Art Palace halls.[66]

Although the Woman's Congress came to an end in late May 1893, Latter-day Saint women from Utah would continue to help showcase their gender, religion, and Territory for the duration of the Chicago World's Fair. Given the warm reception that the Relief Society and YLMIA had received in the White City, a writer for the *Woman's Exponent* editorialized that Mormon women planning to attend the Columbian Exposition should consider packing back issues of the *Exponent* to distribute on the fairgrounds to bystanders interested in learning more about the church. She pointed out that dozens and dozens of gentile women's organizations were distributing their promotional literature to fairgoers. What was keeping Mormon women from doing the same thing on behalf of their faith? "Now the woman's paper is just the right thing for it is still very generally believed that women in this Church are ignorant and in subjection, one copy of the EXPONENT (and it is sold for five cents a copy) is tangible proof to the contrary," she reasoned. "To those who are anxious to do something in a small way to scatter good seed and spread the truth concerning the women of this part of the world, why no surer method could be advocated than to circulate the woman's paper. It speaks for itself and enters where no Mormon Elder would be permitted."[67]

---

65. "World's Congress of Woman," 172.

66. "Editorial Notes," *Woman's Exponent* 21, no. 24 (June 15, 1893): 181.

67. "The Woman's Exponent," *Woman's Exponent* 22, no. 1 (July 15, 1893): 188.

Later that summer, a good number of women from Utah worked tirelessly as hostesses in the Utah Building. And nearly twelve dozen female singers of the Mormon Tabernacle Choir would compete in the Welsh Eisteddfod that September. Mormon matriarchs had found their voice and the world was listening. "Mormon women were not mindless, soulless patsies, obediently bowing to the yoke of Mormon patriarchy and polygamy. They were not oblivious to the non-celestial dimensions of a patriarchal system that did not always fairly or adequately accord them their full dignity as individuals of worth and equality," Terryl L. Givens points out. "These were women of incredible dynamism and capacity, whose submission to the male domination of their religion did not come without a personal sense of pain and injustice, their faith in the essentials of priesthood and polygamy notwithstanding."[68] Latter-day Saint women had come to appreciate that their gender allowed them to break down anti-Mormon prejudice in public spaces in ways that Latter-day Saint men could not in the 1890s.

---

68. Email correspondence with Terryl L. Givens and author, April 23, 2010.

4

Sweet Singers of Zion

THE MORMON TABERNACLE CHOIR
AT THE 1893 WELSH EISTEDDFOD

It is strange to think that the weary, hunted [Mormon]
pilgrims who toiled on foot across the plains of the
Rockies forty-five years ago should now be returning in
Pullmans to contest with the musical societies of the East
for supremacy.*
—*Chicago Inter-Ocean*, 1893

If Brigham Young had told to the brave little column of
devoted Mormons that toiled wearily over plain and
mountain on the long journey to their land of Canaan
beyond the wilderness, that in after years their descendants
would dispute with the Gentiles the palm of musical
cultivation, the assertion would have been a greater test
of faith than the revelation of the Book of Mormon. But
it is a fact that the Mormon church of Salt Lake City is
sending its choir of 250 voices to compete for the largest
prize ever offered in this country for excellence in vocal
music.**
—*St. Louis Post-Dispatch*, 1893

IN AUGUST 1893, two hundred and fifty of The Church of Jesus Christ of
Latter-day Saint's Salt Lake Mormon Tabernacle Choir's best singers (along
with several members of its management and staff) traveled from Utah to
Illinois. There they competed in a Welsh Eisteddfod, a musical competition

---

* Reprinted in Gerald A. Petersen, *More Than Music: The Mormon Tabernacle Choir* (Provo,
Utah: Brigham Young University Press, 1979), 36.
** Reprinted in "Dramatic," *Deseret Evening News*, August 26, 1893.

held in conjunction with the Chicago World's Fair, against the leading choirs of the United States and Great Britain. Performing admirably in the highly contested choral contest, the Tabernacle Choir vaulted their religion into the national spotlight.

Although its journey to the Columbian Exposition in Illinois marked the Tabernacle Choir's first out-of-state performances, the Utah chorus was already well regarded in American musical circles. Thousands of non-Mormons passing through Utah paid voyeuristic visits to the tortoise-shaped Tabernacle and its large choir during the late nineteenth century. The massive 2,648-pipe organ was a significant tourist draw. "Its size alone commanded respect," historian Ronald W. Walker notes.[1] Travelers often recorded their impressions of the Tabernacle and its choir in the heart of Mormondom. A reporter from the *Deutsche Warte* (German Viewpoint), a leading German-language newspaper printed in Chicago, praised the Tabernacle's organ and singers after visiting Salt Lake City in 1891. "The mighty organ sends forth her powerful strains; all at once the noise and hum in the giant assembly cease. The hymn is given out, which, however, is sung by the choir alone. But how it is sung! Grand, powerful, soul-thrilling!" he exclaimed. "That is a choir with none but excellently schooled voices, and we can understand why the Mormons are proud of that music, and why the people of other denominations come Sunday after Sunday to hear it. I assert there are few places in the United States where such a choir can be heard."[2]

Since the beginnings of the church, sacred music has played an important role in Latter-day Saint worship and cultural life. In a canonized July 1830 revelation, the Lord affirmed to Joseph Smith's wife, Emma: "my soul delighteth in the song of the heart; yea, the song of the righteous is a prayer unto me" (Doctrine and Covenants 25:12), after he directed her to compile the first Mormon hymnal. As the Latter-day Saints gathered to, and were driven from, their communities in New York, Ohio, Missouri, and Illinois, they played music to express their joys and sang melodies to lighten their burdens. The creation of bands and campfire dances were regular occurrences in their persecuted populations. Even as the Mormons settled beyond the borders of the United States in 1847, they harmonized hymns as they walked across the breadth of America to the valleys of the Rocky Mountains. Mormon pioneers carted musical instruments alongside their farming implements and pioneer

---

1. Ronald W. Walker, "The Salt Lake Tabernacle in the Nineteenth Century: A Glimpse of Early Mormonism," *Journal of Mormon History* 32, no. 3 (Fall 2005): 199, 229–232.

2. *Deutsche Warte*, September 20, 1891; reprinted in "An Honest Editor," *Deseret News*, October 17, 1891.

housewares in their wagons and handcarts, eager to make music while they were making history. Once in Utah these settlers continued this musical tradition. Welsh Latter-day Saints were largely responsible for the Territory's earliest choirs. "Singing was far more natural for the Welsh than driving a team of oxen across the heartland of America," one historian explains.[3] In fact, after Brigham Young listened to a number of Welsh converts sing a beautiful harmony, he suggested that someday they might be the basis for a larger church choir—a dream that was fulfilled during the American Moses' lifetime.[4]

During the 1852 Latter-day Saint general conference held in Salt Lake City's newly constructed adobe tabernacle, several of these pioneer choruses banded together to form the original Tabernacle Choir. Over the next five decades, these and other Mormon singers were led by conductors John Parry, Stephen Goddard, James Smithies, Charles John Thomas, Robert Sands, George Careless, Ebenezer Beesley, and Evan Stephens. During the 1850s, 1860s, and 1870s, individual Latter-day Saints established musical training schools, including the Deseret Musical Association and the Philharmonic Society, to offer singing classes to eager students. Moreover, most pioneer settlements in Brigham Young's Great Basin Kingdom enjoyed the songs of Zion thanks to local church choruses. In 1876, the growing Tabernacle Choir offered one of the earliest performances of Handel's *Messiah* in western America. During the 1880s the Salt Lake City–based volunteer choir continued to improve. Welshman Evan Stephens finally took over the choir in 1890, immediately increasing the number of its singers to three hundred, many of whom were his former music students. During the final decade of the nineteenth century, the Tabernacle Choir's national reputation was rising, viewed by many as one of the premier choral organizations in the American West, making it a prime candidate for the Welsh musical competition in Chicago.[5]

The Tabernacle Choir's presence in Chicago did more to promote Mormonism than any other single church effort at the Jackson Park fairgrounds. But the singers' experience exposes what has become one of the great ironies of

3. Heidi S. Swinton, *America's Choir: A Commemorative Portrait of the Mormon Tabernacle Choir* (Salt Lake City: Shadow Mountain and Mormon Tabernacle Choir, 2004), 13–17.

4. See Michael Hicks, *Mormonism and Music: A History* (Urbana: University of Illinois Press, 2003), chapter 9, "The Mormon Tabernacle Choir"; Charles Jeffrey Calman, *The Mormon Tabernacle Choir* (New York: Harper and Row, 1979); Petersen, *More Than Music*; and J. Spencer Cornwall, *A Century of Singing: The Salt Lake Mormon Tabernacle Choir* (Salt Lake City: Deseret Book, 1958).

5. Swinton, *America's Choir*, 17–33.

the Mormon public image: many Christian Americans embrace the Mormon Tabernacle Choir but view its sponsoring ecclesiastical institution with suspicion and malice. "Overreaction to and ignorance of LDS religious and political beliefs continued until well after the first United States tours of the Tabernacle Choir, but many of the same people who despised Mormonism divorced the Choir from its namesake church and admitted that the music it produced was more than acceptable," historian Gerald A. Petersen notes. "This separation of Church and music continues today. It is not unusual for a minister or layman of another religion to vigorously attack the Mormons' beliefs while anxiously awaiting his newest recording of the Mormon Tabernacle Choir—and thereafter to use the recording as an example for his own choir to emulate."[6]

Nevertheless, nearly a century after the Mormon chorus was feted in Chicago, choir officials conducted a national survey of radio listeners, which "confirmed that the onetime emblem of the Mormon menace had become an American institution," according to music historian Michael Hicks. The choral group that traces its musical roots to a hobbled-together pioneer choir is now part of America's popular culture. The Tabernacle Choir has received awards from U.S. presidents and had its music anthologized by *Reader's Digest*. Protestant evangelist Billy Graham has praised the award-winning choir. Its image has even been featured on a postal stamp. The choir's *Music and the Spoken Word* weekly radio program has been on the air continuously, longer than any other radio program in America. Hicks makes the case that the Tabernacle Choir singers of Zion have "come to symbolize what seem to many non-Mormons the church's most admirable and even most 'American' traits: cooperation, conservatism, ceremoniousness, and the pursuit of recognition." The church was mainstreamed into America in large measure by its Tabernacle Choir.[7]

The Welsh Eisteddfod at the Columbian Exposition

In the summer of 1891, the Welsh-American National Cymmrodorion Society of Chicago announced it would sponsor and stage a Grand

---

6. Petersen, *More Than Music*, 36.

7. Hicks, *Mormonism and Music*, 166. See Jan Shipps, "Difference and Otherness: Mormonism and the American Religious Mainstream," in *Minority Faiths and the American Protestant Mainstream*, ed. Jonathan D. Sarna (Urbana: University of Illinois Press, 1998), 81–109. The Tabernacle Choir's twentieth-century international excursions have likewise aided the church's assimilation and public image in countries beyond North America (see Cynthia Doxey, "International Tours of the Tabernacle Choir," in *Out of Obscurity: The LDS Church in the Twentieth Century* [Salt Lake City: Deseret Book, 2000], 76–89).

International Eisteddfod at the Columbian Exposition. One journalist explained to his puzzled readers that the Welsh "are passionately fond of poetry and singing, and the music of the harp, and they have acquired an excellence in these directions, superior to the most of the nations and not excelled by any."[8] Of all the Welsh American cultural institutions to showcase, an Eisteddfod seemed the most appropriate and attention garnering. This musical competition was the Welsh claim to cultural fame on both sides of the Atlantic during the second half of the nineteenth century and into the early decades of the twentieth. Still, Welsh American leaders realized a typical Eisteddfod would not suffice: they must make it worthy and fitting of such a cosmopolitan event. So they invited the National Eisteddfod of Wales committee to stage their annual competition in Chicago, rather than in Wales, as was the custom. William Ap Madoc, the group's secretary, prodded his fellow Welshmen living in Great Britain to participate. "Will the Welsh People neglect this grandest and most exceptional opportunity of exhibiting their literary and musical characteristics? 'THEY WILL NOT!' is the united voice of the Cymry [fellow countrymen] of America and their descendents, and we pray that the same will be the voice of Gwalia [Welshmen]," his formal request read.[9] Others in the Welsh American community, including newspapermen, echoed his trans-Atlantic summons. In so doing, they sought to showcase a unified Welsh community and culture in both Western lands.[10]

William Madoc's widely disseminated invitation also outlined the proposed competitions and highlighted the impressive monetary prizes. The Chicago Eisteddfod's main event promised to be the First Grand Choral Contest. All competing choirs were required to have between two hundred and fifty and three hundred coed singers. The first-place chorus was promised a $5,000 purse while the runner-up choir was guaranteed a $1,000 prize. Moreover, the conductors of the winning choirs were assured gold

---

8. Editor, "The Tabernacle Choir at the World's Fair," *Juvenile Instructor* 28 (September 15, 1893): 569; "World Columbian Exposition News," *Chicago Daily Tribune*, July 1, 1893, 1.

9. *The World's Columbian Exposition: International Eisteddvod, Chicago 1893: A National and Eisteddvodic Call and Invitation* (Chicago: Rand, McNally and Company, 1891), 7.

10. Edward George Hartmann, *Americans from Wales* (Boston: Christopher Publishing House, 1967), 139–143. See also Linda Louise Pohly, "Welsh Choral Music in America in the Nineteenth Century" (PhD diss., Ohio State University, 1989). For a history of Eisteddfod in Great Britain, see Margaret Jones, *Eisteddfod: A Welsh Phenomenon* (Aberaeron, Dyfed: Margaret Jones, 1986); and William D. Jones, *Wales in America: Scranton and the Welch, 1860–1920* (Cardiff: University of Wales Press with University of Scranton Press, 1993), 149–153.

medals. The Second Grand Choral Contest was a competition between several fifty and sixty male-voice choruses. The winner would take home a $1,000 award while the runner-up would pocket $500. Again, the winning conductors were promised gold medals. The committee also envisioned a traditional poetry competition and a performance of the ancient bardic ceremony. Expectations ran high in Chicago's Welsh community. To the dismay of Welsh Americans, however, their countrymen back in Great Britain were unmoved by the invitation and refused to relocate its annual Eisteddfod to Chicago. Still, the American committee was successful in convincing the Gorsedd of Bards of Great Britain to hold their yearly contest at the Columbian Exposition. And the Archdruid Clwydfardd agreed to let one of their officials officiate over Gorsedd services during the fair. This enabled the Chicago board to project the appearance that Welshmen on both shores of the Atlantic were working together to promote Welsh culture in the White City.[11]

Having secured at least half of the desired participation from Wales, the National Cymmrodorion Society of Chicago spent the next two years planning what they anticipated to be spectacular events at the fair. Its organizing committee dispatched representatives to the major Welsh communities in America to generate excitement and recruit participation from leading choral societies. It was up to the Welsh American community to showcase their finest singers for the unprecedented competition on U.S. soil. As one historian describes, the stakes were high for a diaspora people who were struggling to project their own ethnic identity and self-worth: "The eisteddfod was not only an 'ancient' Welsh institution which illustrated the antiquity of the Welsh people as a nation and, moreover, one which proved that the Welsh in the United States had maintained their Welshness. It was also a symbol of the worth of the Welsh to American society and a positive force in nurturing their good citizenship."[12] The board and its constituents were very optimistic about what their cultural display would do for their image both at home and abroad. But the Welsh were not the only marginalized American group that leveraged the upcoming Eisteddfod at the Chicago World's Fair to their advantage.

The Latter-day Saints also came to appreciate the public relations utility of the Chicago musical competition. They hoped to convince their fellow

---

11. *International Eisteddvod*, 12; and Jones, *Wales in America*, 153.

12. Jones, *Wales in America*, 154, 157–159.

countrymen that they were as American as any other group within the Union's borders. By the spring of 1891 the Tabernacle Choir's famed Welsh conductor was contemplating his chorus's participation in the Columbian Exposition. Initially, Mormon music virtuoso Evan Stephens did not seriously consider competing in Chicago. "I felt that while my choir was a good one, and we were already familiar with singing considerable of the world's greatest and best music, we were, nevertheless, far too young and inexperienced to enter into competition with old, long-established choirs that had entered great competitions and won many times."[13] But Stephens reconsidered after fellow Welshman William D. Davies, a correspondent for the Welsh-language newspaper the *Y Drych* (The Mirror), published in Utica, New York, toured northern Utah in March 1891 and lobbied for the choir's participation. Davies's impression of Utah and its predominant religionists was shockingly positive. While thousands of Welshman had converted to the church in Wales during the mid-nineteenth century, their fellow countrymen rarely painted them with a favorable—or even tolerable—brush, making Davies's observations all the more noteworthy.[14]

The initial encounter between the Latter-day Saints and the Welsh had begun five decades earlier. Mormon missionaries first arrived in England in 1837, but it took three additional years for them to cross over into Wales, and then another three years to evangelize the Welsh-speaking inhabitants. Latter-day Saint missionary William Henshaw began canvasing the Merthyr Tydfil region of that nation. Thanks to a number of intrepid Mormon missionaries and a receptive Welsh populace, there were over five thousand Latter-day Saints in Wales by 1852. But their numbers dwindled as they immigrated to the United States. Between 1850 and 1862, 2,285 Welsh members of the church gathered to Utah, and many joined the Tabernacle Choir. By the end of the nineteenth century, 6,174 Welsh immigrants and their American-born children lived in Utah out of a total population of 267,160. Only six states—Pennsylvania, Ohio, New York, Illinois, Wisconsin, and Iowa—had more Welsh blood than Utah by 1900. In fact, Salt Lake County had the fourteenth largest Welsh population of any county in America that same year. Welsh visitors to Utah were quick to note the prevalence of

---

13. Evan Stephens, "The World's Fair Gold Medal: Part I," *Children's Friend* 19 (September 1920): 372.

14. Phillips G. Davies, ed. and trans., "William D. Davies Visits the Welsh in Utah in 1891," *Utah Historical Quarterly* 49, no. 4 (Fall 1981): 375.

their countrymen, especially the talented Stephens, who had been born in Wales and converted to the church as a young boy.[15]

While touring the American West, William Davies visited his fellow Welshmen in Utah. In Spanish Fork he proudly noted that of the town's three to four thousand inhabitants, Welsh immigrants and their American-born children made up the "main element of the town" and "many of them are able to read Welsh." He further wrote that his "compatriots are generally in good circumstances. One religious service in Welsh is held every week." In the city of Provo, Davies called on Mormon convert John Jones Davies, a former correspondent to the *Drych* and a well-known Welsh poet. The two men enjoyed a pleasant visit together. The Welsh journalist continued his travels north to Salt Lake City, where he, like many curious tourists of his generation, attended Mormon Sabbath services in a local chapel. Later that afternoon he toured the landmark Tabernacle on Temple Square, recording its construction and seating capacity. Davies also observed the Tabernacle Choir's three hundred and fifty singers and noted with pleasure that its talented conductor was Welsh. Davies then attended a Sunday afternoon choir performance in the Tabernacle and was impressed when its members sang "Worthy Is the Lamb That Was Slain" and selections from Handel's *Messiah*, hymns that typically were performed at an Eisteddfod. Following the Tabernacle Choir's performance, Davies implored Stephens to enter his Latter-day Saint chorus in the upcoming Chicago competition.[16] "He so expressed himself freely, and the idea took hold and spread like a prairie fire, though many of our own good people laughed at the idea of our presumption to enter into contest with the outside world's fine choirs," Stephens recalled.[17]

William Davies published his travelogue upon his return to Pennsylvania, and, to the amazement of his Welsh Protestant East Coast readership, wrote

15. Ronald D. Dennis, "Wales," in *Encyclopedia of Latter-day Saint History*, ed. Arnold K. Garr, Donald Q. Cannon, and Richard O. Cowan (Salt Lake City: Deseret Book, 2000), 1304; and Hartmann, *Americans from Wales*, 94–96. See also Ronald D. Dennis, "The Welsh and the Gospel," in *Truth Will Prevail: The Rise of The Church of Jesus Christ of Latter-day Saints in the British Isles, 1837–1987*, ed. V. Ben Bloxham, James R. Moss, and Larry C. Porter (Solihull, England: The Church of Jesus Christ of Latter-day Saints, 1987), 236–267; Ronald D. Dennis, *The Call to Zion: The Story of the First Welsh Mormon Emigration* (Provo, Utah: Religious Studies Center, Brigham Young University, 1988); and P. A. M. Taylor, *Expectations Westward: The Mormons and the Emigration of Their British Converts in the Nineteenth Century* (Edinburgh and London: Oliver and Boyd, 1965), 248–249.

16. Davies, "William D. Davies Visits the Welsh in Utah in 1891," 374–375, 378–380.

17. Stephens, "World's Fair Gold Medal: Part I," 372.

glowingly of the Latter-day Saints, especially those who shared his Welsh heritage. He declared the Mormon Tabernacle Choir to be the "best church choir in the world" and implied that Evan Stephens's chorus would compete in Chicago. Anticipating challenges to his bold assertion, he added: "In the face of this it is likely that some musicians will smile in doubt and ask with ridicule, 'Who is speaking? And perhaps are there no true roots being evolved in the Seion [Zion] of the Mormons between the rocky wilderness of far Utah?' To those I would say, come and see without the glasses of prejudice on your eyes." Davies further extolled Salt Lake City and its Latter-day Saint inhabitants by praising their pioneer architecture and city planning. He praised the pioneers' industry, making specific reference to the hardships they endured as they wrested an entire civilization from the previously unoccupied valley of the Great Salt Lake. Davies also noted, with considerable pride, that there was a Welsh Saint David's Society in the midst of Mormondom: "I believe that the time will not be long before the good example of the Mormons will cause the Christian world to look on the followers of Joseph Smith as one of the orthodox denominations when they have been completely cleansed from the disgrace of multiple marriages." The Welsh newspaperman, like many Americans to come, separated Mormonism's cultural achievements, especially its celebrated Tabernacle Choir, from its controversial religious reputation that stemmed from the practice of polygamy.[18]

William Davies's exchange with Evan Stephens as well as his Welsh newspaper report had immediate consequences for the conductor and his Tabernacle Choir. A month after Davies's March tour of Utah, the church held its April general conference. A high-ranking church leader informed Stephens that the First Presidency and the Quorum of the Twelve Apostles were weighing the merits of Davies's proposition. After considering the choir's participation, the leaders had determined it should compete at the Chicago Eisteddfod. Taken aback by the sudden turn of events, Stephens questioned his ecclesiastical leader about the financial and logistical challenges of transporting hundreds of singers, not to mention choir staff, to Chicago. The chorus members could not be expected to pay their own fares, he exclaimed. "That has all been considered; it is for you only to select and prepare your singers to try and win," the apostle replied.[19] This appears to be the first time

---

18. Davies, "William D. Davies Visits the Welsh in Utah in 1891," 382–385; and "The Tabernacle Choir," *Deseret News*, June 20, 1891.

19. Stephens, "World's Fair Gold Medal: Part I," 372–373.

the Latter-day Saint hierarchy sensed the public relations value of its Tabernacle Choir. To this point, the choir had only provided inspirational music during church meetings and pioneer community gatherings. The Mormon chorus had never ventured beyond the Territory of Utah as a choral group.

In late May 1891, the National Cymmrodorion Society of Chicago sent Evan Stephens an unsolicited letter formally inviting the Tabernacle Choir to the Columbian Exposition's Eisteddfod. William Ap Madoc referenced Davies's glowing report and his assertion that Mormon leaders were considering entering the choir. "The announcement was exceedingly pleasing to the Cymmrodorion society," the secretary wrote. "I am sure that a word from you on this point would be very acceptable." Madoc further revealed that his committee had recently met and agreed upon a $5,000 grand prize for the main choral competition. After promising to mail the formal "Call and Invitation" prospectus, Madoc concluded to Stephens: "I trust and hope that the *Mirror* reported correctly of your intention of bringing your great choir to compete at the 1893 Eisteddfod."[20] The Mormon conductor and his choir had been gracefully pushed into participation by church leaders and Welsh American representatives.

With nearly two and a half years before the September 1893 competition, Evan Stephens began to prepare his choir and made note of his most qualified singers. Moreover, the *Contributor* periodical kept its Mormon readership apprised of musical developments at the Chicago World's Fair: "The best musical talent of the world will be drawn upon; fine halls will be provided; and something like half a million dollars will be expended to make the musical features of the Exposition a success." The periodical also detailed the proposed construction of a number of buildings, including the Recital Hall, Music Hall, and Festival Hall, where the Tabernacle Choir planned to compete.[21] In addition, Stephens informed his chorus members and the public of the upcoming opportunity to perform at the international exposition. This is not to say, however, that the Tabernacle Choir was focused solely on Chicago. In addition to performing on a regular basis in the Tabernacle, the choir was also gearing up for major performances at the capstone-laying ceremony of the Salt Lake Temple in April 1892 and its

---

20. "The Tabernacle Choir," *Deseret News*, June 20, 1891.

21. "Musical Notes," *Contributor* 13 (November 1891): 53; and "World's Fair Music," *Contributor* 13 (July 1892): 424.

dedication in April 1893. During this time Stephens and his staff and singers prepared extraordinary music and programs for these sacred events. As a result, preparation for the Columbian Exposition was pushed to the backburner.[22]

The choir's demanding performance schedule in Utah was not the only challenge it faced while training for the Chicago competition. How to pay for the massive excursion became a major issue, as Evan Stephens had warned. The national economic depression of 1892–1893 hit Utah hard. Given their church's precarious financial condition, some members questioned whether the choir should be sent to the White City at all. Church finances deteriorated to the point leaders proposed that all singers start saving money to pay for their own fair transportation to Chicago, an idea Stephens rejected. All the singers were volunteers and many were already struggling financially. "Finally it was decided to give it up," Stephens recalled. "We ceased even to think any more about the contest, and devoted our entire energies on the Temple Dedication music."[23] Annoyed by how the matter had been handled, yet also relieved that his choir would not have to compete in Chicago against the leading choirs of America and Britain, Stephens determined to take a leave of absence from the choir and take a vacation to his native Wales that summer. The Latter-day Saint singers would not be heading to Chicago after all.

In late spring 1893, Latter-day Saints were surprised, yet gratified, by the public's positive response to the April dedication of the Salt Lake Temple. Newspapers in the eastern United States, as well as in Europe, feted the church and its sacred structure for its architectural and aesthetic contributions to the American religious landscape. Utah Mormons "were unaccustomed to receiving such praise from the non-Mormon press," two historians explain.[24] Although this sacred event was a boon for future Utah tourism, it is best understood as an accidental polishing—rather than an orchestrated public relations campaign—of the Mormon image. Weeks later, on May 1, 1893, the Chicago World's Fair opened to great fanfare in America and abroad. By early June, some Utahns were questioning the church's decision for the Tabernacle

---

22. Stephens, "World's Fair Gold Medal: Part I," 373; and Swinton, *America's Choir*, 31.

23. Stephens, "World's Fair Gold Medal: Part I," 373.

24. M. Guy Bishop and Richard Neitzel Holzappel, "The 'St. Peter's of the New World': The Salt Lake Temple, Tourism, and a New Image for Utah," *Utah Historical Quarterly* 61, no. 2 (spring 1993): 138.

Choir to not compete in the Eisteddfod. "For the year past the public has heard many intimations to the effect that the Tabernacle choir would in all probability go to Chicago in September next to compete with the leading choirs of the world," one reporter reminded the Utah public of the historic public relations opportunity in Chicago.[25]

Aside from obvious financial concerns associated with such a trip, observers might find it curious that Mormon leaders and laity seemed ambivalent about the opportunity to improve their church's beleaguered public image through its Tabernacle Choir. In the twenty-first century, the church is known for its extensive public relations efforts and visitors' centers, most notably Temple Square in Salt Lake City. But this outward-looking emphasis is largely a twentieth-century innovation. As documented in chapter 1, the church limited the majority of its nineteenth-century public relations efforts to domestic and international evangelizing. Throughout the 1890s, some church officials remained unconvinced that they needed to improve the Latter-day Saint image through self-promotion activities. Nevertheless, they allowed non-Mormon tourists to visit the Salt Lake Tabernacle or walk around the grounds of the Salt Lake Temple. Even more tellingly, the church did not open an information bureau on Temple Square until 1902.[26]

The citizens of Utah were not the only ones disappointed by the turn of events. Upon learning of the Mormon Tabernacle Choir's decision to not complete in the Eisteddfod, several of the National Cymmrodorion Society of Chicago's committee members rushed to Utah to reacquire the chorus's formal participation. Three Welsh representatives attended a Sunday choir performance in the Salt Lake Tabernacle in early June 1893 and afterward lobbied the First Presidency to send the choir to Chicago. President George Q. Cannon asked the Welsh American visitors if they thought the Tabernacle Choir had any prospect of winning the competition. The visitors responded that if the Latter-day Saint chorus sang in Chicago as it had earlier that day it stood an "excellent chance" of winning. But when Cannon posed Evan Stephens the same question, the Welsh director answered with an emphatic "no," as his all-volunteer choir could not possibly be prepared to compete against the leading choirs of America and Wales with fewer than three months to practice. Impressed by the Chicago committee's optimism and unmoved

25. "Tabernacle Choir," *Deseret Evening News*, June 6, 1893.

26. Thomas G. Alexander, *Mormonism in Transition: A History of the Latter-day Saints, 1890–1930* (Urbana: University of Illinois Press, 1986), 239.

by their conductor's pessimism, the First Presidency again debated the best course of action.[27] "There seemed to be a spirit of hope that the way would be opened up and great honor and credit might come to our church through the ability of a leader and sweet singers," Stephens recalled.[28]

In the final decade of the nineteenth century, the beleaguered image of the church needed all the affirmative press the choir could garner. Some positive endorsements had already emerged, which the church leadership saw an opportunity to capitalize on. During the summer of 1893 a number of newspapers celebrated the Tabernacle Choir's reputation. The Denver *Republican* introduced Evan Stephens to its readers as "the accomplished musical director who had risen from the position of a shepherd boy on the hills of Utah to direct the strongest and most talented choir organization between Boston and the Pacific coast."[29] Likewise, a Chicago *Daily Tribune* reporter emphasized that the choir was held in esteem by music aficionados of the East. "Some of the greatest musicians of this country have paid them the most extravagant tributes; among them have been Patrick Gilmore, Myron W. Whitney, Emma Thursby and others. These names will be recognized as competent authorities and they have said the chorus was the best unpaid and regularly organized band of singers in America."[30] These observations from newspapers help explain why the Welsh Americans were so keen to have the highly regarded Utah choral group at their Eisteddfod. Welsh Americans knew that to be considered the best singers nationally, they had to compete against all celebrated contenders, including the Mormons from the West. But it was the St. Louis *Post-Dispatch* that most fully captured the public's fascination with the heretofore-isolated Utah choir: "If Brigham Young had told to the brave little column of devoted Mormons that toiled wearily over plain and mountain on the long journey to their land of Canaan beyond the wilderness, that in after years their descendants would dispute with the Gentiles the palm of musical cultivation, the assertion would have been a greater test of faith than the revelation of the Book of Mormon."[31] Yet now a journey east to compete in the national spotlight was a distinct possibility for the Tabernacle Choir.

---

27. "Tabernacle Choir," *Deseret Evening News*, June 6, 1893.

28. Stephens, "World's Fair Gold Medal: Part I," 373–374.

29. "Trip to Chicago to Compete at the Great World's Fair Musical Contest, 1893," *Denver Republican*, August 31, 1893.

30. "Music by Mormons," *Chicago Daily Tribune*, September 3, 1893.

31. "A Mormon Invasion," *St. Louis Post-Dispatch*, August 20, 1893; reprinted in "Dramatic," *Deseret Evening News*, August 26, 1893.

After the Welsh American committee members returned to Chicago in early June 1893, *Deseret News* editors challenged their readers to support the Tabernacle Choir's opportunity. "Will Salt Lake and the Territory respond to the effort now being made to send the Tabernacle choir to Chicago to compete for the World's Fair prizes?" they questioned. The First Presidency also appointed a committee of eight ecclesiastical and civic leaders—William B. Preston, John T. Caine, Hiram B. Clawson, H. G. Whitney, Charles S. Burton, Spencer Clawson, W. C. Spence, and James Jack—to help evaluate and solve the logistical concerns inherent in sending such a large delegation across the country. "The unanimous opinion was that Utah could not afford to allow this opportunity to pass to show to the outside world something of her musical status and progress; further, that it would do more to advertise the Territory and to reflect more of the real conditions existing here, than any other sort of missionary work that could be attempted," one reporter noted. Like the Welsh Americans, a growing number of church leaders and laity sensed the chance to exhibit in Chicago their religion, culture, and territory to the outside world. Would Mormons answer their curtain call onto the world's stage?[32]

The First Presidency became hopeful that the Tabernacle Choir's presence in Chicago might polish the tarnished image of the church. Forward-thinking George Q. Cannon suggested that the Mormon chorus's participation in the Eisteddfod "is sure to be attended with excellent results. As a missionary enterprise it is likely to be a success, for it will give thousands of people the opportunity of learning a little truth about us, and removing the false ideas which they have entertained concerning us." He continued to extol the benefits:

> Though the Latter-day Saints are better known than they were, many misconceptions concerning us having been removed, still much ignorance prevails, and many people depend entirely upon the newspapers for information about Utah and the Mormon people, they never having seen or had any conversation with a Mormon. To see and hear this famous choir will be a surprise to many. They will hear music beautifully and harmoniously rendered by a body of interesting, good-looking young people of both sexes, whose skill as singers would do credit to the most cultured community on the continent, a body of

---

32. "Choir Arrangement," *Deseret Evening News,* June 7, 1893.

singers whom New York or Boston need not be ashamed. After listening to a concert given by the Tabernacle Choir, the audience must separate with new ideas concerning a people in whose midst such a body of singers has been trained. Their respect for the Latter-day Saints would be increased, and they would feel that a people who had encouraged and sustained the formation of such a choir, could not be the ignorant, inferior people they had been described.[33]

In this statement, Cannon was addressing one of the most devastating non-Mormon misconceptions about Latter-day Saints: that Mormon offspring were genetically and aesthetically inferior to the larger American population. Many Easterners believed the pulp-fiction rumors that caricatured the Latter-day Saints as disfigured sub-Americans. Cannon and his colleagues looked forward to showcasing some of the church's most attractive men and women to dispel these rumors. "The healthy appearance and good looks of the young ladies and gentlemen of the choir make a very favorable impression. The onlookers see they are bright, intelligent and superior-looking, and not such people as too many newspapers would have their readers believe the Mormons to be," he editorialized.[34]

The church's own *Deseret News* began petitioning for the Tabernacle Choir's participation in Chicago. "The entire [Utah] community, we think, will rejoice in the fact that the going of the Tabernacle choir to Chicago is being favorably considered; and all will hope that the necessary arrangements will be made." The reporter then created a link between the choir's anticipated success and the territory's prospects for statehood: "Every citizen of the Territory, especially of this city, is proud of the magnificent choral organization to which we refer. The choir and its gifted leader have been the recipients of the highest praise from tourists and musicians.... These compliments reflect upon the whole community, for only among a music-loving and an appreciative constituency can music itself make headway. The proposed tour would therefore be a progress in which every resident would be directly interested; its triumphs would be triumphs in which we all could share."[35] One church official echoed these sentiments, claiming that both Mormon and non-Mormon residents of Utah were proud of the choir and anticipated its

---

33. Editor, "Tabernacle Choir at the World's Fair," 566–567.

34. Editor, "Tabernacle Choir at the World's Fair," 566–567.

35. "The Choir to Chicago," *Deseret Evening News*, June 7, 1893.

participation in the Eisteddfod would benefit the entire Territory then seeking statehood. Like Welsh Americans, many Latter-day Saints appreciated
being able to represent themselves, rather than relying on the traditional misrepresentations of others.[36]

Four major issues, most of them financial in nature, concerned the First
Presidency and the newly created choir committee. To begin with, the railroads needed to be persuaded to offer discounted rail rates for the large choir
delegation. Transporting over two hundred and fifty people roundtrip between Utah to Illinois was the largest anticipated expenditure. Choir business
managers Hiram B. Clawson and H. G. Whitney spent several weeks and
even made a trip to Chicago to negotiate with the various companies that
provided rail service to the White City. After negotiating with multiple railroads, including the Union Pacific and Rio Grande Western, both of whom
hobbled together the necessary rail connections, the transportation issue was
solved by August 18. Clawson and Whitney also managed to upgrade their
entire group from tourist sleepers to first-class Pullman sleeper coaches for
the entire trip at the same cost, courtesy of the Pullman Company. Church
President Wilford Woodruff later noted these specialty cars as "superb."[37]

In anticipation for the choir's excursion to Chicago, the Union Pacific
Railroad printed advertisements for the trip, detailing the itinerary, titled
The Mormon Church Choir Special: To the World's Fair. The official itinerary
read as follows: The tour would leave Salt Lake City on the Union Pacific
Railroad on Tuesday, August 29, and pass through Ogden, Utah; then
Evanston and Green River, Wyoming. During the early morning of
Wednesday, August 30, it would pass through Rawlins, Laramie, and
Cheyenne, Wyoming, before arriving in Denver, Colorado, that afternoon.
That evening the choir would present a concert at the Trinity Church in
Denver. After the concert, the chorus planned to board its train and travel
on to Kansas City, Missouri, where it would arrive on the evening of Thursday,
August 31. Friday morning, September 1, they were scheduled to make a short
trip on the Missouri Pacific Railway to neighboring Independence, Missouri,
and be back in Kansas City that afternoon for a matinee performance at the

---

36. Editor, "Tabernacle Choir at the World's Fair," 566–567.

37. "The Choir Goes," *Deseret Evening News*, August 18, 1893; Wilford Woodruff, *Wilford
Woodruff's Journal, 1833–1898, Typescript*, ed. Scott G. Kenney, 9 vols. (Midvale, Utah: Signature
Books, 1983–84), August 28, 1893. Woodruff later shared that when he met George Pullman in
Chicago, he learned that Pullman's grandmother was a Latter-day Saint (see Woodruff, *Journal*,
September 7, 1893).

auditorium in Kansas City and then a concert that evening at the same location. After the evening concert, choir members would continue on the
Missouri Pacific Railroad to St. Louis, Missouri, where they would arrive the
morning of Saturday, September 2. That evening they would give a concert at
the Exposition Hall, before boarding the Chicago and Alton Railroad to
Chicago, where they were scheduled to arrive on the morning of Sunday,
September 3. The choir would be lodged at the Columbian Hotel in Chicago
for the duration of their stay. On Tuesday, September 5, they would complete
in the $1,000-prize men's vocal contest, and on Friday, September 8, in the
$5000-prize grand contest of mixed choirs. The Tabernacle Choir was also
scheduled to give a concert at the Central Music Hall on Saturday, September
9, as part of the Utah Day celebrations.[38]

Raising private funds to pay for the entire choir's transportation, as well as
room and board, was the committee's second major hurdle. Ticket sales from
proposed concerts along the way presented an opportunity to cover the
transportation costs. In August, Clawson and Whitney arranged for the
Tabernacle Choir to perform in Denver, Kansas City, St. Louis, and Chicago.
The Denver News advertised the pending choral extravaganza, suggesting that
a "cordial welcome" should be given to the Mormon delegation. When
Clawson and Whitney returned from their negotiation trip to the Midwest,
one church leader expressed confidence that fund-raising was no longer a
critical issue, thanks to the financial concessions negotiated by the two com-
mitteemen and the choir's own fund-raising concerts in Utah. Moreover,
wealthy Utahns promised to cover any budget shortfall, while a series of
planned concerts in Salt Lake City would contribute much-needed cash to
the choir's coffers. Bishop Preston also anticipated that the Tabernacle Choir
would likely win one of the competition's major purses, thereby adding to
their growing travel account.[39]

On the last weekend before the Tabernacle Choir was to depart for the
White City, two fund-raising concerts were held in the Salt Lake Valley. The
first, on Saturday, August 26, at the Saltair amphitheatre, featured the choir as
well as popular soloists. "The quartette from Rigoletto, the prison scene from
Trovatore, a ladies' chorus of forty, and the Hallelujah chorus will be features

38. The Mormon Church Choir Special (Omaha: Union Pacific, 1893).

39. "The Tabernacle Choir," Deseret Evening News, August 3, 1893; and "The Choir Goes,"
Deseret Evening News," August 18, 1893.

of the program," read an advertisement in the *Deseret News*.[40] The following Sunday evening was the final pre-trip concert at the Tabernacle on Temple Square. Local church leaders in the Salt Lake Valley were encouraged to finish their Sabbath services early so all who wanted to attend could wish the Tabernacle Choir singers "Godspeed." At this concert the choir performed the same musical selections it planned to sing on the journey to the Midwest. The Union Pacific Railroad even offered discounted rail rates to those who hoped to travel from outlying communities to Salt Lake City to attend the concert. These and other fund-raising events helped push the choir over the financial hump.[41]

Third, should the choir, which by then totaled nearly four hundred, send only their two hundred and fifty best singers to Chicago? The committee's challenge was to convince about one hundred and fifty longtime choir members that their services would not be needed in Chicago, since only two hundred and fifty could perform, according the National Cymmrodorion Society's Eisteddfod guidelines. Committee member John T. Caine gathered the entire choir into the Tabernacle and explained the staffing dilemma. To their credit, the singers agreed to the conditions. But it was not until the middle of August that Stephens announced in the *Deseret News* which lucky sopranos, altos, tenors, and basses—selected for their singing ability—would be heading to Chicago. One can only imagine the highs and lows felt by the hundreds of singers when they saw—or did not see—their name on the list.[42]

Fourth, would the singers be willing to perform many promotional concerts to and from Chicago, on top of offering several performances at the Columbian Exposition, without pay? The committee sought to convince choir members to perform over a dozen paid concerts without individual remuneration. The church and the Utah community would pay for roundtrip travel to and from the fair, as well as room and board in Chicago; choir members had to agree to perform in these planned concerts. Despite the arduous preparation and performances, to say nothing of the fatigue of traveling, Caine explained that choir members would be free to enjoy the fairgrounds while in Chicago—they could do as they pleased during their down time. Choir members were later delighted when the fair's director general George

---

40. "The Choir," *Deseret Evening News*, August 22, 1893.

41. "Tabernacle Choir Concerts," *Deseret Evening News*, August 25, 1893.

42. "Choir Arrangement," *Deseret Evening News*, June 7, 1893; "The Choir to Chicago," *Deseret Evening News*, June 7, 1893; and "Who Was Earlier?" *Deseret Evening News*, August 19, 1893.

R. Davis generously provided complimentary World's Fair passes, valid during the entire duration of their stay in Chicago, to each traveling member.[43]

By mid-August, things were looking up for the choir: the railroads had offered the hoped-for concessions, the prospects for concert ticket sales and additional fund-raising looked bright, choir members had committed to sending only their finest singers (although many were disappointed), and the selected singers did not expect to be paid for their participation. With the First Presidency again convinced that it was in the church's public relations interests for its Tabernacle Choir to compete at the Eisteddfod, Stephens began training his chorus with his personal sheet music but was obliged to request additional music from the East Coast. As the competition was only a month away, the choir rehearsed day and night for two weeks straight. Stephens decided he needed to inspect the competition venues, so he and assistant Horace S. Ensign traveled by train to Chicago, leaving Joseph J. Daynes, the choir's organist, responsible for rehearsals in his absence. When Stephens and Ensign arrived in the Windy City, they were greeted by William Ap Madoc, who showed them around the fairgrounds and the Festival Hall. Stephens wrote that Madoc was "a gentleman of highest attainments as a scholar and musician, who ever after proved a most constant friend to us and our people." Stephens also commented on the Chicagoan Welsh societies that treated him and Ensign "so royally and kindly, that half of the dread of my competition experiences to come had vanished before our return." The show would go on after all.[44]

Not all in the Salt Lake community, however, were excited about the possibility of the church putting its best foot forward onto the national and international stage in the White City. Some evangelical Christians decried the Tabernacle Choir's pending public relations tour. "Warning to the Citizens of Salt Lake City! Take steps and assist the people of the Eastern United States in preventing the Mormon Tabernacle Choir from doing any business there," they wrote in a widely distributed notice. "It is a shame for those people who practice morality, to accept [the Tabernacle Choir's] trip. Likewise, for any Christian Church. If the government accepts their trip it will be a Mormon-government and turn the people into the same,

---

43. "Choir Arrangement," *Deseret Evening News*, June 7, 1893; "The Choir to Chicago," *Deseret Evening News*, June 7, 1893; and "The Choir Goes," *Deseret Evening News*," August 18, 1893.

44. Evan Stephens, "The World's Fair Gold Medal: Part II," *Children's Friend* 19 (October 1920): 420–421.

in spite of other countryes [*sic*]."⁴⁵ These Protestants feared the Mormons might improve their image by such a visit and thus propel Utah toward statehood—the antithesis of what these Protestants hoped for. They were afraid that once Utah shed its territorial status, the church would reassert control over America's newest state.

En Route to the White City

On Monday, August 28, 1893, Mormon choir members assembled in the Tabernacle to receive their berth assignments and tickets for the trip. The entire train consisted of eleven cars, including eight Pullmans for the singers, a day coach for overflow, a baggage car, and a private car labeled "Pickwick" for the First Presidency. About four hundred people traveled in the delegation, including special correspondents from Utah's major newspapers.⁴⁶ "The members are all in excellent spirits, these being abundantly fortified by the good wishes and strong hopes of the many thousands of friends to be left behind, while a carefully selected escort representing every department of life in our busy community will lend buoyancy to the excursionists while dissipating as much of the tedium of travel as possible," one reporter said of the final preparations. He continued, "All the elements necessary to such an experience are with them—excellent company, good cheer, good health, relaxation from daily routines, sight seeing, business and pleasure so skillfully interwoven as to prevent either from becoming so conspicuous and continuous as to be tiresome, a noble errand, and the best wishes of the kindest community in the world."⁴⁷

The following day, the Tabernacle Choir, its management and staff, and the First Presidency pulled out of Salt Lake City bound for Chicago. Over three thousand supporters lined up at the Union Pacific depot to wish their religion's and Territory's representatives goodbye (figure 7). "The crowd was so large that it was only with the greatest difficulty that passengers were able to elbow their way to their respective cars," one newspaper correspondent noted.⁴⁸ As the singers boarded the train cars they all wore identifying badges

45. Reprinted in Petersen, *More Than Music*, 35–36.

46. "Making Ready to Go," *Deseret Evening News*, August 28, 1893.

47. "Au Revoir to the Choir," *Deseret Evening News*, August 29, 1893. The *Deseret News* sent H. G. Whitney, the *Salt Lake Tribune* sent E. K. Gillespie, the *Salt Lake Herald* sent Clark Whitney, and the *Ogden Standard* also sent a reporter.

48. "Off for Chicago," *Deseret Evening News*, August 29, 1893.

FIGURE 7 Mormon Tabernacle Choir departing for the Chicago World's Fair, Union Pacific Railroad depot, Salt Lake City, August 29, 1893, courtesy of the Church History Library, The Church of Jesus Christ of Latter-day Saints, Salt Lake City, Utah.

that pictured the Salt Lake Temple and Tabernacle and featured the phrase "Mormon Tabernacle Choir." Choir members also carried with them stacks of promotional literature on Utah to be distributed at the fair. These singers were to be walking advertisements for both the church and for Utah Territory. The trains themselves were draped with massive banners on both sides, spanning three car lengths, that proclaimed the train was transporting the "Mormon Tabernacle Choir," "Two Hundred and Fifty Voices," and "En route to Chicago to Sing at the Fair." "Utah's sweet singers will advertise this Territory as it has never been advertised before," Church President Wilford Woodruff exclaimed. Such a departure scene "was a most memorable one and without a parallel in the history of the West." The popular Saltair band celebrated the choir sendoff with music.[49]

The Latter-day Saint delegation left Utah and traveled through Wyoming. "The progress of the train thus far has been like a triumphal procession," an observer explained.[50] The previous day the singers' train had been greeted by large crowds at the Ogden train depot; at the train's first stopover in Evanston, Wyoming, nearly a thousand well-wishers, including the mayor and a brass

49. "Off for Chicago," *Deseret Evening News*, August 29, 1893; Woodruff, *Journal*, August 29, 1893.

50. "Speeding Along," *Deseret Evening News*, August 30, 1893.

band, swarmed around the station. The choir responded by performing two numbers from their train cars before continuing on to their next destination. That first night, as the train passed through Rock Springs, Wyoming, the choir was awakened at midnight by a large crowd who were singing as the train passed by at full speed. The Tabernacle Choir also serenaded well-wishers after breakfast in Cheyenne, Wyoming.

From Cheyenne, the Mormon delegation traveled southeast to Denver, Colorado, the site of their first fund-raising performance. Hiram B. Clawson and H. G. Whitney had arranged for the choir to offer a benefit concert at Denver's Trinity Methodist Episcopal Church to help defray tour costs. The performance was a smashing success as the predominantly Protestant audience seemingly focused on the Latter-day Saint musical prowess, not its theology. Moreover, five hundred people had to be turned away due to lack of seats. The choir grossed a prearranged 80 percent of the $1,200 collected in ticket sales. "Denver Stormed and Captured by the Tabernacle Choir," proclaimed the *Deseret News*. Even conductor Evan Stephens was overwhelmed by the public's response in Denver: "We have never, even at home, received a warmer recognition; we were encored from first to last, and the programme was lengthened until nearly 12 o'clock."[51] Local papers echoed his sentiments. "Never was the attractive power of song more strikingly illustrated in Denver than in the concert given by the celebrated Mormon Tabernacle Choir," the Denver *Republican* exclaimed. "The audience filled the building, packed the sidewalks, lingered on the outside and when unable to gain admission, by reason of the dense crowd within, hung on the outside to catch the echoes of the sounds from within." The audience left convinced that the Mormons "would carry off the laurels at Chicago."[52] The manager of the concert hall eagerly offered the choir a return concert with the same financial terms.

Flush with success in Colorado, the Mormon chorus boarded their Pullman cars and headed east. The train arrived outside Kansas City, Missouri, late on the evening of Thursday, August 31, but choir members slept in their sleeper cars. When the Utah visitors awoke the next morning, they were greeted by a committee of prominent Missourians. "As the handsome train pulled into the Union depot the platforms of the cars were crowded and bright faces appeared

51. "Triumph Number One," *Deseret Evening News*, August 31, 1893.

52. "This Time a Friendly Mob," *Kansas City Times*, September 1, 1893; and "Trip to Chicago to Compete at the Great World's Fair Musical Contest, 1893," *Denver Republican*, August 31, 1893.

at the windows. Many for the first time found themselves in Jackson County, which, to them, is sacred soil, and they were anxious for a glimpse of what they have been taught to believe will finally be the early paradise of the Saints," one Missourian wrote.[53] Choir members were then escorted by the mayor of Kansas City to neighboring Independence, Missouri. President Wilford Woodruff noted: "The Mayor had lost one Arm in the Armey [*sic*]. But the one arm left he kindly gave to me while I was with Him."[54] The Utah travelers were stunned to find the town arrayed in festive decor. Fifty handsome carriages transported the entire group up a slight hill to the temple site, where they were joined by thousands of local citizens. One church leader called it a "pilgrimage."[55]

This reception was all the more remarkable as Missouri mobs had illegally driven Latter-day Saints from their farms and homes in this area back in the 1830s. "No reference was made either on the part of visitors or citizens to the old-time troubles except in the *Times* today which pleasantly heads its two-column illustrated article 'this time a friendly mob,'" a Kansas City *Times* journalist wrote.[56] Once the First Presidency was seated on the stage, the town's mayor welcomed his Mormon guests to their old area. "To you, American Freemen, visitors from the far west, from a land of fruits and flowers, I am here as the representative of the citizens of Independence , Mo. A broad, open people, free from bigotry, generous, law abiding, God fearing and lovers of liberty," he declared. "We extend to you the right hand of fellowship and a hearty welcome within our limits. Hoping that the memory of this day may be ever garnered in each heart and treasured there as a gem of one of the most happy events of our lives."[57] There is little doubt that these Latter-day Saints disputed this reporter's characterizations of Missourians, but the choir delegation was still gracious and overwhelmed by the hospitality. Many years had passed since a large group of Latter-day Saints (not including members of the Reorganized Church of Jesus Christ of Latter-day Saints and other "Mormon" offshoots) had stood on Missouri soil.

53. "This Time a Friendly Mob," *Kansas City Times*, September 1, 1893.

54. Woodruff, *Journal*, September 1, 1893.

55. Brian H. Stuy, ed., *Collected Discourses Delivered by Wilford Woodruff, His Two Counselors, the Twelve Apostles, and Others*, 5 vols. (Burbank, Calif.: B. H. S. Publishing, 1987–1992): 5:106.

56. "This Time a Friendly Mob," *Kansas City Times*, September 1, 1893.

57. "In Jackson County," *Deseret Evening News*, September 1, 1893; and "Mormons on Sacred Soil," *Kansas City Star*, September 1, 1893.

Following the mayor's welcome, Presidents Woodruff and Cannon thanked the assembled crowd for their warmth and hospitality. Afterward, the Tabernacle Choir sang "Light and Truth," and then soloist R. C. Easton sang "Oh My Father," a special hymn to the Latter-day Saints. According to one reporter, Easton sang the hymn "in such a pure tone and fine enunciation that tears fell from the eyes of many." He also noted the deference and esteem shown to the church's fourth prophet, Wilford Woodruff, who as a young man had been driven from Missouri to neighboring Illinois six decades earlier. "He has seen and taken part in all the severe trials endured by the Mormons in founding their colony in Utah and witnessed the close of the struggles which drove the Mormons from the town he visited today."[58] Another local newspaper rehearsed Woodruff's previous associations with Independence, Missouri, during the 1830s.[59] In his journal, President Woodruff reflected on how things had changed in Missouri after six decades: "I went through Jackson County with Harry Brown in 1834 on a Mission to the Southern States. At that time we had to keep secreted so the people would not know that we were in the County as our lives would be sacrafized [sic] if they knew that two Mormon Missionaries were in the County. Now the Mayor of the City of Independance [sic] Comes & greets us with the warmest reception. How Great the Contrast. We give God the praise."[60]

Before leaving the hallowed temple site to visit with the adjacent splinter group known as the Reorganites (there were about eight hundred followers living in the area), choir members tried to memorialize the morning's experience by taking some of the sacred ground with them. "Scores picked pebbles and tore off twigs from the trees and shrubs to carry away as sacred relics," one Missourian recorded.[61] That afternoon the Latter-day Saint delegation returned to Kansas City, where they performed two concerts, grossing an additional $1,800 in ticket sales. That evening the group boarded their Pullman cars and bade farewell to newfound admirers.[62]

The following morning, the Tabernacle Choir arrived in St. Louis, Missouri, their final stop before Chicago. Once more they were celebrated by local dignitaries and citizens. The mayor threw a reception on the floor of the

58. "Mormons on Sacred Soil," *Kansas City Star*, September 1, 1893.

59. "This Time a Friendly Mob," *Kansas City Times*, September 1, 1893.

60. Woodruff, *Journal*, September 1, 1893.

61. "This Time a Friendly Mob," *Kansas City Times*, September 1, 1893.

62. "St. Louis Also Captured," *Deseret Evening News*, September 2, 1893.

Merchant's Exchange, which also was attended by three thousand non-Mormon well-wishers. The male choir members delighted the crowd by singing several songs impromptu. That afternoon, their hosts treated all the singers to a free steamboat ride up and down the Mississippi River. As an added bonus, the choir managers distributed the complimentary World's Fair passes, thanks to Davis, to all the choir members so they could enjoy the exposition at their leisure, thus saving the choir $1,000 in ticket fees for their six-day visit to Chicago. That evening the Tabernacle Choir performed another concert to a sold-out audience numbering over three thousand five hundred people, netting their travel fund another $1,500 in receipts. The *Deseret News* trumpeted the choir's triumphs in St. Louis. "The success there was astonishing, and almost bewildered the choir. The reception at the Merchants' Exchange and the praise uttered there for the singing gave an enormous impetus to the box office," one Latter-day Saint correspondent gushed.[63] Another Mormon noted: "At night the crush and brilliance in the great, broad vestibules and the mammoth music hall were overpowering. Wealth, fashion and culture were out in force, and the managers said it included the most distinguished critics of the city. From first to last the program was given an ovation."[64]

The Missouri press likewise extolled the Mormon chorus. According to the St. Louis *Republic*, "The right of the big stage was a sea of white costumes interspersed sparsely with the color of bouquets and badges and relived by brilliant eyes and many hued hair. On the left were the black regulation suits and white bosoms of the men shining under faces of strength and intelligence.... Taken altogether the singing of the Mormon Tabernacle choir was a decided success."[65] The competing St. Louis *Globe Democrat* was even more complimentary and thoughtful of the Latter-day Saints. "Many men, still in middle life, can remember when the Mormon bands, driven from the Mississippi valley, turned their eyes to the great west and began the long journey that ended in the valley of Salt Lake," one reporter reminisced. "Although the railroads have practically abolished space and made Salt Lake City and St. Louis next door neighbors, the fact is not so well appreciated and the thrill of surprise was felt at the announcement that a large band of accomplished singers from the Mormon Tabernacle Choir would appear in St. Louis, en route to Chicago, there to contest for a prize of substantial

---

63. "Choir at the Fair," *Deseret Evening News*, September 5, 1893.

64. "St. Louis Also Captured," *Deseret Evening News*, September 2, 1893.

65. "Mormon Tabernacle Choir," *St. Louis Republic*, September 3, 1893.

proportions."[66] With the city of St. Louis won over to the choir, the delegation once again boarded the train to head east to Chicago.

The Tabernacle Choir's pending arrival in Chicago was heralded in the local papers. "In a magnificent train of Pullman cars 250 of Utah's bravest sons and fairest daughters, the pick and flower of Mormondom, the Territory's sweetest singers, will arrive in Chicago tomorrow morning. This aggregation of vocalists is Utah's chief and grandest contribution to the World's Fair," the Chicago *Daily Tribune* announced. "Never before has a musical organization of this size ever traveled half way across a continent either for the purpose of giving entertainments or to engage in a contest: To bring so large a number of people a distance of 2,000 miles to a fete of this kind was an enterprise of stupendous and costly magnitude."[67]

But it was not the enormous size or even the celebrated musical talent of the choir that captured the public's imagination. Most Chicago residents and cosmopolitan fairgoers simply wanted to see what an "exotic" Latter-day Saint looked like up close and in person. "An unusual interest is felt by all people in this choral society, even those not musically inclined. This is, in a large measure, due to the knowledge that its members are all Mormons and there is a natural and overwhelming curiosity to know what manner of creature a real live flesh and blood Mormon is," one Chicagoan explained. Thankfully, the reporter had the good sense to argue that, "Among these curious ones there will be not a little disappointment when they discover that these musical Mormons are just the same as other people; that they are in no way outré or different from those of other religious beliefs. They have no eccentricities of manners or costume. The men are manly; the women are sweet, womanly, real pretty many of them, and are accomplished in the arts of millinery."[68] That same day the Chicago *Inter-Ocean* likewise noted: "There was a curiosity to this choir, as there was a novelty about Mormons, singers though they are, appearing in a contest."[69]

The Grand Eisteddfod

The Latter-day Saint delegation arrived in Chicago on the morning of Sunday, September 3, 1893. "We reached Chicago half past 8 And the Choir had to be

---

66. "The Mormon Concert," *St. Louis Globe Democrat*, September 3, 1893.

67. "Music by Mormons," *Chicago Daily Tribune*, September 3, 1893.

68. "Music by Mormons," *Chicago Daily Tribune*, September 3, 1893.

69. *Chicago Inter-Ocean*, September 3, 1893.

GEORGE Q. CANNON.   WILFORD WOODRUFF.   JOSEPH F. SMITH.
                        THE FIRST PRESIDENCY
            SAINSBURY   Of The Church of Jesus Christ of Latter-Day Saints.
            AND   Photographed April 6th 1893
            JOHNSON.   SALT LAKE CITY, UTAH.
                        COPYRIGHT BY S. & J.

FIGURE 8 The First Presidency (from left to right: George Q. Cannon, Wilford Woodruff, and Joseph F. Smith) of the Church of Jesus Christ of Latter-day Saints in Salt Lake City, April 6, 1893, courtesy of the Church History Library, The Church of Jesus Christ of Latter-day Saints, Salt Lake City, Utah.

taken to the various Hotels," President Wilford Woodruff noted. "The Labor was vary [*sic*] great Esspecially [for] the femals [*sic*] as they were faint for the want of food. We finally went to the Montreal Hotel. We had a Difficulty about our trunks and Baggage."[70] But the Mormons were greeted with the exciting news that they would be singing second during the grand contest that Friday evening. Moreover, their conductor Evan Stephens was invited to lead the Hallelujah Chorus, comprised of all the choirs enrolled in the competition. Stephens and the Tabernacle Choir were also asked to provide music for

70. Woodruff, *Journal*, September 3, 1893.

the dedication of the Liberty Bell the following Saturday.⁷¹ The Chicago *Daily Tribune* noted that all three members of the First Presidency—Wilford Woodruff, George Q. Cannon, and Joseph F. Smith (figure 8)—had accompanied the choir to Chicago: "It is not often these Mormon leaders come East, and probably never before have all been away from home at the same time. This pilgrimage is to see the Fair."⁷² The reporter was right. In fact, Cannon was the only member of this First Presidency who had ventured beyond the Great Basin desert to the east in decades.

Not surprisingly, Mormon officials visited the Utah Building exhibit at the fair first thing Monday morning. That afternoon, they met with Apostle Heber J. Grant, who had just returned from New York, where he had met with Wall Street financiers to help stave off the church's pending bankruptcy. "He says the financial outlook is immensely improved," one of the leaders noted with relief. But President Woodruff confided in his diary that the bridge loans were obtained "at a fearful per cent."⁷³ The Mormon delegation spent the rest of Monday touring the fairgrounds on their complimentary passes. One leader exclaimed of the White City: "It was a vary [*sic*] grand scene. A man would want a Month to go through this fair ground & to do Justice in Examining what the Grounds Contain." He later wrote: "I visited the fine Arts building. Went through it And it was like a sea of sculpture & Art Painting. It was immens [*sic*]. Then I visited the streets of Cario [*sic*]. Saw the Camels & Asses & Belowan [*sic*] Arabs & Turks & their Harams [*sic*]. I visited their Temple. Saw 10 Mummies. Heard a Lecture of the Temple. I then went through the old Moorish Palace. It was about the grandest affair I Ever saw."⁷⁴

The Latter-day Saints in the White City were again delighted—and likely astonished—with their public reception beyond the borders of Utah. One Utahn correspondent shared the Tabernacle Choir's "royal treatment" and was particularly gratified by the kindnesses extended by the fair's management, especially its director, General Davis. The Latter-day Saints reciprocated his warmth. Later that week the choir gathered in the rotunda of the fair's Administration Building and feted Davis with the song "America." Upon hearing the hundreds of voices below, the director came to his balcony and basked in the musical tribute. Following the serenade, Davies received his

---

71. "Mormon Singers Here," *Chicago Times*, September 5, 1893.

72. "Mormon Dignitaries at the Fair," *Chicago Daily Tribune*, September 5, 1893.

73. Woodruff, *Journal*, September 4, 1893.

74. "Mormon Dignitaries at the Fair," *Chicago Daily Tribune*, September 5, 1893, and "Choir at the Fair," *Deseret Evening News*, September 5, 1893.

Mormon guests downstairs. Orson F. Whitney, a Latter-day Saint dignitary, presented Davies with a handsome, handcrafted mahogany cane and expressed his church's gratitude. "The cane is an emblem of support, and as you look upon this and perhaps lean upon it in future years, may it serve to remind you, by its symbolism, of the support of our friendship and admiring sympathy,— those kindly feelings which we now entertain for you, and of which I doubt not you will ever be the recipient." Following Whitney's remarks, Davies accepted the gift and offered a few remarks on "his good will toward the people of Utah." The choir responded by singing "Light and Truth." Davies then met with the First Presidency and other church leaders in his office.[75]

The Welsh Americans' long-awaited Grand Eisteddfod commenced on Tuesday, September 5, to great fanfare and celebration, including a Welsh parade down the Midway Plaisance. Well-known Welshmen had crossed the ocean to witness the spectacle of their diaspora countrymen in America: "The cream of Welsh America contributed either as guests of honour, conductors, adjudicators or committee members."[76] Over the four-day festival, approximately forty thousand Welsh attended the World's Fair. "There were Welshmen from Wales, Welshmen from the coal mines of Pennsylvania, Welshmen who play the harp at the court of Queen Victoria, Welshmen and Welshwomen from the temple of the Mormons at Salt Lake City, Welshmen who sing like the larks of their native land, and who bring back to present memory strange echoes of the Druids of old," a Chicago reporter wrote.[77] One historian characterized the Chicago Eisteddfod as "an Alpine peak on the landscape of the Welsh experience in America," for several reasons. First, no other Eisteddfod had been staged on such a massive level in the world. Second, preparations overtook the Welsh American community for the two years leading up to the actual event. Third, the Eisteddfod encouraged the same community to evaluate its progress in America.[78]

During the first week of September, the Welsh and their national revival performances garnered a great deal of attention and newsprint in Chicago papers, as well as Welsh-language papers on both sides of the Atlantic. The Chicago *Tribune*, along with a number of other local and Utah dailies, kept readers apprised of the results in the White City, temporarily turned Wales. Readers in Utah were especially interested as members of the Tabernacle

75. "From the Fair Grounds," *Deseret Evening News*, September 14, 1893.

76. Jones, *Wales in America*, 148–149, 161.

77. "Welsh Bards Meet," *Chicago Tribune*, September 6, 1893, 3.

78. Jones, *Wales in America*, 148–149.

Choir were participating in the three key vocal competitions. All of the major contests and performances took place in the Festival Hall, which could accommodate a large audience. Following the opening ceremonies on Tuesday, the Welsh American and British choirs commenced the clash of choruses. Tuesday afternoon was the men's grand choral competition, pitting seven male choruses of fifty to sixty voices each against one another for $1,500 in prize money. The Rhondda Glee and the Penrhyn Male Choir, both from Wales, took the first and second prizes. On Wednesday, four female choirs competed for a smaller purse of $450. The Cardiff Ladies Choir took the first place prize in the women's grand choral competition. The choral contest was put on hold on Thursday, when the Welsh committees and supporters celebrated the grand day of the bardic chair ceremony.[79]

The fourth and final Eisteddfod session—the long-awaited chief choral competition of mixed voices—took place that Friday. A number of highly regarded choruses, including the two hundred and fifty-mixed voice Tabernacle Choir, battled for $6,000 in prize money, including the $5,000 grand reward. The competing choirs gathered before a sold-out crowd of about ten thousand audience members at Festival Hall, and drew lots to see which chorus would sing first. The Welsh choir from Scranton, Pennsylvania, drew the first lot and opened the competition to great acclaim. During their rival's performance, Evan Stephens had his singers wait in the building's basement, where they gathered for group prayer. When it was the Mormon Tabernacle Choir's turn, Stephens led them to the stage, all of the women in white dresses and the men in black suits (figure 9). "As we appeared and charmed the great throng with our modest, clean, orderly sight, a great wave of applause greeted us from every part of the house," Stephens recalled. His choir opened with "Worthy is the Lamb" to cheers from the crowd, followed by "Blessed are the Men who Fear Him." Of this latter piece, Stephens noted that it "went evenly and fair, but requiring a softer tone quality, the hoarseness of some of the singers made it difficult to control, and render the more tender passages just as we should have done." Their final number "Now the Impetuous Torrents Rise" was likewise a bit uneven, in Stephen's estimation, although it was performed "very well indeed."[80] The Tabernacle

---

79. "Choir at the Fair," *Deseret Evening News*, September 5, 1893; "Welsh Bards Meet," *Chicago Tribune*, September 6, 1893, "Welsh Week in Music," *Chicago Tribune*, September 3, 1893, Jones, *Wales in America*, 159–161.

80. Evan Stephens as quoted in Ray L. Bergman, *The Children Sang: The Life and Music of Evan Stephens with the Mormon Tabernacle Choir* (Salt Lake City: Northwest Publishing, 1992), 122–124.

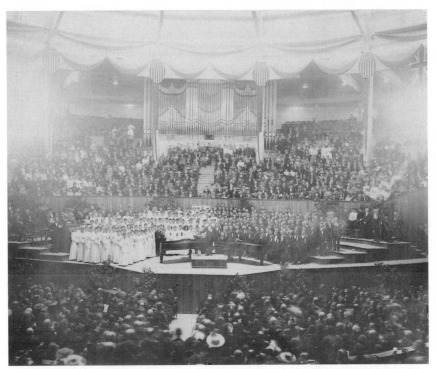

FIGURE 9 Mormon Tabernacle Choir performing at the Welsh Eisteddfod in Festival Hall, Chicago, September 8, 1893, courtesy of the Church History Library, The Church of Jesus Christ of Latter-day Saints, Salt Lake City, Utah.

Choir's three choral arrangements lasted about twelve minutes. They were followed by other chorus who offered their own renditions of these three pieces. Once all of the choirs had competed, Stevens was given the honor of conducting the "Hallelujah Chorus" for the entire gathering of singers and audience members.

With the choral competitions completed, the waiting game began to learn which choir had captured the brass ring. One Mormon observer wrote: "The general opinion was that the $5000 prize would be divided between two of us, as the rules allowed in case of equal merit, and that the third would receive the second prize of $1000."[81] Several musical judges assured Tabernacle Choir singers they would at least share the first prize, so expectations ran high in the Latter-day Saint camp. Later that day, all the Eisteddfod participants gathered as Dr. Henry Gower announced the winners. "Taking all things together the two choirs which sang with few-

81. "The Great Contest," *Deseret Evening News*, September 8, 1893.

est faults and most excellencies were, first the Choral Union, from Scranton, and the Tabernacle Choir, from Salt Lake City," he declared. The Utah chorus took only the silver medal. One reporter shared the resulting scene: "Pandemonium broke loose. After the Welsh and Pennsylvanians had exhausted themselves, one of them cried 'Three cheers for the Mormons!' and a chorus of shouts arose." After the Scranton choir received its $5,000 purse, Evan Stephens graciously accepted the second place check for $1,000 on behalf of the Tabernacle Choir. Although the Utah singers had hoped to win the grand prize, most were still euphoric about their runner-up victory and generous purse.[82] But some church officials were suspicious of the judging: "I think without Doubt that our Quire [*sic*] was the Best & should have had the first Prize But the Quire that took the first Prize was Welsh and the Welsh furnished the Money And it Could hardly be Expected that they would give it to a Mormon Quire Though one of the Judges said the Salt Lake Quire ought to have it," President Wilford Woodruff complained.[83]

Although the Eisteddfod was now over, the weekend's festivities were just beginning for the representatives of the church and Utah Territory. A Friday-evening reception at the Utah Building, hosted by the Utah territorial governor and church leaders, kicked off the festivities. "The place was thronged with notables and refreshments were served by a dozen of Salt Lake's fair daughters, all arrayed in white. There was plenty of music and sociability unlimited," one reporter noted.[84] The party lasted until midnight. The high-point of the revelry occurred when Horace Whitney arrived at the Utah Governor's reception and again publicly announced the choir's runner-up victory to "a storm of enthusiasm." One Latter-day Saint explained: "There had been many fears that we would obtain nothing more than honorable mention, especially as the two Scranton choirs were recruited by foreign singers as well as both held a heavy percentage of Welsh. Up till now every prize, big and little, had gone to the sons or daughters of Cambria and our choir's jubilation is all the heavier accordingly."[85]

Saturday morning marked the celebration of "Utah Day," an official World's Fair holiday commemorating the forty-third anniversary of Utah's

82. "The Great Contest," *Deseret Evening News*, September 9, 1893.

83. Woodruff, *Journal*, September 8, 1893.

84. "It Was Utah's Day!" *Deseret Evening News*, September 9, 1893.

85. "The Great Contest," *Deseret Evening News*, September 9, 1893.

gaining U.S. territorial status. To celebrate, "Utah will entertain with the aid of the great Mormon choir." Exposition organizers had scheduled the holiday to coincide with the Tabernacle Choir's presence in Chicago, in an ongoing attempt to drum up attendance and gate receipts. In addition to "Utah Day," Saturday also commemorated Grand Army Day, California Day, Civil Engineers' Day, and Transportation Day in the White City. The Tabernacle Choir had at last enabled the church, in terms of its cultural institutions, to shed its sullied image and sparkle on stage of public opinion.[86]

Exhibiting Mormonism

The Church's preeminent "Cinderella" moment of the nineteenth century came on Saturday, September 9, 1893, when the Tabernacle Choir was invited to provide dedicatory music for the official placement of the Liberty Bell, a prized relic of Americana, at the Columbian Exposition. The Associated Press reported that Utah's celebrated Tabernacle Choir would perform at the patriotic dedication. That afternoon the Mormon chorus continued to serenade Chicago as they celebrated the Utah Territory's enabling act at Festival Hall. Between three and four thousand people attended the performance to listen to the choir and observe Latter-day Saint leaders in person. To the audience's delight, the Mormon chorus sang a stirring rendition of the "Star-Spangled Banner," after which territorial dignitaries and church leaders offered patriotic remarks, which merited more applause. The Festival Hall, with its Mormon-American entertainers, was the place to be that day in the White City.

That evening, the Tabernacle Choir presented a farewell concert in the Central Music Hall. In attendance were the First Presidency, Governor Caleb West of Utah, as well as other dignitaries including George Fowler, and George W. Pullman. The chorus responded with a number of requested encores and enjoyed heartfelt applause. In fact, several of the Scranton Welsh

86. "Fair Notes," *Deseret Evening News*, September 8, 1893. In the weeks preceding the arrival of the Latter-day Saint delegation, for example, the Columbian Exposition celebrated West Virginia and Delaware Day (August 23), Illinois Day (August 24), Colored People's Day (August 25), Missouri Day (August 26), Grocer's Day (August 30), Netherlands and Ottoman Empire Day (August 31), Nicaragua Day (September 1), Catholic Education Day and Sportsman's Day (September 2). ("Utah," *Deseret Evening News*, September 9, 1893; "Coming Events of Importance," *Chicago Daily Tribune*, August 16, 1893, 1; and "Exposition Notes," *Chicago Daily Tribune*, September 1, 1893, 2.)

American singers mused that if the Mormons had sung as well during the competition there would have been no question that the visitors from Utah would have taken the top prize. Following the performance, a prominent concert promoter lobbied the choir's management to return to Utah via the East Coast, promising audiences in the leading concert halls of New York City, Washington, D.C., Boston, and Philadelphia. But the Tabernacle Choir's managers turned down this generous offer as their singers were already committed to performing in Omaha and Denver during their return to Utah.[87]

Back in Utah, the Latter-day Saints took stock of their choir's participation in the fair in local papers, church periodicals, and personal writings. "The appearance of our choir was most impressive. They evoked very favorable comment. Despite any prejudice there may have been against them as Mormons, their appearance and singing made them friends. They did not fail to call forth respect and praise," President Cannon editorialized. "It will contribute, with other influences which are operating, to make our people better known and understood. That the Latter-day Saints in Utah should send a choir to the World's Fair to compete with the world's best singers and carry off the second prize is a triumph of no ordinary significance, and foreshadows many grand triumphs yet to come."[88] Likewise, an editorial in the *Contributor* proclaimed: "It must be gratifying to every resident of our beautiful Territory to know of the success which has followed our choir in its recent trip to Chicago and the World's Fair."[89] President Woodruff proudly noted the church's accomplishments in the White City: "The Mormon Quire [*sic*] took the 2d Prize in the Chicago fair in Contesting against the world. W. Woodruff G Q Cannon & J F Smith as the Presidency of the Church was Received with open Arms at the Chicago fair by the Leading Men of the world. Even the Mayor & Citizens of Jackson County Entertained us & made us welcome."[90]

The fairy tale-like successes of the previous week, including the Tabernacle Choir's award-winning choral performance and their dedicatory music for the Liberty Bell, made the Latter-day Saints and other Utahns proud. By

---

87. "It Was Utah's Day!" *Deseret Evening News*, September 9, 1893; "Hasting Homeward," *Deseret Evening News*, September 12, 1893; and "Mormon Choir Gives a Concert," *Chicago Daily Tribune*, September 10, 1893, "The Great Contest," *Deseret Evening News*, September 9, 1893. See also, "The Great Contest," *Deseret Evening News*, September 8, 1893.

88. Editor, "Tabernacle Choir at the World's Fair," 569.

89. "The Successful Trip of Our Tabernacle Choir," *Contributor* 14 (October 1893): 600.

90. Woodruff, *Journal*, December 31, 1893.

means of the Tabernacle Choir, the geographically and religiously marginalized Mormons had successfully wrapped themselves in patriotic trappings of red, white, and blue. Such a confluence of events could not have been imagined a few years earlier, when Congress seized the church's assets and passed laws that caused many leaders and ordinary members to go on the "underground" due to federal prosecution of Mormon-sanctioned plural marriages. Consequently, heretofore-loathed Latter-day Saint leaders and laity were overwhelmed by the kindness and acceptance they received from the "Gentile" world on this trip to the Eisteddfod.

"Since 1890 LDS leaders have single-mindedly sought to convince their fellow Americans that the Saints are culturally mainstream and politically committed to the nation's values and purpose," historian Stephen A. Marini insightfully argues. "The principal public vehicle for this complex legitimation strategy has been the Tabernacle Choir, and it has been extraordinarily successful at its appointed task."[91] He rightly emphasizes that although the choir's appointed role has always been its musical offerings for church meetings, its primary mission, since the Manifesto of 1890, has been to create a new and improved image of the church. Thanks in large measure to the Tabernacle Choir, the Chicago World's Fair seemed to mark a new dawn for the public image of the church, at least as a cultural institution, but this optimistic view would be tempered by the reception of the church at the Parliament of Religions, which began days later near the exposition fairgrounds.

---

91. Stephen A. Marini, *Sacred Song in America: Religion, Music, and Public Culture* (Urbana: University of Illinois Press, 2003), 222.

5

Mormonism's Blacksmith Orator

BRIGHAM H. ROBERTS AT THE WORLD'S PARLIAMENT OF RELIGIONS

The gathering at the Art Institute is a parliament of religions—not a parliament of Christians or a parliament of monogamists. The people in attendance knew what they might expect when they accepted invitations to the congress. If they desired to hear only what was entirely agreeable to them they might better have stayed away. The slight put upon Elder [Brigham] Roberts was unjustified and will detract from the value and the reputation of the whole gathering.*
— *Chicago Herald*, 1893

I hold the smiling, benevolent mask of toleration and courage, behind which the Parliament has been hiding, in my hands, and the old harridan of sectarian bigotry stands uncovered, and her loathsome visage, distorted by the wrinkles of narrow-mindedness, intolerance and cowardice, is to be seen once more by all the world.**
—BRIGHAM H. ROBERTS, 1893

ON THE MORNING of September 11, 1893, just as the silver-medaled singers of the Mormon Tabernacle Choir disembarked from their Pullman train cars in Salt Lake City, another auxiliary congress of the Chicago World's Fair commenced in Chicago. Years earlier, at the same moment that the Welsh American committee began planning their singing spectacular, a number of spiritual-minded managers of the Columbian Exposition created the General

---

* Reprinted in Gerald A. Petersen, *More Than Music: The Mormon Tabernacle Choir* (Provo, Utah: Brigham Young University Press, 1979), 36.

** Reprinted in "Dramatic," *Deseret Evening News*, August 26, 1893.

FIGURE 10 Brigham Henry Roberts, Mormonism's "Blacksmith Orator," courtesy of the Church History Library, The Church of Jesus Christ of Latter-day Saints, Salt Lake City, Utah.

Committee on Religious Congress Auxiliary to coordinate the inaugural World's Parliament of Religions. This organizing committee posted over three thousand copies of its preliminary invitation to representatives of all religions around the globe in June 1891. But in contrast to the Welsh Eisteddfod committee, which lobbied Mormon leaders to send their famed choir to compete in Chicago, officials of the Parliament of Religions board made certain that no invitation was mailed to the headquarters of The Church of Jesus Christ of Latter-day Saints in Salt Lake City. The committee instead privileged the representatives of the many denominations and branches of what were then considered the world's ten great religions—Buddhism, Christianity, Confucianism, Hinduism, Islam, Jainism, Judaism, Shinto, Taoism, and Zoroastrianism—at the end of the nineteenth century, despite the church's claim to be a restoration of primitive Christianity. Protestant delegates were loath to admit the "heretical" Mormons to their gathering. Viewed by most American Protestants as neither a wholly Christian (insider) nor totally heathen (outsider) spiritual tradition, Mormons were relegated to an invisible (bystander) role at the historic religious congress. But one Latter-day Saint leader—Brigham H. ("B. H.") Roberts (figure 10)—was unwilling to play this pressured part in the unfolding religious drama in the White City. The church's "blacksmith orator" made sure the world knew of his religion's slight in Chicago.[1]

Scholars can learn a great deal about the prevailing Protestant establishment in Gilded Age America by analyzing which religious groups were barely represented—or not exhibited at all—at the Parliament of Religions and by studying the reasons for their exclusion, according to historian Richard Hughes Seager. In addition to the Latter-day Saints, who received no invitation, Native Americans and African Americans were represented only in a handful of presentations during the entire congress. International exclusions included the so-called primitive religions, except for several paternalistic papers on these tribal faiths offered by Euro-American attendees. Moreover, the religions of Africa and Latin America were barely exhibited at the Parliament. Islam had only two spokesmen. But securing representation was only half the battle for these non-Christian delegates once they arrived in the White City.[2] "The Parliament was an aggressively Christian event, born of American Protestant Christian confidence in its superiority and organized around unquestioned Christian assumptions of the nature and function of religion," historian Judith Snodgrass explains. "It was governed by a set of rules for controlling discourse so permeated with Christian presuppositions that they effectively reduced all other religions to inadequate attempts to

1. Roberts, "Christian Treatment of Mormons," 750–766; and Davis Bitton, "B. H. Roberts at the World Parliament of Religion," *Sunstone* 7 (January/February 1982): 46–51. See also Jan Shipps, *Mormonism: The Story of a New Religious Tradition* (Urbana: University of Illinois Press, 1985), chapter 4.

2. Richard Hughes Seager, ed., *The Dawn of Religious Pluralism: Voices from the World's Parliament of Religions, 1893* (La Salle, Ill.: Open Court, 1993), 7–8. See also Richard Hughes Seager, "Pluralism and the American Mainstream: The View from the World's Parliament of Religions," *Harvard Theological Review* 82, no. 3 (July 1989): 301–324.

express the Christian revelation."[3] Latter-day Saint representation was not wanted nor solicited by the organizers of the 1893 Parliament.

In hindsight, this study of Mormonism at the Parliament, taken together with the experience of other Latter-day Saints at the Chicago World's Fair, helps illuminate several larger issues. First, it provides religious studies scholars and historians with a rich (and largely unknown) case study demonstrating, in the words of Seager, "the ongoing process of revisioning religion in American history."[4] Roberts and his fellow Latter-day Saints were denied the right to exhibit their faith in the main Columbus Hall because Protestant organizers determined that the church did not qualify as a "religion," largely on the grounds of its practice of plural marriage. This helps set the stage to explain how and why Latter-day Saint leaders subsequently attempted to exhibit Mormonism as an advanced cultural institution, rather than focusing on its religious differences to the outside world. Second, we learn how the fates of two men, one a Mormon and the other a Muslim, became intertwined in Chicago. Neither man could get an unprejudiced hearing in the Protestant-organized gathering because of the presence of the other. Third, scholars can learn how and why the Parliament of Religions radically altered the Mormon mental map of non-Christian religions, in contrast with that of other American Christians. When individuals, peoples, and nations encounter one another—especially under unprecedented circumstances like the 1893 Parliament—few walk away unaffected by the meeting. This especially held true for the Latter-day Saints in Chicago. While they sought to reshape outsider perspectives on their religion by exhibiting their own faith, the Mormons were also influenced by the representation of other religionists in the White City.[5]

Genesis of the 1893 Parliament of Religions

Charles Carrol Bonney, a Swedenborgian attorney, is considered the father of the Parliament of Religions. A searching soul who explored the varieties of the religious experience during his life, Bonney first dreamed of an international gathering of religionists in Chicago after learning about the proposed Columbian Exposition. "While thinking about the nature and proper charac-teristics of this great undertaking, there came into my mind the idea of a com-prehensive and well-organized Intellectual and Moral Exposition of the

3. Judith Snodgrass, *Presenting Japanese Buddhism to the West: Orientalism, Occidentalism, and the Columbian Exposition* (Chapel Hill: University of North Carolina Press, 2003), 1.

4. Seager, *Dawn of Religious Pluralism*, 8.

5. Seager, *Dawn of Religious Pluralism*, 8.

Progress of mankind, to be held in conjunction with the proposed display of material forms," he reminisced. Unable to shake his impression, Bonney shared his concern with Walter Thomas Mills, editor of the *Statesman*, who encouraged him to draft a proposal that embraced the spiritual as well as the temporal concerns and achievements of humankind. Bonney argued in 1889 that the penultimate congress of the Chicago World's Fair "should not be the exhibit then to be made of the material triumphs, industrial achievements, and mechanical victories of man, however magnificent that display may be. Something higher and nobler is demanded by the enlightened and progressive spirit of the present age." Rather the "crowning glory" of the international spectacle should focus on the "world of government, jurisprudence, finance, science, literature, education, and religion should be represented in a Congress," he wrote. The life of the mind and the heart needed to stand on equal—if not higher—footing than the industrial attainments of Western civilization.[6]

Bonney's avant-garde proposal struck a responsive cord with the informed public and organizers of the Columbian Exposition. They agreed that the mental and religious life of men and women deserved to be showcased alongside of emerging technologies and human constructions. Within weeks Bonney was enthroned as the chairman of an ever-expanding committee charged with the implementation of his grand vision. Over the next year, Bonney and his colleagues created a number of special subcommittees to oversee the various congresses. In October 1890, these men formally created the World's Congress Auxiliary of the World's Columbian Exposition, with Bonney serving as its president. Their organization oversaw over two hundred committees, managed by sixteen hundred group representatives. Bonney handpicked John Henry Barrows, minister of Chicago's First Presbyterian Church, as chairman of the General Committee on Religious Congress Auxiliary. In response, Barrows selected fifteen local clergymen, one Roman Catholic and fourteen Protestants of different stripe, to help plan and execute the unprecedented religious congress. In the minds of many, the resulting Parliament of Religions proved to be the crowning jewel of the entire Columbian Exposition. Over the next several years, Barrows and Bonney worked hand in hand to showcase the contributions of America's Protestant Establishment, which they and, for the most part, their committees represented.[7]

---

6. Charles Carrol Bonney, "The Genesis of the World's Religious Congresses of 1893," *New-Church Review* 1 (January 1894): 79.

7. Bonney, "Genesis of the World's Religious Congresses of 1893," 80–81; Richard Hughes Seager, *The World's Parliament of Religions: The East/West Encounter, Chicago, 1893* (Bloomington: Indiana University Press, 1995), 47.

Desirous of assembling the most inclusive body of religionists in the history of the world, Barrows's committee mailed over three thousand invitations to Christian and non-Christian religious leaders around the globe. "Believing that God is, and that he has not left himself without witness; believing that the influence of religion tends to advance the general welfare, and is the most vital force in the social order of every people, and convinced that of a truth God is no respecter of persons," the summons began, "we affectionately invite the representatives of *all faiths* to aid us in presenting to the world, at the exposition of 1893, the religious harmonies and unities of humanity, and also in showing forth the moral and spiritual agencies which are at the root of human progress."[8]

Copies of the ecumenical text made their way around the world, by land and by sea, to the heads of Protestant, Catholic, and Orthodox ecclesiastical organizations, as well as to leaders of Buddhist, Hindu, Muslim, and other religious traditions. But the global response was mixed. Some religious leaders favored such a pluralistic gathering, while others eschewed its theological designs and implications. A debate soon arose in religious circles about the propriety of holding such a religious congress in conjunction with the Columbian Exposition. Yet in the end, the committee's proposed Parliament of Religions gained extraordinary support in a number of spiritual communities, including the non-polygamy-practicing Reorganized Church of Jesus Christ of Latter Day Saints (the Community of Christ since 2001).[9] The LDS Church, however, was the single American religious group that was completely denied the promised hospitality from the beginning. Barrows's advisory board never mailed an invitation to Latter-day Saint leaders in Utah.

Nevertheless, after reading about the proposed religious congress in a newspaper, Elder Brigham H. Roberts, a member of the First Council of the Seventy and one of the church's most capable and vocal apologists, saw a unique public relations opportunity in Chicago. Born in England in March

---

8. John H. Barrows, ed., *The World's Parliament of Religions: An Illustrated and Popular History of the World's Parliament of Religions, Held in Chicago in Connection with the World's Columbian Exposition*, 2 vols. (Chicago: Parliament Publishing Company, 1893), 1:10–61; emphasis added. Two additional published sources of the Parliament proceedings are Walter R. Houghton, ed., *Neely's History of the Parliament of Religions and Religious Congresses at the World's Columbian Exposition*, 2 vols. (Chicago: Neely Publishing, 1894); and J. W. Hanson, ed., *The World's Congress of Religions: The Addresses and Papers Delivered before the Parliament* (Chicago: W. B. Conkey, 1894).

9. Joseph Smith III, president of the Reorganized Church of Jesus Christ of Latter Day Saints in 1893, and a number of his church colleagues also were present at the Parliament. They kept their membership abreast of the proceedings through several letters later published in the *Saints' Herald* periodical. (Roger D. Launius, *Joseph Smith III: Pragmatic Prophet* [Urbana: University of Illinois Press, 1988], 296.)

1857, Roberts immigrated to the United States with a Mormon pioneer company. He overcame innumerable childhood challenges, including extreme poverty and abuse. Once in Utah, he earned his daily bread as both a miner and a blacksmith. He also excelled as a student at the University of Deseret and served a domestic mission for the church. Roberts became a member of the press, a renowned speaker, and a celebrated mission president in the American South. Most important to this story, he was an outspoken polygamist with three wives in 1893. For years, Roberts had defended the practice of plural marriage through the spoken word and printed page. He had even taken flight to England in December 1886 to evade U.S. marshals trying to convict him for unlawful cohabitation in Utah. Roberts spent the next two years in exile editing the England-based *Millennial Star* and helping oversee the Mormon evangelism of Great Britain. Finally, in fall 1888, he returned to Salt Lake City and was called as a Latter-day Saint General Authority. The following year, Roberts served a four-month prison term for his practice of polygamy. This humiliating experience further strengthened Roberts's belief that he and his religion had been unjustly treated at the hands of American officials who sought to restrict his religious liberties.[10] As with many Latter-day Saints who had sacrificed dearly to practice polygamy, Roberts was surprised when he learned of Church President Wilford Woodruff's September 1890 Manifesto prohibiting additional Mormon plural marriages.[11]

While working as the associate editor of the Salt Lake *Herald*, Roberts published an editorial in July 1891 suggesting that the church should lobby to become involved in both the Parliament of Religions and the overarching World's Columbian Exposition. He argued that the Chicago gathering might provide an unprecedented opportunity for Latter-day Saints to showcase their history, theology, and cultural contributions to the national and international religious community. After describing the upcoming religious

10. Truman G. Madsen, "B. H. Roberts," in *Encyclopedia of Latter-day Saint History*, ed. Arnold K. Garr, Donald Q. Cannon, and Richard O. Cowan (Salt Lake City: Deseret Book, 2000), 1034–1035. Roberts married Sarah Louisa Smith on January 24, 1878; Celia Ann Dibble on October 2, 1884; and Margaret Curtis Shipp in April 1890, just months before the 1890 Manifesto that prohibited future polygamist unions within Mormonism. (See Truman G. Madsen, *Defender of the Faith: The B. H. Roberts Story* [Salt Lake City: Bookcraft, 1980], chapter 8, "Exile in England" [160–181] and chapter 9, "Castle Prison" [182–198].)

11. Ronald W. Walker, ed., "B. H. Roberts and the Woodruff Manifesto," *Brigham Young University Studies* 22, no. 3 (Summer 1982): 363–365.

congress to his mostly Mormon readers, Roberts then advocated official Latter-day Saint participation: "Mention of this great religious congress reminds us that Mormonism is an American product, one of which all the inhabitants of the earth have heard, and about which they all have a curiosity if not an interest."[12] As the Latter-day Saints had long bemoaned the negative portrayals of their faith and the misrepresentation of their religious practices in the press and in public opinion, it was up to them to take advantage of the present opportunity to begin to reshape the negative image of the church, Roberts believed. He argued that it was time for the Latter-day Saints to tell their own story, especially since his fellow church members had complained for years that they never had a public platform to counter the misrepresentations of their enemies.[13]

In hindsight, Roberts was naively optimistic that a religious tradition like Mormonism, with its unique American origins and history, "could not well be denied a hearing in its own behalf in the religious congress, unless, indeed, a narrow and most ungenerous prejudice should prevail in the councils of those having the arrangement and management of the congress." Still, he warned that "if a sectarian bigoted prejudice should bar the Mormon Church from a hearing in the congress, there is still the bar of public opinion in the world." (Events in September 1893 proved Roberts prophetic on both accounts: the church was denied a hearing at the Parliament, and America's press proved to be an ally in shaping public opinion in the aftermath.) Roberts suggested that the church arrange for an exhibit-hall display at the larger exposition, where it could build a podium for leading Latter-day Saint apologists who might offer a lecture series on the church. Moreover, Roberts wanted church leaders to establish an information bureau on the Mormon faith within the gates of the exposition, where official representatives could sell literature and engage interested observers in religious conversation. Church leaders might even publish a special exposition periodical detailing Latter-day Saint beliefs, which could be distributed to fairgoers. "Much bitterness exists in religious circles against Mormonism and its devotees; yet when people of the world become conversant with the former and familiar with the latter,

---

12. B. H. Roberts, "A Religious Congress," *Salt Lake Herald*, July 15, 1891.

13. Roberts would later complain that the church was falsely accused of "shunning such opportunity for comparison and contrast" with other religions and made reference to his attempt to gain Mormon representation at the Parliament. (See his article, "The Claims, Doctrines, and Organization of The Church of Jesus Christ of Latter-day Saints," *Improvement Era* 1, no. 9 [July 1898]: 664–680.)

their prejudices are softened and their bitterness vanishes," Roberts asserted that July.[14] Yet his follow-up proposal generated little excitement among Latter-day Saints in Utah, who were seemingly focused on preparing exhibits for Utah Territory, rallying women's participation for the feminist congress, and gearing up for the Welsh musical competition.

Three months after Roberts issued his initial proposal, in an October 1891 general conference meeting of male priesthood holders, he again tried to convince Mormon leaders and laity about the public relations opportunities within the upcoming Parliament. Perhaps because they had yet to receive a formal invitation soliciting their contribution, his colleagues did not share his enthusiasm. Roberts let another six months pass before he again lobbied for his losing cause. During the priesthood gathering of the April 1892 general conference, he again made it clear why Latter-day Saints should not pass up the opportunity to exhibit Mormonism in Chicago, in whatever capacity permitted by exposition leaders. This time church leaders reluctantly organized a group to consider Roberts's proposal, but as is often the fate of causes consigned to committee study, nothing ever happened. He recalled that "the general feeling prevailed that the matter was unimportant, and therefore no preliminary steps were taken looking to the representation of the Church, either in the exposition in the World's Columbian Exhibition proper or in the Parliament of Religions."[15]

Latter-day Saint leaders remained unconvinced of the utility of such a religious congress through the first half of 1893. Self-conscious that their church was the only religious group in America that had not been included, the First Presidency determined not to plead for an invitation, for the time being. It would not be until *during* the Columbian Exposition that church leaders began to appreciate it was somewhat within their control to determine how the church was exhibited to the world at such a sophisticated event.[16]

Despite exhibiting general apathy towards the pending Parliament of Religions in Chicago, Latter-day Saints in Utah were increasingly aware of the particulars of the approaching religious congress, thanks to Roberts and a series of *Deseret News* articles that praised the declared goals of inclusiveness.

---

14. Roberts, "A Religious Congress."

15. B. H. Roberts, "The Church of Jesus Christ of Latter-day Saints at the Parliament of Religions: II. Preliminary Agitation," *Improvement Era* 2, no. 9 (July 1899): 675.

16. Roberts, "Preliminary Agitation," 675.

"In this assembly the representatives of each religion will be given full liberty to set forth the doctrines, principles and cardinal truths of their beliefs. They can even go further and show how far humanity has been or will be benefited by their theology, but controversy and criticism are sternly to be prohibited. The idea is in truth grand, poetic, sublime," declared an April 1892 editorial.[17] One week later another announcement celebrated the religious congress in the same paper.[18] That November an additional editorial echoed the claims of the first, with a decidedly Latter-day Saint slant on the utility of the Parliament: "Can it be that the world at last has become conscious of its helpless condition and is willing to investigate the possibility of saving the various fragments of religion from total destruction? Has the time come for the 'warriors of the cross' to transform their swords into implements of peace, preparatory to the dawning of the day of universal brotherhood?" Perhaps the church might shine when placed alongside the religious organizations of the world, the writer suggested.[19]

Once the Chicago World's Fair opened in May 1893, hundreds of Latter-day Saint fairgoers began questioning their church's decision not to participate in its congresses, like the Welsh Eisteddfod and the upcoming Parliament. On July 10, 1893, one month after they agreed to send the Mormon Tabernacle Choir to the Welsh Eisteddfod at the Chicago World's Fair, Presidents Wilford Woodruff, George Q. Cannon, and Joseph F. Smith finally attempted to secure Latter-day Saint participation at the Parliament of Religions through a direct appeal to Bonney. "We are given to understand that an invitation is extended to all denominations of Christians and to all religions of the earth" to air their beliefs in Chicago, their letter began. The church's "success in the face of the stupendous opposition it has encountered gives it the right to be heard in such an assembly by its own accredited representatives. All this we believe will be patent to you, and we therefore respectfully ask that the privilege be accorded us of sending a delegation to represent the Church of Jesus Christ of Latter-day Saints at the World's Religious Congress," they emphasized. The First Presidency concluded their letter by requesting further details: "You will pardon our lack of information on the subject since none of the literature treating of the movement has been forwarded to us."[20] Of course they

17. "A World's Parliament of Religions," *Deseret Evening News*, April 8, 1892.

18. "A Congress of Thinkers," *Deseret Evening News*, April 16, 1892.

19. J. M. S., "Religious Congress," *Deseret Evening News*, November 19, 1892.

20. Roberts, "Preliminary Agitation," 676; and "World Congress of Religions," *Messages of the First Presidency*, comp. James R. Clark, 6 vols. (Salt Lake City: Bookcraft, 1965), 3:248–250 (July 10, 1893).

knew full well they had been slighted, as they posted their letter to Chicago, just two months before the Parliament was to begin in the White City. What remained to be seen was how the First Presidency's eleventh-hour appeal would be handled by Bonney and Barrows's organizations.

After waiting ten days for Bonney's response, the First Presidency dispatched Roberts by train to Chicago to meet face-to-face with exposition and Parliament officials. Adhering to nineteenth-century protocol, the Mormon envoy packed letters of introduction from prominent Utahns to exposition leaders he hoped to meet and lobby in Chicago. One of the references was from Moses Thatcher of the Quorum of the Twelve Apostles, to his relative Solomon Thatcher Jr., a non-Mormon who was a commissioner of the Chicago World's Fair and whose wife was on the exposition's Lady Board of Managers. Roberts departed solo from Salt Lake City on July 20, and arrived five days later in Chicago. Once in the White City he sought out Thatcher, who kindly arranged for an interview between him and Colonel George R. Davis, director general of the exposition, to see if space was still available for a Mormon information bureau, the church's first objective. Roberts recalled that Davis was cordial but explained that all the spaces in the Liberal Arts Building already had been reserved. Because Mormon leaders had not acted until weeks before the Parliament was to begin, contrary to Roberts's urgings, the church missed out on the opportunity to represent itself in the greater exhibition, just as Roberts had feared. In the meantime, many other religions hosted informational booths at the world's fair and denominational congresses at the Parliament.[21]

Disappointed yet undaunted by the news from Colonel Davis, Roberts turned his attention to his church's second objective: gaining Mormon representation at the Parliament. After exerting much effort and enduring many delays, Thatcher arranged for Roberts to meet with Charles Carrol Bonney. Unlike Davis, who had treated Roberts warmly, Bonney dispensed with pleasantries and admitted to Roberts that he had not yet replied to the First Presidency's letter, as the Parliament's committee was conflicted about the proper response to the undesirable Mormons. "There was a very general opinion that the [LDS] Church ought not to be admitted to representation for the reason that it would doubtless prove to be a disturbing element in the Parliament, and it was doubtful in [the committee members'] minds if any good would come from [the church's] admission," Roberts later fumed.

---

21. Roberts, "Preliminary Agitation," 677–678. For a biographical sketch of George R. Davis, see *The Biographical Dictionary and Portrait Gallery of Representative Men of Chicago, Iowa and the Columbian Exposition* (Chicago: American Biographical Publishing, 1893), 12–15.

Chagrined, he asked the president of the Columbian Exposition why Barrows's committee believed Latter-day Saints would disturb the Parliament. Bonney replied because of the continued Protestant outrage over the Mormon practice of plural marriage. Roberts countered that the Latter-day Saints should be allowed to present their faith to dispel such religious intolerance, regardless of past or current religious practices. A defensive Bonney conceded that "common fairness" necessitated Mormon participation in the religious congress.[22]

Bonney then went on the offensive, cross-examining Roberts through a series of pointed questions: "How would you answer the objection urged against the representation of your Church in the Parliament, because of its belief and practice of polygamy?" Roberts replied that such objections should be ignored, pointing out that most of the Asian religions (Hinduism, Islam, Confucianism, and Judaism) and foreign nations represented at the Parliament also practiced polygamy in the past or at least countenanced concubinage currently, yet they were not kept from addressing the Parliament. If the organizing committee was willing to admit "unchristian and polygamous religions from the East they ought not to bar those that were considered unchristian and polygamous from the West." Roberts then pointed out that the church and its leaders had officially discontinued the practice of taking additional plural marriage three years previously, in October 1890, rendering it a moot concern in 1893. Moreover, he made it clear he did not plan to discuss polygamy in his paper to be given in the Hall of Columbus. Roberts further pointed out to Bonney that anti-Mormons accused the Utah-based church of evangelizing only the "ignorant and that it would not dare to come in contact with the enlightenment of our age and civilization." Given the stated objectives of the Parliament and its claims to tolerance, it "would be inconsistent with the character of the great gathering and come with bad grace" to exclude the Mormons from participating. Non-Mormon Thatcher agreed that the Latter-day Saints deserved a hearing on this point.[23]

Bonney finally promised the duo that he would bring the matter again before the Parliament's organizing committee. Roberts impetuously asked if he could be in attendance when the committee discussed his proposal. Bonney replied in the negative but instructed Roberts to put on paper why the Latter-day Saints should be allowed to address the attendees and to outline his proposed comments on the church, a request that Bonney and

22. Roberts, "Preliminary Agitation," 678–679.

23. Roberts, "Preliminary Agitation," 679–680.

Barrows made of no other religion before or during the Parliament. As required by Bonney, Roberts drafted a letter justifying why the Latter-day Saints should get a hearing at the Parliament and outlined his proposed remarks. He divided the latter into seven main sections: church history, summary of its articles of faith, the organization of the church, the domestic work of the church, the foreign evangelism of the church, and a conclusion describing the church's contribution to humanity. Roberts then delivered both documents to Bonney's office for official review. But after a week and a half of fruitless waiting for a response in Chicago, Roberts determined to return to Utah by train, having failed to achieve either of the First Presidency's objectives. As things stood, the church would not be represented at either the exposition or the Parliament. Before departing, however, Roberts wrote one more letter to Bonney, informing him of his pending return to Utah and how he could be contacted in Salt Lake City, if and when Barrows's committee ever made a decision.[24]

The historical record is largely silent about why Bonney, a liberal-minded Swedenborgian, was opposed to the inclusion of the Latter-day Saints in the religious congress. Perhaps he harbored animosity toward Joseph Smith, the founder of the church, who some have suggested borrowed from the cosmology and theology of Emanuel Swedenborg. Or maybe Bonney believed members of his own extended family had been deluded by the Latter-day Saints and persuaded by its leadership to relocate to the mountain deserts of the American West. A number of Bonney's relatives converted to the church and gathered with the Latter-day Saints, breaking up his immediate kinship networks. His maternal uncle and aunt, Joseph and Sally Murdock, embraced the Latter-day Saint message when a Mormon elder evangelized the citizens of Hamilton, New York, in 1836, and performed several miraculous healings. A number of townsfolk, including several of Bonney's cousins, likewise joined with the Latter-day Saints. Four years later, they moved to Nauvoo, Illinois, to be near the religion's founder, Joseph Smith; following his 1844 assassination, most Mormons resettled in the Salt Lake Valley. Several of Bonney's cousins became well-respected, local Mormon leaders. Bonney, in contrast, moved from Hamilton to Peoria, Illinois, at age nineteen, and subsequently converted to Swedenborgianism. Whether this religious rupture of family relationships soured Bonney on the church is unknown, but he was not the first

24. Roberts, "Preliminary Agitation," 680–682.

American to blame the Latter-day Saints for geographically splintering his relations.[25]

While Bonney's rationale for prejudice against the Latter-day Saints remains murky, John Henry Barrows was an outspoken opponent of the church. Bonney's handpicked committee chair was born in 1847, the same year that the Latter-day Saints were driven from the United States into Mexican territory. After studying theology at Olivet College, Yale Divinity School, Union Theological Seminary, and Andover Theological Seminary, Barrows was ordained a Congregational minister in 1875. For the next six years, Barrows held pastorates at the Maverick Church, East Boston, and the Eliot Church, Lawrence, Massachusetts. He then served as pastor of Chicago's First Presbyterian Church between 1881 and 1896.[26]

Barrows began his crusade against the church when he visited his brother Walter, who was serving as a Congregational Church pastor and as president of the board of trustees for the Salt Lake Academy, an evangelical Protestant institution bent on the destruction of the church and the practice of polygamy.[27] During his stay in Utah and the West, John Barrows gave a number of speeches condemning the Mormon faith. He also authored an anti-Mormon circular for Colorado College titled "Christian Education for the Mormons." The published pamphlet is full of contempt and anger toward Latter-day Saints, whom he, like his colleagues, viewed as the vilest of sinners. "Their doctrines are abominable.... This system ought to be wiped out. We send the gospel to

---

25. For an overview of Bonney's life and theology, see *Biographical Dictionary and Portrait Gallery*, 224–228; and George F. Dole, *With Absolute Respect: The Swedenborgian Theology of Charles Carroll Bonney* (West Chester, Penn.: Swedenborg Foundation, 1993). On Mormonism and Swedenborgianism, see Richard Lyman Bushman, *Joseph Smith: Rough Stone Rolling* (New York: Knopf, 2005), 198–199; and Catherine L. Albanese, *A Republic of Mind and Spirit: A Cultural History of American Metaphysical Religion* (New Haven, Conn.: Yale University Press, 2007), 139–144. George A. Thompson, *Advancing the Mormon Frontier: The Life and Times of Joseph Stacy Murdock, Pioneer, Colonizer, Peacemaker* (n.p.: George A. Thompson, 1980), 2–7; and Andrew Jenson, *Latter-day Saint Biographical Encyclopedia*, 4 vols. (Salt Lake City: Andrew Jenson History Company, 1920), 3:173–174. I thank Glen Cooper for providing me with much of the Bonney family biographical data, but I alone am responsible for my conclusions. Bonney's Columbian Exposition papers were lost. (See Seager, *World's Parliament of Religions*, 177.)

26. For an official biographical sketch of Barrows, see *Biographical Dictionary and Portrait Gallery*, 137–140. See also John Henry Barrows, Papers Finding Guide, Oberlin College Archives. Mary Eleanor Barrows, *John Henry Barrows: A Memoir* (Chicago: Fleming H. Revell, 1904), 134–135.

27. For a sample of Walter M. Barrows's anti-Mormon rhetoric, see his *The Mormon Problem* (Boston: Frank Wood, 1878); "Mormonism: A National Shame and Peril," *Home Missionary* 52, no. 5 (September 1879): 113–116; and *How Shall the Mormon Question be Settled?* (Chicago, 1881).

Turkey and India; and we are lacking in our duty to our country if we do nothing to promote Christianity in Utah, and heal this plague spot by touching it with pure gospel instruction."[28] Barrows's contempt for the church continued long after the 1893 Parliament of Religions. In 1900, while serving as president of Oberlin College, he became a founding member of the Utah Gospel Mission Executive Committee, "an interdenominational organization incorporated in January 1900 with the stated purpose of mounting a national crusade against Mormonism." Barrows labored on the committee until his early death from pleuropneumonia in 1902.[29] Barrows wore his anti-Mormonism on his sleeve as a badge of evangelical courage and Christian orthodoxy. He was likely the chief agitator within the organizing committee who lobbied against Latter-day Saint participation in the congress.[30]

Opposition to the church's participation in the Parliament of Religions was not merely a grassroots campaign by low-level Parliament committee members. The anti-Mormon cause was championed by the organization's leadership: both Bonney and Barrows fought Mormon involvement from their gathering's genesis. Having the president of the World's Congress Auxiliary and the chairman of the Parliament's organizing committee fundamentally set against the church was a major hurdle—one church leaders eventually found insurmountable. While both Barrows and Bonney swam in the mainstream of late nineteenth-century American Protestant thought with regard to the Mormon tradition, the two men were uniquely positioned to act on their anti-Mormon prejudice in the White City.

Weeks after B. H. Roberts returned to Utah, and many days since he had abandoned hope that the church would be allowed representation at the Parliament of Religions, he received a conciliatory letter from Bonney dated August 28, 1893. After apologizing for his tardy response to the First Presidency's missive of July 10, Bonney revealed that Barrows was now willing to accept

28. See "Barrows Full of Anti-'Mormonism,'" *Deseret Evening News*, August 18, 1881; and "The Object in View," *Deseret Evening News*, August 20, 1881. John H. Barrows, *Christian Education for the Mormons* (N.p., 1878), 2.

29. See Utah Gospel Mission Collection, Center for Archival Collections, Jerome Library, Bowling Green State University, Bowling Green, Ohio; and Brendan Terry, "Evangelizing Mormondom: John Danforth Nutting and the Utah Gospel Mission, 1900–1949" (Honors thesis, Brigham Young University, 1992). See also Jana Riess, "Heathen in Our Fair Land: Anti-Polygamy and Protestant Women's Missions to Utah, 1869–1910" (PhD diss., Columbia University, 2000).

30. Barrows's personal papers were ruined by a 1923 fire in Berkeley, California, and his files relating to the Parliament were mistakenly destroyed at the University of Chicago. (See Seager, *World's Parliament of Religions*, 177; and Oberlin College Archives finding guide.)

Roberts's proposed paper on the church for presentation in the main assembly room of the religious congress. The president of the Columbian Exposition concluded his note by asking Roberts to pass along his regards to the church's governing body. As fate would have it, however, Presidents Woodruff, Cannon, and Smith had already departed from Salt Lake City as part of the Mormon Tabernacle Choir entourage to Chicago's Eisteddfod, just days before Bonney's letter arrived in Utah. Seeking official direction in the absence of the First Presidency, Roberts consulted with President Lorenzo Snow of the Quorum of the Twelve Apostles, the highest ranking church official not attending the Columbian Exposition with the Tabernacle Choir. Snow encouraged Roberts to prepare the accepted paper and hand deliver it to Bonney or Barrows in Chicago, rather than trusting the mail. "If you merely send your paper they will pigeon-hole that, but if you go down for the purpose of reading it they will not pigeon-hole you so easily," Snow reasoned.[31] Roberts was skeptical of his forthcoming reception in Chicago by the Parliament's organizers, yet excited by the renewed opportunity to try to secure representation for his religion in the White City.

Roberts arrived in Chicago by train on September 8, a mere three days before the Parliament commenced, but just in time to witness the Tabernacle Choir's triumphs with hundreds of other Latter-day Saints. That weekend Roberts made his way to Barrows's office to personally hand over a draft of his paper on the church, as directed by Lorenzo Snow. Barrows "seemed both somewhat surprised and annoyed at seeing me, and reminded me of the very guarded promise made by Bonney of the acceptance of my paper," Roberts recalled. The two men soon engaged in a heated debate about whether the church should be represented at the Parliament, contesting the same ground Roberts had covered with Bonney during his July trip to Chicago. "Feeling somewhat impatient at the treatment accorded the Church I represented," Roberts continued, "I took occasion to remind the reverend gentleman that there was a public opinion that beyond all question would pass upon the unfairness of a rejection of the application of the Mormon Church for hearing in that Parliament, and that if we were not granted the right of a hearing, the world at least should know of the narrow, sectarian bigotry which had denied to us that right." The fiery interview ended following this threat. But Barrows conceded to review Roberts's paper on Mormonism and pledged to let him know the following day its status for presentation.[32]

31. Quoted in Roberts, "Preliminary Agitation," 682–683; and Andrew Jenson, *Church Chronology: A Record of Important Events Pertaining to the History of the Church of Jesus Christ of Latter-day Saints* (Salt Lake City: Deseret News, 1899), 203 (August 29 and September 8, 1893).

32. Roberts, "Preliminary Agitation," 684.

The Mormon delegate returned to Barrows's office the next morning to hear the decision of Barrows's committee. When Roberts arrived, Merwin-Marie Snell, Barrows's personal secretary, informed Roberts that the chairman was out but that Roberts could wait until Barrows returned. Roberts (a Mormon) and Snell (a Roman Catholic) hit it off in Barrows's office, both having felt the weight of the Protestant establishment against their respective faiths. Roberts was delighted to learn that Snell was a professor of comparative religions and an editor of the *Oriental Magazine*. In addition to studying Asian religious traditions, Snell shared that he also had investigated the church.

In Barrows's absence, Snell divulged to Roberts how unfairly the Latter-day Saints had been treated in the private congress committee meetings. "He gave me some very interesting accounts of the stormy discussions that had taken place with reference to this subject. Among other things he said that it had developed that from the earliest agitation of the propriety of holding the Parliament it had been at least tacitly understood that the Mormon Church would not be admitted," Roberts noted. Snell further revealed that he had personally argued for the Latter-day Saints' right to be heard alongside all other religions, an opinion he would soon advocate in public. Roberts accepted Snell's exposé as to why the church had not received any information on the Parliament or an invitation from the organizing committee. As Roberts and Snell concluded their conversation, Barrows came through the door of his office with several Asian Parliament delegates in tow. Unaware of Snell's damning disclosures, Barrows nevertheless declared that although he had not yet read Roberts's paper on Mormonism he had distributed copies to several of his colleagues who judged it "altogether unobjectionable in its character."[33] Roberts would be allowed to deliver his address after all.

Opening of the Parliament of Religions

The inaugural World's Parliament of Religions (figure 11) commenced on Monday, September 11, 1893, with great fanfare. "An event of world wide historic interest, and one without previous counterpart in the history of the world,

---

33. Roberts, "Preliminary Agitation," 684–685. During the Parliament, Roman Catholic Merwin-Marie Snell stepped up as an unlikely supporter for the Latter-day Saints and other minority faiths traditionally marginalized by the American Protestant establishment. As historian Matthew J. Grow argues, "Late-nineteenth-century Catholics adopted a militant stance towards Mormonism," making Snell a notable exception. (Matthew J. Grow, "The Whore of Babylon and the Abomination of Abominations: Nineteenth-Century Catholic and Mormon Mutual Perceptions and Religious Identity," *Church History* 73, no. 1 [March 2004]: 156.)

FIGURE 11 The main assembly of the World's Parliament of Religions, Columbus Hall, Chicago, September 1893, taken from Barrows, *World's Parliament of Religions.*

took place here today. It was the assembling of the parliament of religions, a gathering of representatives of all the great beliefs on the earth," a reporter for the *Deseret News* exclaimed. The Utah journalist was moved by the unprecedented gathering of global religious leaders and representatives. The pageantry, especially the native Asian, Middle Eastern, and Islander costumes, added to the spectacle: "The occident in severely plain garments touch elbows not only on the platform but in the great audience with the brilliantly costumed orient." The journalist further exclaimed that followers of "Jehovah, Christ, Confucius, Buddha, Muhammad" were present as well as delegates from "China, Japan, India, Turkey, the islands of the sea, Catholic and Protestant Europe, and of the Hebrews of the world." Most impressive was the gathering's beginning, an ecumenical invocation led by the Catholic Cardinal James Gibbons.[34]

While seated in Columbus Hall that magnificent morning, Roberts played back in his mind his earlier conversation with Barrows. The chairman had promised only that his "paper would be read," Roberts recalled, which caused him to fear that a non-Latter-day Saint might be assigned to read his paper on the church. Roberts wrote Bonney a short note seeking clarification. "I am left in a little uncertainty as to whether I am to be permitted to read my own paper or you would have it read by someone else," the Latter-day Saint representative asked. "Now, in order that there may be a perfect understanding between us on that, to me, very important matter, I write you this note to say, that under no circumstances could I consent to have my paper read by any

34. "Parliament of Religions: The Occident and Orient Meet to Discuss Their Creeds," *Deseret Evening News,* September 11, 1893.

person but myself.... The disadvantage at which the Church I represent would be placed by having an unsympathetic person read its paper is too obvious to need comment."[35] Three days later, Bonney sent Roberts a message making clear that that he would be able to read his own paper. The church would get a hearing in the main congress Hall of Columbus, or so it seemed.

The next two and a half weeks of congress meetings were unprecedented in the Western world in terms of the comparative study of religion and ecumenical outreach. "Delegates presented some 216 papers in which they advocated a wide variety of theologies, philosophies, creeds, and religions and explored the relationship between religion and music, literature, ethics, morality, ritual, history, and art," Richard Seager describes.[36] The Buddhists were represented by sixteen papers, the Hindus by thirteen, and the Jews by eleven. Presentations on Confucianism, Taoism, Shinto, Jainism, Islam, and Zoroastrianism were also heard by the crowds in Chicago. Delegates from seventeen nations offered remarks, flavoring the religious congress with international seasoning. Asian Indians presented eighteen papers, Japanese seventeen, British sixteen, French five. Moreover, representatives from Armenia, Belgium, Canada, Germany, Greece, Russia, Switzerland, Syria, Thailand, and Turkey each took their turn behind the congress's podiums. There were about fifty "Unitarians, freethinking liberals and naturalists, Swedenborgians, Quakers, Shakers, and other sectarians," twenty-seven "Catholics, Armenians, and Orthodox," and eleven Jewish delegates. The Asian delegation numbering thirty was split between twelve Buddhist delegates, eight Hindu delegates, and a smattering of other Asian representatives. According to Seager's calculation, these 118 "non-evangelicals" accounted for 61 percent of the total number of Parliament presenters. Awash in a sea of non-Christian faith, it is noteworthy that the Parliament organizers hoped to sideline the Latter-day Saints, whom they viewed as non-Christian, during Chicago's international Pentecost.[37]

While waiting to occupy center stage at the Parliament on behalf of his beleaguered flavor of Christianity, Roberts and several of his Mormon associates, including the entire First Presidency, attended a daily stream of

---

35. Roberts, "Christian Treatment of Mormons," 752.

36. Seager, *World's Parliament of Religions*, 50.

37. See F. Max Muller, "The Real Significance of the Parliament of Religions," *Arena* 61 (December 1894): 1–4. See also John P. Burris, *Exhibiting Religion: Colonialism and Spectacle at International Expositions, 1851–1893* (Charlottesville: University Press of Virginia, 2001); Seager, *World's Parliament of Religions*; Eric J. Ziolkowski, ed., *A Museum of Faiths: Histories and Legacies of the 1893 World's Parliament of Religions* (Atlanta: Scholars Press, 1993); and Seager, *Dawn of Religious Pluralism*, for a discussion of its significance to the scholarly study of religion.

congress sessions to learn about other religions. A handful of Latter-day Saints were present during two of the non-placid moments of the gathering. The first was caused by a Japanese Buddhist delegate, Hirai Kinzo. As Buddhologist James E. Ketelaar describes, Barrows initially disallowed Hirai's address as too provocative for the Chicago assembly and urged him to present a more conventional essay on religious unity. So when Hirai made his way to the dais clutching his earlier inflammatory paper, Barrows confronted him center stage and tried to stop him from proceeding. A furious Hirai verbally exploded within earshot of the audience: "Why do you try to prevent me from speaking? By what rights do you violate my freedom of speech? What authority do you claim to interfere with the speeches of members of this Parliament?" Barrows recoiled and the Japanese representative proceeded with his remarks titled "The Real Position of Japan towards Christianity," a tirade against the "abusive, high-handed, self-righteous, bigoted, and racist attitudes of the Christian missionaries in Japan as well as the political inequities perpetrated upon the nation of Japan by the so-called Christian nations." The largely Western audience erupted with applause, although private reactions varied among the Christian denominations. Not surprisingly, Barrows did not record his confrontation with Hirai in his official proceedings. Barrows and his committee were hoping to avoid such embarrassing moments when American Protestantism, which they believed was the ultimate culmination of all world religions, was exhibited in anything but the best light. The Protestant-minded committee dreaded public antagonists like Hirai.[38]

---

38. James E. Ketelaar, "Strategic Occidentalism: Meiji Buddhists at the World's Parliament of Religions," *Buddhist-Christian Studies* 11 (1991): 48. See also Ketelaar's "The Reconvening of Babel: Eastern Buddhism and the 1893 World's Parliament of Religions," chapter 4 in *Of Heretics and Martyrs in Meiji Japan: Buddhism and Its Persecution* (Princeton, N.J.: Princeton University Press, 1990), 136–173. Andrew Jenson, *Autobiography of Andrew Jenson* (Salt Lake City: Deseret News Press, 1938), 208–209 (September 17, 1893). President George Q. Cannon (who was also present at the Parliament) later editorialized of Hirai's paper: "He holds the mirror up to professed Christians. He enables the American people to look at themselves as a Christian nation." Cannon then suggested that the same paper "is not without its profit to us as Latter-day Saints. We make high-sounding professions. Do they correspond with our conduct? Are we consistent? In our treatment of others especially those not of our faith or whom we may think of inferior races to ourselves do we carry into practical effect our professions and teachings? These are questions each of us can ask himself." (Editor, "The Parliament of Religions," *Juvenile Instructor* 28 [October 1, 1893]: 607–608.) See also Vidi, "A Progressive People," which editorializes about the parliamentarian comments of Buddhist delegate Ashitsu Jitsuzen in the same *Juvenile Instructor* issue, 595–597. Barrows was not adverse to editing his collection of Parliament texts that did not meet his approval, as also evidenced by his excising of the remarks of African American delegate Fannie Barrier Williams, who took Christianity to task for its past sanction of slavery (see Umar F. Abd-Allah, *A Muslim in Victorian America: The Life of Alexander Russell Webb* [New York: Oxford University Press, 2006], 222).

As with other Christian attendees, Roberts and members of the First Presidency were awed by the international spectacle at the World's Fair and astonished by the richness of the Asian religions they encountered within the walls of the Hall of Columbus, including Hirai's Buddhism. George Q. Cannon, for instance, observed that "some things...are going to puzzle this parliament," at least the Christian contingent, who believed that Jesus Christ had taught novel doctrines during his mortal ministry. "But here come the Buddhists and the followers of Confucius," he noted, "and they prove that long before the Savior was born many of the truths which He proclaimed were taught by their leading men." Cannon correctly surmised that this anachronistic Christian worldview was "likely to furnish good ground for infidelity and for men thinking that after all there is not so much in this Christian religion as those who advocate it assume; because if Buddha and Confucius knew these truths, where are the claims of the Christians that the Savior was the first to introduce them in His sermon on the Mount?" Many Christians at the Parliament were, in fact, puzzled over these seeming anachronisms of truth.[39]

From the church's 1830 founding until the 1893 Parliament, Latter-day Saint leaders generally employed the "light and spirit of Christ" theory to account for Christian parallels in non-Christian religions. According to this early explanation, "the spiritual influence which emanates from God is not confined to selected nations, races, or groups. All men share an inheritance of divine light. Christ himself is the light of the world. Even those who have never heard of Christ are granted the spirit and light of Christ."[40] As such, God inspired the founders of Buddhism, Islam, Hinduism, Taoism, Confucianism, Shinto, Jainism, Sikhism, Zoroastrianism, and other Asian faiths, to bless all his earthly children. While Joseph Smith was almost certainly ignorant of Asians and their religions, the Latter-day Saint prophet brought forth a number of new scriptures that provided a theological framework for mapping non-Christian, non-Western religions, such as Buddhism and Shinto. According to the Book of Mormon, "the Lord doth grant unto all nations, of their own nation and tongue, to teach his word, yea, in wisdom, all that he seeth fit that they should have" (Alma 29:8) and "the Spirit of Christ

---

39. Brian H. Stuy, ed., *Collected Discourses Delivered by Wilford Woodruff, His Two Counselors, the Twelve Apostles, and Others*, 5 vols. (Burbank, Calif.: B. H. S. Publishing, 1987–1992): 3:355.

40. Spencer J. Palmer, *Religions of the World: A Latter-day Saint View* (Provo, Utah: Brigham Young University, 1988), 197.

is given to every man, that he may know good from evil" (Moroni 7:16; see also Doctrine and Covenants 93:2; John 1:9). In 1832, Smith further revealed that "the Spirit enlighteneth every man through the world, that hearkeneth to the voice of the Spirit. And every one that hearkeneth to the voice of the Spirit cometh unto God, even the Father" (Doctrine and Covenants 84:45–47). Thus, the light and spirit of Christ theory became the leading Mormon explanation for the existence and value of Asian religions during the nineteenth century—until the Chicago gathering.[41]

As in the case of other Christians formally introduced to non-Christian traditions at the Parliament, some Latter-day Saint leaders reformulated their theological response to Eastern religions. Previously they had to explain only how truth existed in other religions. Now they had to account for striking Christian parallels in those same faiths. In other words, the Parliament prompted a Latter-day Saint rhetorical shift from the light and spirit of Christ theory to a diffusionary hypothesis, a theology better suited to account for Christian parallels in non-Christian religions. The diffusion theory proposes that all religions can trace their beginnings to the Christian gospel as originally taught to Adam and Eve by God. Rather than advocating an evolutionary "fulfillment" model, which was quite in vogue in the late nineteenth century, Latter-day Saints viewed the gospel of Jesus Christ in an anti-evolutionary framework. They rejected the developmental claims characteristic of fulfillment inclusivists that suggested nineteenth-century Christianity was the pinnacle of human religious progress. Instead, Mormons advanced a declension model, asserting God had revealed the saving mission of Jesus Christ to Adam and Eve, who then taught it to their children and their children's children. But their descendants had apostatized, resulting in spiritual darkness until God had seen fit to restore that spiritual light. Thus, humanity experienced a number of dispensations of gospel truth followed by apostasy and hopes for future renewal. In short, Mormons dated Christianity at least four thousand years earlier than other Christians did. By moving back the origins of the gospel of Jesus Christ to the time of Adam and Eve, Mormons avoided the timing issue of Christian parallels found in non-Christian religions, parallels that disturbed other Christian Parliament attendees. In brief,

---

41. See my essay, "Joseph Smith and Nineteenth-Century Mormon Mappings of Asian Religions," in *Joseph Smith: Reappraisals after Two Centuries*, ed. Reid L. Neilson and Terryl L. Givens (New York: Oxford University Press, 2009), 209–220, for a comparison of nineteenth-century Mormon and Protestant views of Eastern traditions.

post-Parliament Latter-day Saint rhetoric evidences a shift from the light and spirit of Christ rationalization to a diffusionary explanation.[42]

Attendance at the Parliament of Religions would radically alter the Mormon mental map of non-Christian religions and their adherents, more than any other nineteenth-century encounter between Latter-day Saints and Asians. At the same time as Latter-day Saints were trying to get other religionists to take a fresh look at post-polygamy Mormonism, they were confronted, along with many of their fellow Christians, with the upstanding morality and shared truths of the religions of Asia. After listening to several of the speakers at the Parliament, Mormon historian Andrew Jenson noted in his diary "I cannot deny that some lofty and excellent thoughts were made by these able speakers on religious points."[43] Another church leader who attended the Parliament later wrote of the Asian delegates: "The Buddhists and the Shintovists [*sic*] and the believers in Confucius have a great many truths among them, and they are not so imperfect and heathenish as we have been in the habit in this country of believing them to be."[44] Not only were the Mormons in Chicago to teach, they were there to learn.

After attending the Parliament, Cannon and Roberts advocated diffusion theory. In 1896, Roberts argued that Mormonism, like mining quicksilver, is the force that can unite and blend all truth. He recalled his own experience in Chicago, where he had the "opportunity of listening to an explanation of the religion of Brahma, of the Buddhist religion, of the Philosophy of Confucius and Zoroaster, and of the Mohammedan religion, and in short, of nearly all the religions." Roberts admitted to being "very much astonished at the amount of truth to be found in all these systems of religion." He related how

---

42. Some eighteenth-century Deists advanced their own version of "primitive monotheism" or "original monotheism," although it differed from the later Christ-centered Latter-day Saint theological position. (See Samuel Shuckford, *The Sacred and the Profane History of the World Connected*, vols. 1 and 2, 3rd ed. [London: Printed for J. and R. Tonson, 1743].) Peter Harrison describes primitive monotheism in his book *"Religion" and the Religions in the English Enlightenment* (Cambridge: Cambridge University Press, 1990), 139–146. Wilhelm Schmidt, a non-Mormon critic of evolutionism, argued a similar original monotheism theory, but not until the first decades of the twentieth century. According to Eric Sharpe, Schmidt's "overriding concern was to demonstrate that the older [the] stratum of human culture, the more clearly can one discern in it clear evidence of the worship of a Supreme Being" (Eric J. Sharpe, *Comparative Religion: A History* [New York: Charles Scribner's Sons, 1975], 182–184). See also W. Schmidt, *The Origin and Growth of Religion: Facts and Theories* (London: Methuen and Company, 1930); Palmer, *Religions of the World*, 194.

43. Jenson, *Autobiography*, 208–209.

44. Stuy, *Collected Discourses*, 3:355.

writers including Robert Ingersoll, David Hume, and Voltaire "have undertaken to prove that Christianity was not an original religion with Jesus Christ,
that is, they insist that Jesus Christ copied his precepts, his ordinances, and
the religious and fundamental truths of his religion from the religions of the
orient."[45] At the Parliament the similarities between Christianity and Asian
religions puzzled many Protestant theologians. Echoing Cannon, Roberts
employed the diffusion theory to account for these Christian parallels. He
contended that Latter-day Saint scriptures, including the Bible, Book of
Mormon, and Pearl of Great Price "teach the antiquity of the Gospel" and
explain the "fragments of Gospel truth held by the religions of the Orient, of
India, Persia, Egypt and some portions of Japan and of China." Neither
Cannon nor Roberts again used the light of Christ theory to map Asian religions after their close encounter in Chicago, instead espousing a diffusionary
explanation. The Latter-day Saints left Chicago with new ideas and fewer stereotypes about other religions.[46]

Roberts also was in attendance when Muslim representative Alexander
Russell Webb, a Caucasian convert to Islam, made his highly debated presentation, "The Spirit of Islam," in the Hall of Columbus. His presentation
overshadowed even Hirai's diatribe against Christian missionaries. Webb
remained on safe ground in the beginning as he described the history and
basic tenets of Islam. He lost his footing with the mostly Western audience
when he offhandedly broached the Muslim practice of polygamy. He had
the audacity to suggest in Victorian America that although Islam did not
inculcate plural marriage, "polygamy is no curse. A man can be a good,
honest Christian and yet be a polygamist."[47] While Webb was not an
advocate of polygamy, "he argued that Westerners were ignorant of how it
was actually practiced in the Muslim world and that their categorical condemnation of it was self-righteous and hypocritical in view of the problems

---

45. Quoted in Stuy, *Collected Discourses*, 5:155.

46. Stuy, *Collected Discourses*, 5:155.

47. Latter-day Saints in Utah were aware of Webb and his *Moslem World* periodical prior to
the Parliament. See "Mohammedanism in America," *Juvenile Instructor* 28 (July 1, 1893): 413–
414. For early American views on Islam, see Thomas S. Kidd, "'Is It Worse to Follow Mahomet
than the Devil?' Early American Uses of Islam," *Church History* 72, no. 4 (December 2003):
766–790; "Discourses on Religion of Islam," *Chicago Tribune*, September 21, 1893, 9; and
"Islam is Preached," *Chicago Tribune*, September 21, 1893, 9; "The Religious Congress," *Deseret
Evening News*, September 29, 1893.

that surrounded the marital and sexual practices of their own societies," his biographer explains.[48]

A reporter for the San Francisco *Argonaut* wryly pointed out that Webb's discussion of Muslim polygamy should not upset "the moral sensibilities of the wealth of Christian populations of New York, Chicago, and San Francisco, where, we understand, practical polygamy and even polyandry, are not altogether unknown."[49] One Parliament historian writes tongue-in-cheek that the largely Christian audience reacted to Webb's statements on plural marriage as if they were ignorant of Old Testament luminaries David and Solomon, who were both polygamists and leaders of the Israelite nation.[50]

The 1893 Parliament was neither the first nor the last public occasion that antagonistic Protestants tarred Islam and Mormonism with the same black brush. "Mormonism arose within a North American culture emanating from European Christian civilization, which had nourished anti-Islamic attitudes that were redirected against Mormonism," Near Eastern historian Arnold H. Green describes. "The Joseph Smith–Muhammad analogy developed through three phases correlating with, respectively, anti-Mormon polemics, Orientalism, and pseudosociology."[51] To begin with, Roman Catholics charged Protestant Reformers with being religious heretics and imposters like Muhammad, a medieval indictment labeled

---

48. Abd-Allah, *Muslim in Victorian America*, 239–241. This hypocrisy was not lost on Latter-day Saints in Utah. One Utahn argued: "Coming down to the essence of the matter, if Mr. Webb's statement is false, then the only conclusion to be drawn is that no Mohammedan can be a good, honest gentleman. Nor is this all. Many of the heroes who in the books most revered by all Christians are held out as patterns of the highest standard must be denounced, *and the descent of our Savior Himself must be traced through an ancestry consisting of 'no good, honest gentlemen.'* Surely no Christian is prepared to accept that conclusion. Would it not be better, even for those who profess an ultra-morality, to admit that the peculiar doctrine has had its benevolent mission to perform at some stages of the world's civilization?" "The Religious Congress," *Deseret Evening News*, September 29, 1893; emphasis added.

49. As quoted in Abd-Allah, *Muslim in Victorian America*, 241.

50. Abd-Allah, *Muslim in Victorian America*, 241.

51. Arnold H. Green, "Mormonism and Islam: From Polemics to Mutual Respect and Cooperation," *Brigham Young University Studies* 40, no. 4 (2001): 199–203. See also his "The Muhammad–Joseph Smith Comparison: Subjective Metaphor or a Sociology of Prophethood?" in *Mormons and Muslims: Spiritual Foundations and Modern Manifestations*, rev. ed., ed. Spencer J. Palmer (Provo, Utah: Religious Studies Center at Brigham Young University, 2002), 111–133. See also Timothy Marr, *The Cultural Roots of American Islamicism* (New York: Cambridge University Press, 2006), chapter 4, "'Turkey Is in Our Midst': Mormonism as an American 'Islam'"; and J. Spencer Fluhman, "Anti-Mormonism and the Making of Religion in Antebellum America" (PhD diss., University of Wisconsin at Madison, 2006).

"cryptomohammedanism." The theological descendants of these early Protestants, now the religious establishment in America, ironically redirected this same accusation in opposition to the small, but growing Mormon religious minority as early as 1830.

Early critics of the church, including Abner Cole, Alexander Campbell, Pomeroy Tucker, James Gordon Bennett, E. D. Howe, and even Thomas B. Marsh, employed this anti-Mormon polemic—that Joseph Smith was a latter-day Muhammad in Christian America—viciously and consistently. This latest iteration of cryptomohammedanism eventually made its way into many anti-Mormon articles, pamphlets, and books; moreover, these attacks expanded the simile to embrace the whole of Islam and Mormonism. But as Green makes clear, "This larger superstructure rested on the original foundation: like Muhammad, Joseph Smith was an ignorant, devious, violent impostor."[52]

Eventually, the Joseph Smith–Muhammad comparison moved into the European observation of the Near East, known today as "orientalism." For example, renowned explorer Richard F. Burton toured the Utah capital of the church in 1860, sixteen years after Joseph Smith's assassination, yet still imagined the theological fingerprints of Muhammad all over Salt Lake City and its majority religion, especially when it came to the practice of plural marriage. Burton's sensational travel account *City of the Saints*[53] likely influenced British historian D. S. Margoliouth, who later penned *Muhammad and the Rise of Islam*,[54] which exploited the same comparative trajectory of the founders of Islam and Mormonism. Celebrated German historian Eduard Meyer continued in this vein in his book *Ursprung und Geschichte der Mormonen* ("Origin and History of the Mormons"), the most extensive comparative treatment yet between Muhammad and Joseph Smith.[55] Over time, anti-Mormon polemics and orientalism moved to, in Green's view, "the pseudosociology stage [which] represented a dialectical synthesis of the first two," by which Christian sociologists sought to discredit both religious founders.[56]

---

52. Green, "Mormonism and Islam," 201.

53. Richard F. Burton, *City of the Saints: And Across the Rocky Mountains to California* (New York: Harper & Brothers, 1862.)

54. D. S. Margoliouth, *Muhammad and the Rise of Islam* (London, 1905).

55. Eduard Meyer, *Ursprung und Geschichte der Mormonen* (Halle a.S., M. Niemeyer, 1912).

56. Green, "Mormonism and Islam," 202.

All three of these described phases of anti-Islamic and anti-Mormon thinking contributed to the now-intertwined fates of Webb and Roberts at the religious congress. Yelling "fire" in the crowded Chicago hall might have created less of a stir than the mere mention of the explosive word *polygamy*, which conjured up reminders of the still-distressing "Mormon Question" in America. "The reading of [Webb's] paper was an exceptional event in the proceedings of the Parliament, for the fact that it was attended with strong and even violent and impatient expressions of disapproval on the part of the hearers," Barrows later editorialized in his anthology of speeches. "At the outset of the paper . . . these demonstrations, in the form of hisses and cries of 'Shame!' were so emphatic that the speaker seemed deterred from pursuing the line of discourse on which he had entered." Barrows appeared outraged that the taboo subject of polygamy was broached in front of the main assembly.[57] But Richard Seager questions Barrows's recollection of Webb's comments and the audience's response. "Newspapers reproduced the talk with parentheses showing cries of approval and disapproval, with applause outnumbering hisses and boos three to one (indeed, twice hisses and cries of 'shame' were heard together with applause.)" Seager further notes that Barrows expunged Webb's discussion of polygamy in his official proceedings.[58] Moreover, as biographer Umar F. Abd-Allah points out, Webb never intended to discuss plural marriage in this, the first of his two scheduled speeches: "Since Barrows chaired the first session, it is quite possible that Barrows himself prompted Webb to begin his speech by addressing the issue of polygamy."[59]

Why might the Protestant chairman of the Parliament do such a provocative thing? One possibility is that Barrows, anticipating a firestorm of controversy over the mere mention of Muslim plural marriage, hoped to use the incident to disqualify Roberts and his pending presentation on the church, a

---

57. Barrows, *World's Parliament of Religions*, 1:127. Barrows goes on to say, "Concerning this solitary incident of the kind in the whole seventeen days, three remarks require to be made: 'It was a sudden, unpremeditated outburst of feeling, which the conductors of the Parliament exerted themselves not in vain to repress. It was occasioned, not by any doctrinal statement, but by what was taken for an attack on a fundamental principle of social morality. As soon as the speaker turned from this to a more appropriate line of discourse, he was heard with patient attention and even with applause'" (127–128).

58. Seager, *Dawn of Religious Pluralism*, 279. See also reports in *Daily Inter-Ocean*, September 21 and 22, 1893, reproduced in Seager, *Dawn of Religious Pluralism*, 279–280.

59. Abd-Allah, *Muslim in Victorian America*, 238, 240.

religion infamous for its own allowance of polygamy. In any event, that is exactly what happened. That afternoon, as the commotion over Webb's address subsided, Barrows met with his committee, which determined to un-invite Roberts to address the large gathering on the church in the Hall of Columbus. "Webb's paper on polygamy had aroused such a decided opposi-tion to a free discussion of polygamy, the members of the congress decided that an apostle of Mormonism would be out of place at the congress," the Chicago *Herald* documented the next day.[60] Neither man could get an unprej-udiced hearing in the largely Protestant gathering because of the presence of the other. Roberts's religion, with its polygamist baggage, hampered Webb's reception in Victorian America; and Webb's remarks on Muslim polygamy disqualified Roberts's participation in the same Progressive Era milieu. Regardless of how Barrows subsequently framed and recounted the incident in his Columbian Exposition history, Webb's controversial comments doomed Mormonism's chance to get an impartial investigation during the remainder of the Parliament. Ironically, American Protestants at the Parliament gave a much warmer reception to the Asian representatives of non-Abrahamic (and non-Christian) religions like Hinduism and Buddhism than to Euro-American delegates of Islam and Mormonism.[61]

Barrows sent Roberts a message inviting him to read his already vetted paper (that made no mention of polygamy) in Hall Three, a side room, the following Monday. Already defensive over his previous treatment at the hands of the Parliament's organizers, Roberts was furious to learn of Barrows's administrative about-face regarding his religion's representation. He was well aware that Hall Three was merely a side committee room with space for only two hundred seats. "In a fundamental way," Seager explains, "if one was not among the speakers or the 3,000 observers in the Hall of Columbus in the Chicago Art Institute (or in the Hall of Washington in the case of overflow-ing crowds), one was not at the World's Parliament of Religions."[62] Barrows himself referred to Hall Three as a place "where papers of a more scientific and

---

60. *Chicago Herald*, September 26, 1893, as quoted in "The Religious Congress," *Deseret Evening News*, September 29, 1893; "Parliament Notes," *Chicago Daily Tribune*, September 24, 1893.

61. See also Sarah Miglio "Encountering Islam: Mohammed Alexander Russell Webb and the 1893 World's Parliament of Religions," paper presented at the annual meeting of the American Society of Church History, January 2007, copy in my possession.

62. Richard Hughes Seager, "The Two Parliaments, the 1893 Original and the Centennial of 1993: A Historians View," in *The Community of Religions: Voices and Images of the Parliament of the World's Religions*, ed. Wayne Teasdale and George F. Cairns (New York: Continuum, 1996), 25.

less popular character were read."[63] In Roberts's view the church was once again being kicked to the curb of public opinion. It was the Hall of Columbus or bust for his religion. Having come so far, yet seemingly being denied his desired prize just at the moment that it seemed within his grasp, Roberts came out swinging. That Thursday he dashed off a note to Barrows in which he agreed to present his approved paper on the church in Hall Three as long as doing so would not bar him from also delivering the same address before the entire congress audience in the Hall of Columbus. Angered by this defiant response, Barrows stopped Roberts as the two passed each other in the hall. Barrows made it clear that Hall Three was the only place that Roberts and his religion would be granted a public platform. "The conversation was very hurried, but there was no mistaking the intention of the managers of the Parliament to thus get rid of what they evidently regarded a very troublesome church and representative," Roberts recalled.[64] The First Presidency's representative was right.

The next day Roberts vented his outrage over the way he and his church had been treated by supposedly open-minded Parliament organizers in a letter to Barrows and his committee. He rehearsed everything that had transpired during both of his trips to Chicago on behalf of the First Presidency and described how he had jumped through every hoop that Bonney and Barrows had placed before him. Yet his religious tradition had been denied equal representation. "I may be pardoned for saying that to ask me to read my paper there and let that be the only hearing that 'Mormonism' has, looks very like an attempt to *side track the Church* I represent," Roberts exclaimed, "while the Parliament preserves a reputation for broad-minded toleration that could not even exclude a 'Mormon,' while, as a matter of fact, it hears of him either not at all or else only as in a corner." The church's apologist continued his perceived litany of abuses by pointing out that Hall Three, "whatever be said in praise of the meetings held there, is not the Hall of the Parliament of Religions, nor the platform from which the great religious sects and faiths have spoken—Christianity, Judaism, Islam, Buddhism. Nor has there appeared in the [news]papers any account of its proceedings." Roberts then informed Barrows that he planned to withdraw his paper in formal protest. For Roberts, if Mormonism could not be heard in the Hall of Columbus, "she will be content with the distinction of being the one voice in all the world that

63. Barrows, *World's Parliament of Religions*, 1:152.

64. Roberts, "Christian Treatment of Mormons," 753.

could not be heard in such an assembly, and will seek other means for expressing her views."[65] His was not an idle threat.

From Barrows's perspective, Roberts's status continued to degenerate from
nagging nuisance to irrepressible interloper. And it further deteriorated as the
religious gathering concluded. Feelings of relief, more than thoughts of retali-
ation, likely soothed Barrows's mind. The Mormon problem seemed to have
passed and the overall congress already was being celebrated as a positive
turning point in the religious history of the world. Needless to say, Barrows did
not respond to Roberts's scathing missive. Roberts, on the other hand, sought
justice in the court of public opinion, which was well beyond the control of
Bonney, Barrows, and their Protestant-dominated committees. Roberts
continued to attend the Parliament sessions, to ensure that he was always available if the opportunity arose to represent his faith. Barrows would not have the
opportunity to say Roberts was not available for comment. In addition,
Roberts sought out his new ally Merwin-Marie Snell, complained about the
church's treatment by the Parliament's leaders, and explained why he had with-
drawn his paper on the church, which deserved better than a hearing in Hall
Three, Roberts contended. Snell, a Roman Catholic, agreed.[66]

During the previous week of the Parliament, Snell had encouraged his
Chicago audience to thoroughly investigate other religious traditions before
passing judgment. "The prejudices and animosities which perpetuate religious disunion are in a large proportion of cases the result of gross misconceptions of the true character of the rival creeds or cults," he argued. "The
anti-Catholic, anti-Mormon, and anti-Semitic agitations in Christendom,
and the highly colored pictures of heathen degradations in which a certain
class of foreign missionaries indulge, are significant illustrations of the malig-
nant results of religious ignorance." To make his point he further contended:
"No one would exclude the Church of the Latter-Day Saints from the family
of the world's religions who had caught the first glimpse of its profound cos-
mogony, its spiritual theology and its exalted morality." According to Snell,
studying religion scientifically would enable all religions—including the
Mormon faith—to be welcomed at ecumenical gatherings such as the present
congress. No religions "need to feel out of place; none of them need sacrifice
their favorite tenets, and none of them should dare to deny to any of the
others a perfect right to stand upon the same platform of intelligent and

65. Roberts, "Christian Treatment of Mormons," 755.

66. Roberts, "Christian Treatment of Mormons," 756.

impartial inquiry and to obtain a free and appreciative audience for all that they can say on their own behalf," he concluded.[67] Bonney, Barrows, and like-minded Protestants, of course, disagreed. Not surprisingly, Snell's defense of the church and other non-mainline strands of Christianity never made it into Barrows's "official" collection of the proceedings. The chairman only abstracted Snell's comments and made no mention of his biting critique of anti-Catholicism, anti-Mormonism, or anti-Semitism.[68]

On Sunday, September 24, while chairing a Parliament session, Snell publicly expressed his outrage over how Bonney and Barrows had behaved toward Roberts and the church, noting the First Presidency's delegate had pulled his paper in official protest. Snell also shared with his audience what he had previously divulged only to Roberts—that when Barrows's committee was planning the congress it had come to a tacit consensus that the church would not be allowed to participate in the Parliament. Snell also related that Bonney and Barrows had personally assured Roberts that he could read his prepared statement in the Hall of Columbus. But now Roberts was being denied that opportunity. He further pointed out that—with the exception of the church—not one other American religion, or its representatives, was barred from participation at the Parliament, a committee decision he considered, with obvious hyperbole, to be "the darkest blot in the history of civilization." Moreover, "this ineradicable blot seems to have been due to contemptible ignorance of the religion," he exclaimed.[69] One Chicago reporter reconstructed the heated dialogue that ensued between Snell and members of his audience:

"Are you a Mormon?" asked a ministerial-looking man who occupied a front seat.
"I'm a Mormon this afternoon," was the answer [of Snell].
"Were you yesterday?"
"That makes no difference, I am now."
Continuing Mr. Snell said, the Mormon Church had suffered through the preposterous ignorance and prejudice of other religious bodies. The same was true of the Catholic Church, "I never saw a Protestant," said he, "whose mind was not full of lies about the Catholic Church."

---

67. Houghton, *Neely's History of the Parliament of Religions*, 1:260–261.

68. See Barrows, *World's Parliament of Religions*, 2:1347.

69. Roberts, "Christian Treatment of Mormons," 756.

"What's that? What's that?" Interrupted the ministerial-looking gentleman
again, "You say you never saw a Protestant whose—"
"Yes, I say I never saw a Protestant whose mind was not full of lies about the
Catholic Church."
At this point another gentleman in the audience arose and took exceptions to
the interruptions. The little wave of excitement passed over and Mr. Snell
was allowed to proceed quietly with his talk.[70]

Roberts and the church had found an outspoken advocate in Snell. The
next morning the *Chicago News* reported the Roman Catholic's remarks
under the blaring headline: "SPOKE FOR MORMONISM: SECRETARY
SNELL STIRS UP THE PARLIAMENT OF RELIGIONS. DECLARES
THAT FAIR PLAY WAS NOT ACCORDED THE CHURCH OF
LATTER-DAY SAINTS." Barrows's own secretary, the journalist noted,
"jumped into the breach" in defense of the church and its ill-treatment at the
hands of the Parliament committee. "Mr. Snell was full of religious fair play,
besides possessing a quantity of knowledge about the Church of Jesus Christ
of Latter-day Saints," he described. "What the meeting lacked in numbers it
made up in spice."[71] The Mormon controversy, it appears, was not again
addressed in any of the sessions during the final days of the religious congress.
Roberts never presented his speech on the church in Hall Three or the Hall of
Columbus.[72]

Closing of the Parliament of Religions

The Parliament of Religions concluded on September 27, 1893, after seventeen
days of religious discussions, presentations, and networking events. During
the final plenary session, Bonney addressed the large audience in the Hall of
Columbus and reflected on the apparent triumphs of the historic gathering.
"These Congresses have been successful far beyond anticipation; that they
have transformed into enduring realities the hopes of those who organized

---

70. Roberts, "Christian Treatment of Mormons," 756–757.

71. *Chicago News*, September 25, 1893; and "Addresses by German Ministers," *Chicago Daily
Tribune*, September 25, 1893. See also *Chicago Herald*, September 26, 1893, as quoted in "The
Religious Congress," *Deseret Evening News*, September 29, 1893.

72. Roberts later published his submitted—yet never presented—paper in his "The Paper on
Mormonism," 831–840; and his *Defense of the Faith and the Saints*, 2 vols. (Salt Lake City:
Deseret News, 1907), 1:5–22. It makes no mention of polygamy.

and conducted them, and that they will exercise a benign and potent influence on the welfare of mankind through the coming centuries," he declared were simply "established facts." He then congratulated his fellow organizers and everyone who participated in the groundbreaking ecumenical spectacle that had relatively few administrative hiccups.[73] Bonney added: "If some Western warrior, forgetting for the moment that this was a friendly conference, and not a battle field, uttered his war-cry, let us rejoice that our Oriental friends, that a kinder spirit, answered, 'Father, forgive them, for they know not what they say,'" in response to the behavior of one Protestant agitator.[74]

Bonney also used his closing remarks to justify why he, Barrows, and their committees had excluded one philosophical group and a single religious sect from participation. "If the so-called Secularists or Freethinkers were denied admission to the Religious Congress, it was not from any personal ill-will, but because they had no religious faith to affirm, and no religious achievements to set forth," he explained. Rather than making a similar argument about Mormonism—that it was not a "real" religion—a claim that Roberts and Snell had protested both in private and public, Bonney used a more emotional argument: "If the Mormon Church was not admitted to the Parliament of Religions, it was not because of any discrimination against its religious faith, but for the reason that its disclaimer of a practice forbidden by the laws of the country had not become sufficiently established to warrant such admission." Nevertheless, Bonney claimed that in both situations "the action of the World's Congress Auxiliary was in conformity with the highest rules of charity and justice."[75]

Seated in the Hall of Columbus, a seething Roberts determined not to let Bonney have the final whitewashed word on how the Parliament's leadership had dealt with the church behind closed doors. As he had warned Barrows, Roberts would plead his religion's case before the court of public opinion. That afternoon, Roberts contacted Chicago's leading newspapers, seeking a forum to air his grievances. He convinced the editors of the Republican *Inter-Ocean* to publish what he regarded as "a faithful history" of his experiences at the Parliament in the form of an open letter to Bonney and Barrows. Roberts's

---

73. Charles Carroll Bonney, *World's Congress Addresses* (Chicago: Open Court Publishing Company, 1900), 77–81. See also Barrows, *World's Parliament of Religions*, 1:185.

74. The offensive individual was almost certainly the Rev. Joseph Cook, who was "narrow, dogmatic, uncharitable, and discourteous to non-Christians at the Parliament" (Seager, *Dawn of Religious Pluralism*, 50–51).

75. Bonney, *World's Congress Addresses*, 77–81; Barrows, *World's Parliament of Religions*, 1:185.

bombshell appeared in newsprint the following day. After detailing Bonney and Barrows's unfair handling of the church and its representatives, Roberts concluded his scathing rebuke in crescendo. "Gentlemen, you should have extended a hearty invitation to the 'Mormon' Church to participate in your Parliament, and give her representative a full and fair hearing, not in some out-of-the-way corner, but in general Parliament. You should have done that if for nothing else than to have had the joyful news proclaimed that polygamy had been discontinued by the 'Mormons,'" he wrote. "If you thought us in error, as Christian ministers, you should have been anxious to learn and have the world find out wherein we were in error, that you, as lovers of human souls could find out where we were wrong, and then in kindness and for our good show us our error—and what could have been better for you Christians than to have exposed our error from our own statement of our faith, and then reclaimed us? But you have missed your opportunity."[76]

Roberts's public denunciation of Bonney, Barrows, and the Parliament made waves in a sea of faith. A condensed version of his letter was distributed nationally by the Associated Press, which garnered a good deal of editorial attention, particularly in Chicago's newspapers.[77] "This was most discourteous treatment.... The gathering at the Art Institute is a parliament of religions—not a parliament of Christians or a parliament of monogamists," the Chicago *Herald* editorialized on October 3. "The people in attendance knew what they might expect when they accepted invitations to the congress. If they desired to hear only what was entirely agreeable to them they might better have stayed away. The slight put upon Elder Roberts was unjustified and will detract from the value and the reputation of the whole gathering."[78] The Chicago *Daily Tribune* likewise advertised Roberts's charges against Bonney and Barrows. "All the religions of the world—oriental and occidental, known and unknown, white and black, from idolatry to atheism—have been heard," its reporter summarized. "But the doctrine of the Latter Day Saints, as preached under the anti-polygamy laws of the United States, were completely ignored by the officials of the Congresses at the Art Institute."[79] There is no known record of Bonney or Barrows ever responding in print to Roberts's charges.

76. Roberts, "Christian Treatment of Mormons," 765–766.

77. Joseph Smith, Jr., *History of The Church of Jesus Christ of Latter-day Saints*, ed. B. H. Roberts, 2nd ed., rev., 7 vols. (Salt Lake City: Deseret Book, 1971), 6:240–241.

78. *Chicago Herald*, October 3, 1893; reprinted in *Deseret News Weekly*, October 7, 1893.

79. "Mormon Church is Aggrieved," *Chicago Daily Tribune*, September 28, 1893.

The disappointment that Latter-day Saint leaders felt after their religious tradition was sidelined at the Parliament reinforced what most of them already suspected: that anti-Mormons in powerful places would continue to thwart their theological attempts to assimilate into Christian America. But in Chicago they also came to appreciate that American Christians were willing to embrace the Latter-day Saints as cultural contributors. On the one hand, the territorial representatives from Utah, the women of Mormondom, and the Tabernacle Choir enjoyed international acclaim and commendation. But on the other hand, Roberts and the church were ostracized by the Parliament of Religion's organizing committee. Just after the men and women of Utah, especially the Tabernacle Choir singers, sparkled on the world's *cultural* stage, a Mormon official was denied access to the globe's *religious* platform. Juxtaposing these overlapping experiences helps scholars better understand the limits of religious tolerance in late nineteenth-century America. Not only would the Protestant establishment continue to define the concept of "religion," but it also would seek to control how minority American faiths like Mormonism publicly exhibited themselves to the world. Nevertheless, the Mormon successes—and struggles—at the larger Chicago World's Fair pushed church leaders to seek to escape these imposed confines and to exhibit thereafter their ecclesiastical institution as embodying a culturally advanced society.

6

After the Chicago World's Fair

EXHIBITING MORMONISM IN AMERICA, 1893–1934

> It was known to the officials of this [ecumenical]
> organization that Brother [Brigham H.] Roberts had
> been in Chicago forty years ago, and had not been
> permitted to speak in the general assembly. In the
> introduction that was given to him this fact was referred
> to as indicative of the change in public opinion.*
> —GEORGE S. ROMNEY, 1933

> Since a tree is known by its fruit…the [LDS] Church
> cannot be a wicked institution if its members are an
> upright, honourable people of proven integrity.… This is
> the key to a variety of activities engaged in by officials
> and organizations of the Church. With what results?—a
> better understanding by the people generally of the
> principles and objectives of the Church. Evil-minded
> people had spread abroad so much intense prejudice
> against them that the delivery of the Gospel message
> through our missionary methods has been seriously
> handicapped. In defense the Church has been forced to
> use available publicity means, with excellent results.**
> —JOSEPH F. MERRILL, 1934

JUST WEEKS AFTER Brigham H. Roberts and The Church of Jesus Christ of
Latter-day Saints were denied formal representation at World's Parliament of
Religions, the overarching Columbian Exposition came to an unfortunate

---

* George S. Romney, in Conference Report, October 1933, 40.

** Joseph F. Merrill, "Tabernacle Choir at Chicago Fair," *Millennial Star* 96, no. 36 (September
6, 1934): 568–569.

end. Fairgoers were horrified when a disgruntled resident of Chicago murdered Mayor Carter H. Harrison, Sr., on October 28, 1893, three days before the fair's planned closing ceremonies. In response to the tragedy, the Exposition's commissioners determined to shut down the fairgrounds on Monday, October 30. That evening at 6:00 P.M., a blast of field guns signaled the official end of the White City. "The Utah building and mining and agricultural pavilions closed with the booming of cannon, and the day ended to our representatives with a quiet sociable at the commissioner's office. All expressed satisfaction at the manner in which Utah had been brought to the notice of the world," Latter-day Saint George Pyper described. "During the past six months this Territory has been better advertised than ever before. The entire contingent from Utah have talked themselves hoarse and distributed much literature, and the value to the Territory has been double the amount expended."[1] The next morning workers streamed into the uninhabited sites, packing up and carrying off all of the state and territory exhibits for shipment back to their native homes. Within days all of the contents of the Utah Building were packed and ready for rail transport back to Utah. By the second week of November, all of the Utah leaders and staffers of the Utah delegation were home in Utah, along with the Territory's crated exhibits. Almost overnight, the White City boomtown devolved into a ghost town.

Latter-day Saints were thrilled with their church's reception in Chicago, despite the Parliament of Religions scandal. Members of the First Presidency were delighted by their experiences beyond the Mormon corridor in the West. "At Chicago everything went off in the most pleasant manner. It would be difficult to ask for kinder treatment; ... I am thankful to see people free from prejudice; to see them look at the Latter-day Saints as they truly are; to see us in our true light, and recognize the fact that we are struggling, with them, in our way, to advance the human family and to make progress," President George Q. Cannon noted to a gathering of church members upon his return from Chicago. He then shared his optimism towards the improving Mormon image, skirting the subject of Roberts's treatment in Chicago. He noted that there seemed to be a "spirit of progress abroad in the world" and that the Columbian Exposition had enabled the Latter-day Saints to demonstrate how they were part of this larger trajectory of improvement as a church and a people. Yet Cannon was aware that

---

1. "Closing of the Utah Exhibit," *Millennial Star* 55, no. 50 (December 11, 1893), 801.

image-making was generally a drawn-out process and that it would be a long while before the church truly came out of obscurity to the world. "Of course, we need not expect that there will be any very great hurry in acknowledging our worth or recognizing us in our true character. The air has been filled with misrepresentation. The very atmosphere has been so beclouded with falsehood and misrepresentation that it has been almost impossible to see us through it. But it is gradually clearing up, and men and women are beginning to look at us with different lights and to acknowledge that indeed the Latter-day Saints are accomplishing a great work," the First Presidency counselor summarized.[2]

Striving for elusive Utah statehood and working toward a respectable American identity, Mormon leaders and Utah Territory officials who ventured to the Columbian Exposition became convinced of the image-shaping utility of such cultural gatherings. Latter-Day Saint administrators realized they could, to a degree, shape and broadcast their own image and message to the non-Mormon world. While in Chicago, especially after the way Charles C. Bonney and John H. Barrows sidelined Roberts at the Parliament of Religions, they sensed the importance (from a public relations perspective) of deemphasizing their church's polarizing spiritual beliefs and practices and emphasizing their religion's cultural contributions.

Subsequently, Mormons sought to present themselves, rather than be exhibited by others, which resulted in a bifurcation of the Mormon image in American thought that still lingers. By the first decade of the twenty-first century, Latter-day Saints are commonly viewed by their fellow Americans with both admiration and disapproval. They are thought to have exceptional families, to lead healthy lifestyles, and to be patriotic neighbors and law-abiding citizens; but they are seen by many as weird cultists, religious fanatics, and even non-Christians. Mormon leaders and laity would spend the next century after the Columbian Exposition trying to refashion their public image in America (figure 12). A paradox of this assimilation strategy, which began in 1893 in Chicago, is that Mormonism was subsequently mainstreamed into American culture as a *religion* because of its *nonreligious* achievements to the nation. In other words, the church was eventually integrated into Americana in spite of, *not because of,* its religious contributions.

2. Brian H. Stuy, ed., *Collected Discourses Delivered by Wilford Woodruff, His Two Counselors, the Twelve Apostles, and Others,* 5 vols. (Burbank, Calif.: B. H. S. Publishing, 1987–1992), 3:350–351.

FIGURE 12 The Bureau of Information of The Church of Jesus Christ of Latter-day Saints on Temple Square, Salt Lake City, courtesy of the Church History Library, The Church of Jesus Christ of Latter-day Saints, Salt Lake City, Utah.

Mormon Participation in Utah-Centered Exhibits at American Fairs, 1893–1907

The Columbian Exposition marked a turning point in Mormon community-relations activities by prodding General Authorities to focus on the education of the public in addition to its evangelistic enterprises. During the summer of 1893, over seven thousand Latter-day Saints made their way to the Chicago World's Fair both as tourists and exhibitors of their faith and the Utah Territory. Hundreds were involved in preparing and staffing exhibits for the official Utah Building at the Jackson Park Fairgrounds, representing the interests of Latter-day Saint ladies at the World's Congress of Representative Women, competing in the Welsh Eisteddfod, and attending the inaugural World's Parliament of Religions. The church would thereafter balance its evangelistic efforts with its promotional activities. Official church involvement helped leaders appreciate that they needed both converts and friends to fulfill its larger mission. As a result, Latter-day Saints participated in many subsequent American expositions, generally in conjunction with representatives of their home state of Utah. Between 1893 and 1907, church delegations visited a number of these domestic fairs, along with their fellow Mormon and non-Mormon Utahns. But it was not until the 1909 Alaska-Yukon-Pacific Exposition held in Seattle, Washington, that the Utah-based church and its members transitioned from "state-centered to Church-centered" participation in world fairs.[3]

Five years after the Columbian Exposition delighted fairgoers in Chicago, another major American fair opened in Omaha, Nebraska. Geographically speaking, the 1898 Trans-Mississippi and International Exposition was the world's fair held nearest to Utah. Having achieved statehood in 1896, Utah leaders determined to represent their newly recognized state at the Midwestern fair. In 1897 the Utah state legislature debated what level of financial support to give to its delegation for the exposition, ultimately settling on a mere $2,000. Church leaders likewise hoped to represent the church in Omaha, a city they had helped settle in 1846 in neighboring Council Bluffs or Winter Quarters. By this time, the Mormons appreciated the utility of such cosmopolitan gatherings and anticipated the attention they would likely receive as representatives of the pioneering spirit of the American West. But when Church President Wilford Woodruff passed away in early September 1898, the Latter-day Saints scaled back their participation. Still, Mormon leaders Lorenzo Snow, George Q. Cannon, and Joseph F. Smith traveled with Latter-day Saint Utah governor Heber M. Wells and a number of other Utah dignitaries by train to Omaha to help celebrate "Utah Day" at the fair on October 20. "Utah has nobly contributed a large share towards this progress. Her day at the fair ought, therefore, to be one of the memorable ones, and we have no doubt it will be made such. The interests of the State at the exhibition are in good hands, and visitors will find the Utah section, one to be proud of," a Latter-day Saint reporter noted.[4]

St. Louis, Missouri, another important staging area for the mid-nineteenth-century Mormon pioneer exodus, was the site of the 1904 Louisiana Purchase Exposition. By the turn of the twentieth century, St. Louis had over 575,000 citizens, making it the fourth-largest city in the United States,

---

3. Gerald J. Peterson, "History of Mormon Exhibits in World Expositions" (Master's thesis, Brigham Young University, 1974), 21, 30.

4. "Utah's Day at Omaha," *Deseret Evening News*, October 17, 1898.

behind New York, Chicago, and Philadelphia. Utah officials erected a modest state building on the fairgrounds, much to the delight of local Latter-day Saints who had lived for years on the periphery of Mormondom. "For the St. Louis members, the fair and the Utah State Pavilion were an opportunity to meet hundreds of Saints visiting from the West. Thus for a brief moment, branch members felt that even though their numbers were small, they were part of something much larger," two historians explain.[5] Noted Utah photographer Charles R. Savage visited the St. Louis fair and described Utah's building to his fellow Latter-day Saints back West: "Visitors from Utah generally went to the state building. It was a neat and attractive structure wherein you could inscribe your name and rest yourself. It kept the name of our state before the people although it did not possess any particularly attractive features in itself. It was an object of much curiosity." He further noted that Utah's exhibits were appealing and garnered a number of awards: "Citizens of Utah had every reason to be proud of them. The agricultural exhibit had a reproduction of Little Zion Valley, showing the farms enclosed by high mountains. This pretty little nook is found on one of the forks of the Virgin River, above Springdale, in southern Utah. The educational and mineral exhibits were first class."[6]

The state of Utah came away from the St. Louis World's Fair with a number of awards. Its exhibits in the Educational Palace, directed by Horace H. Cummings, Frances N. Eddy, and F. M. Driggs, beat out dozens of other state educational institutions. "The jury of awards has given us three bronze medals, two silver medals, one gold medal, and one grand prize, which will be ours unless the superior jury makes any changes, which they are not apt to do unless by giving us more," Professor Cummings wrote of their success in Nebraska. "It seems a marvel to me when I think what a humble beginning we had here, how we have gained favor until everybody in the Palace of Education speaks of Utah educational conditions with the greatest respect, and the jury of awards has given us such fine recognition."[7] Utah also received prizes for its

---

5. Fred E. Woods and Thomas L. Farmer, *When the Saints Came Marching In: A History of the Latter-day Saints in St. Louis* (Orem, Utah: Millennial Press, 2009), 70–72.

6. Charles R. Savage, "The World's Fair at St. Louis," *Juvenile Instructor* 40, no. 7 (April 1, 1905): 194. See also Charles R. Savage, "The World's Fair at St. Louis," *Juvenile Instructor* 40, no. 8 (April 15, 1905): 225–227; Editors, "At the Louisiana Purchase Exposition," *Improvement Era* 8, no. 2 (December 1904): 94–97.

7. "Utah Schools at the World's Fair," *Improvement Era* 8, no. 1 (November 1904): 75–76.

mining, metallurgy, agricultural, and irrigation displays. In fact, the Mormon-dominated state did so well, in terms of medals won, the leaders of other states levied complaints against the Utah delegation and its exhibits in St. Louis. Utahn Samuel T. Whitaker pled his state's case before the fair's International Jury of Awards committee for two hours and was relieved when the committee allowed his delegation to retain their numerous honors.[8]

While the Louisiana Purchase Exposition continued to delight fairgoers in Missouri, organizers of the 1905 Lewis and Clark Centennial Exposition finalized their fair preparations. By early twentieth century, Portland, Oregon, had emerged as one of the Pacific Northwest's economic centers, in large mea-sure because of the convergence of the Northern, Southern, and Union Pacific Railroad lines within its boundaries. Seeking to bolster the prominence of Portland, and its surrounding Oregonian attractions, promoters of the fair decided to highlight the contributions of early American explorers Lewis and Clark, who had reached the Pacific Ocean in 1805, a century earlier. The Portland cultural celebration promised to be the biggest and most spectacular fair yet on American soil. "The Exposition will thus stand preeminent over all its predecessors, in extent, and magnitude, as well as in expenditure. The chance of a life time, to see the peoples and displays of all countries, and of every stage of civilization in the world, will here be offered to the visitor," one Mormon writer shared with his fellow church members. "As the pioneers of Utah early crossed the great west and raised the stars and stripes in a foreign land across the borders of the Purchase, and as the Church had some of its most wonderful experiences therein, it is specially fitting that our citizens join the celebration."[9] Given their recent public relations coups at the St. Louis fair, representatives of both the church and the state of Utah were anxious to be involved in the forthcoming Oregon exposition. And church periodicals and local newspapers kept Latter-day Saints in Utah and the surrounding states apprised of the events at the Portland fairgrounds.

Utah's delegation, acting under the direction of Latter-day Saint Spencer Clawson, constructed an impressive building on the fairgrounds, much to the

8. "Utah at the World's Fair," *Improvement Era* 8, no. 2 (December 1904): 154–155.

9. "The Louisiana Purchase Exposition," *Improvement Era* 6, no. 8 (June 1903): 622–625. For more information on the Lewis and Clark Centennial Exposition, see Henry E. Reed, comp., *Oregon, A Story of Progress and Development, Together with an Account of the Lewis and Clark Centennial Exposition* (Portland, Oreg.: F. W. Bates and Company, 1904); and Robert Rydell, "Visions of Empire: International Expositions in Portland and Seattle, 1905–1909," *Pacific Historical Review* 52, no. 1 (February 1983): 37–65.

delight of the Utah Mormons who converged on the Rose City. "Crowning the eminence rising from Guild Lake and beyond the Idaho Building stands the graceful Utah Building, showing the enterprise of her people and the products of the state" is how one popular exposition guidebook described the Utah edifice.[10] "The Utah building was naturally a place where the Utes were interested. On the border of the lake was our Information Bureau where the Church works and Utah curios were on sale. On an elevation near by was our state building, and near it was that of Idaho. Crowds were in daily attendance and the display was in every way credible to the commission in charge. The varied products of the state were artistically arranged," Mormon photographer Charles R. Savage described. "Our school exhibit was meritorious in every way and received numerous medals for superiority. In the rear of the building was a stamp mill showing the methods of treating ores. Each visitor received a souvenir in the shape of a bottle of quartz or ore reduced to powder. Utah silk and honey showed up very credibly, as well as the ores from different mines. Residents of Utah were made to feel at home. The attendants were courteous and entertaining."[11] Another Utah Mormon paid similar tribute to the efforts of the Utah delegation. "Our State's display of minerals, products of the soil, and educational methods and advancement, merits mention with the best. Considering, also, the population of this state, the number of visitors to the fair from here must be highly satisfactory to its leaders."[12] Before the Lewis and Clark Exposition came to a close, fair officials honored the Mormons and the State of Utah with medals for their participation, especially for their singing, mining, agricultural, and educational exhibits.[13]

But the participation of the famed Ogden (not Salt Lake) Mormon Tabernacle Choir provided the biggest boon to Mormon image-making at the Lewis and Clark Centennial Exposition. Months earlier, National Irrigation Congress Chairman C. B. Boothe contacted leaders of the church in hopes of having either the Salt Lake or Ogden choral group perform at its

10. Robert A. Reid, *Sights and Scenes at the Lewis and Clark Centennial Exposition, Portland, Oregon* (Portland, Oreg.: Bushong and Company, 1905), N.p.

11. Charles R. Savage, "The Lewis and Clark Exposition," *Juvenile Instructor* 40, no. 23 (December 1, 1905): 722.

12. Joseph Ballantyne, "Utah at the Lewis and Clark Exposition," *Improvement Era* 8, no. 12 (October 1905): 914.

13. Joseph F. Smith, Jr., "The Lewis and Clark Centennial Exposition," *Improvement Era* 8, no. 10 (August 1905): 719–720; and Edward H. Anderson, "Utah and the Portland Fair," *Improvement Era* 9, no. 1 (November 1905): 78.

annual meeting, held in conjunction with the Portland fair. For years both Mormon singing groups had battled for dominance in the Utah choir scene. After raising the necessary $10,000 dollars to pay for upfront travel costs, the two-hundred-member Ogden choir was selected to represent the church. Under the direction of Joseph Ballantyne, the choir traveled to Oregon by train to participate in the Portland fair. The choral group offered their first performance on Monday, August 21, 1905, to a sellout crowd of 2,500, including a stirring rendition of the "Irrigation Ode," composed by Mormon musician John J. McClellan. The Ogden Tabernacle Choir received a five-minute standing ovation from their audience at the conclusion of their performance. Once the applause had died, Irrigation Congress Chairman Richardson praised the Latter-day Saint singers still on stage: "I want to tell you that this is the greatest two hundred voice chorus in the United States.... I also want to remind you that this marvelous music has come from 'Mormon' throats, that every singer in the choir is a 'Mormon,' and that collectively they have come to help this congress out, to show the people of Portland and the Lewis and Clark Exposition what they can do."[14] That Tuesday and Wednesday evenings, the choir again performed sold-out concerts in the Rose City.

Choir director Ballantyne reflected on his Mormon choir's success in Portland. "Probably one of the greatest tributes paid the chorus and soloists was the fact that more than one thousand persons were turned away from the last concert on Wednesday night. Numerous offers of advanced prices were made for admission, but could not be gratified. It was certainly an ovation seldom accorded musicians in the great centers of musical activity in the world. Not only did the chorus find its way into the hearts of the public and press, but the soloists and accompanist—artists every one—of whom we feel justly proud, were given enthusiastic receptions," he noted. Ballantyne took special pride in social invitations extended to him and the members of his Ogden choir, including invitations by the president of the Portland Fair, the governors of California, Utah, and Washington, the president of the Portland Commercial Club, and others. "I am so grateful that the impression we created was a favorable one. It does seem to me that the great masses can be reached through the realm of art, when, at times, all other resources fail. I am especially grateful that there are times, in the history of the Latter-day Saints, when strong intellectual and artistic appeals can be made to the world," he

---

14. Joseph F. Smith, Jr., "The Ogden Choir at the Fair," *Improvement Era* 8, no. 12 (October 1905): 955–956. See also Ballantyne, "Utah at the Lewis and Clark Exposition," 914–916.

concluded. Ballantyne was especially gratified to observe that his fellow Mormons were making meaningful contributions to America's arts and cultural scene.[15]

America's next major world's fair, the Jamestown Tercentennial Exposition, was held on the Virginia shore between April and December 1907. It commemorated the passage of three hundred years since the founding of Jamestown, the original English settlement in the New World. Latter-day Saints were made aware of the plans for the East Coast fair in church periodicals and local newspapers in Utah, although the church limited its involvement to sending a few leaders as official representatives. In an official circular, the Jamestown committee highlighted what they viewed as the main feature of the exposition: the military might of the United States. Organizers invited the world's major nations to send their warships to the Virginia coastline, where they could participate in military exercises and naval maneuvers. "President [Theodore Roosevelt] reviewed the ships of the Atlantic fleet and the visiting war vessels from foreign nations, anchored in three lines in Hampton Roads. It was the greatest naval display ever witnessed in American waters. In the first line were twelve foreign ships, British, German and Austrian; in the second, sixteen American battle ships; and in the third, twenty-two cruisers, monitors and torpedo craft," one Latter-day Saint correspondent noted of the opening ceremonies, which were attended by former Utah governor Arthur L. Thomas.[16] Members of the American press, however, expressed their disapproval that war, rather than peace, was to be showcased at the exposition. The Jamestown Exposition got off to a bad start in the eyes of the American public and never fully recovered.

The Virginia world's fair struggled to live up to national expectations. Even the *Deseret News* weighed in on the reasons for its struggles in several 1907 editorials. Reporters noted that the downpour of springtime rain made the exposition access roads difficult to travel and the fairgrounds a muddy mess. Moreover, visitors were upset by the militaristic flavor of the exposition. That public proposals to hold a peace conference instead of the military displays were rejected by the fair's management team showed them to be out of touch with popular American sentiment of the day. To make matters worse,

---

15. Ballantyne, "Utah at the Lewis and Clark Exposition," 916–917.

16. Edward H. Anderson, "The Jamestown Exposition," *Improvement Era* 9, no. 11 (September 1906): 908; *Jamestown Exposition, opens April 26, closes November 30, 1907, Hampton Roads, Virginia* (Norfolk, Virginia: Jamestown Exposition Company, 1907), 3; and Edward H. Anderson, "Jamestown Exposition," *Improvement Era* 10, no. 9 (June 1907): 637–638.

the national railroads, due in part to recent interstate commerce legislation, did not offer the press the expected rates to travel to the fair, so they did not go en masse and promote the fair as expected; all these factors combined to stifle attendance and mar the fair's image. An editorial reported that due to lower-than-anticipated gate receipts the Jamestown Exposition would not be able to break even financially and might not be able to pay back its loans to the federal government. Nevertheless, the same writer expressed hope that the exposition could be salvaged, or at least that the upcoming Utah Day at the fairgrounds might be a success. "We hope that the attendance will increase. The birth of the Republic, as the settlement of Jamestown may be called, is well worth celebrating. A trip to the South will be interesting and instructive. There will be a Utah day, and we hope its observance will be a credit to the state."[17]

Despite the shortcomings of the Virginia exposition, Utahns were pleased how the State was showcased on October 15, 1907. A number of prominent civic and Latter-day Saint leaders, including Governor John C. Cutler, former governor Arthur L. Thomas, together with other Mormon and non-Mormon Utah citizens, made their way to the Jamestown fairgrounds for the festivities. John J. McClellan, the Salt Lake Mormon Tabernacle Choir's organist, together with the choir's violinist Willard E. Weihe, delighted the crowd with their music. Tributes were paid to Utah's sons and daughters by Virginia's Lieutenant Governor J. Taylor Ellyson, and Director General Alvah H. Martin said that Utah was the only one of the western states that had made an appropriation for representation at the Exposition and sent a delegation for the observance of a state day. Governor Cutler from Utah praised the Jamestown Exposition and its organizers for their good work in honor of the founders of the American nation, and they expressed appreciation that Utah Day was being properly celebrated on the fairgrounds. He also described the similarities between Virginia's founding by British colonists and Utah's settlement by Mormon pioneers. Cutler described the many contributions of Utah to the larger Union and emphasized that the Latter-day Saints were "good, worthy, honest, intelligent American citizens."[18] Arthur L. Thomas, Utah's inaugural governor after statehood, offered the event's closing remarks. He lauded the citizens

17. "The Jamestown Fair," *Deseret Evening News*, June 22, 1907; "A Financial Loss," *Deseret Evening News*, October 15, 1907.

18. "Came from Utah to Observe Day," *Norfolk Landmark*, October 16, 1907, as cited in the Journal History, October 16, 1907, p. 11, Church History Library; Edward H. Anderson, "Utah at the Jamestown Exposition," *Improvement Era* 11, no. 2 (December 1907): 158–159.

of Utah and their contributions to the larger nation and congratulated the Utahn musicians Professors John J. McClellan and Willard Weihe for their wonderful musical contributions to the fair during the Utah Day celebrations and at other recitals.

A post–Utah Day editorial in the Salt Lake City–based *Inter-mountain Republican* lauded the state of Utah at the Jamestown Exposition. It compared the success of the Mormon pioneers in colonizing Utah and the failure of the English colonists to establish permanent settlements in Virginia in Jamestown. "We are additionally pleased at the appearance of Utah in Jamestown, because the founders of Utah did not fail. They probably faced far more discouraging conditions than those on the James. They met Indians in whose breasts burned fires never known to Powhatan. They braved trials in crossing the desert to which the voyage across the ocean and the tramp to Jamestown could not be compared. They carried with them women and children, and when they had no bread, they ate roots and berries," the writer continued. "There never has been in American history a better example of human resolution and fortitude, of courage and persistence—or of success—than that which these people who made Utah gave to the world. And where the strong men of Captain John Smith's band retreated before difficulty, the makers of this state stood their ground, and won from hostile nature a commonwealth and a capital!"[19] This meant a lot to the Mormons and the other Utahns still seeking for legitimacy in the Union, just within two decades of the Manifesto and just after the Reed Smoot trial.

Mormon Participation in Church-Centered Exhibits at American Fairs, 1909–1916

A watershed moment in the official church participation in world's fairs occurred at the 1909 Alaska-Yukon-Pacific Exposition in Seattle, Washington. Since the 1893 Chicago World's Fair, church representatives had partnered with the territory or state of Utah (where its members still constituted a majority) to represent their ecclesiastical and civic accomplishments in state-centered exhibits. But this changed in 1909, when the church sponsored its own series of displays, completely apart from the state of Utah, marking a new official approach to the exhibition of Mormonism. Historian Gerald J. Peterson flags the importance of this Latter-day Saint "transition from

19. "Utah at Jamestown," *Inter-mountain Republican* (Salt Lake City), October 19, 1907.

state-centered to Church-centered exhibits" in his study of Mormon involve-ment in world's fairs and expositions.[20] The likely catalyst for this shift was an invitation from the federally sponsored Smithsonian Institute to church leaders, asking them to participate in the Seattle celebration. Specifically, the Washington, D.C. based cultural organization hoped that the Mormons would showcase their own contribution to the colonization of the American West. Beginning with Richard T. Ely's 1903 *Harper's Monthly* article on the Mormon cooperative economic system in Utah, the Latter-day Saints were starting to be feted for their earlier pioneering efforts. "This recognition by the government is but giving credit where it is due, and after many years of waiting is keenly appreciated by every Latter-day Saint, and should be by ever lover of justice," Melvin J. Ballard, president of the Northwestern States Mission, noted. "This action by our great government is a signal which should be heeded by all men everywhere to come up from the small, petty prejudice, lose their hatred and malice and for once acknowledge that there is virtue in 'Mormonism.'"[21] Not surprisingly, the children and grandchildren of the original pioneers were delighted to be so celebrated.

The Latter-day Saint exhibits at the Seattle fair were simple but effective in garnering positive publicity and generating good will for the Mormons. One wall featured a map of the western United States that showcased the 1846 march of the Mormon Battalion and the 1847 pioneer exodus trail and high-lighted the hundreds of towns and communities that Latter-day Saints set-tled. A highlight of the display was a gleaming plaster of paris model of the Salt Lake Temple, which was lit internally so it glowed as passersby made their way through the exhibit. Mormon representatives also built a scale model of the landmark Salt Lake Tabernacle, which they displayed adjacent to the mock up of the Salt Lake Temple. They designed the Tabernacle model so that there was a cut-away view that showcased the interior and the ingenious construction of the roof. Both the temple and tabernacle were surrounded by explanatory texts detailing their construction and purposes. Two nearby display cases housed artifacts from the pioneer trek, including the primitive odometer constructed in 1847 by Mormon leaders to measure the distance from the Missouri River to their ultimate colonization point in the Salt Lake Valley. Also showcased was the "Bulletin of the Plains," a bleached buffalo

---

20. Peterson, "History of Mormon Exhibits," 30.

21. Melvin J. Ballard, "The Church at the Seattle Exposition," *Liahona: The Elder's Journal* 7, no. 6 (July 31, 1909): 90.

skull that had inscribed upon it "Pioneers camped here June 3rd, 1847, making 15 miles today. All well. Brigham Young." Another display highlighted a number of Mormon Americana artifacts, including the architectural schematics for the Salt Lake Temple, the printing presses that produced the first copies of the Book of Mormon and the *Deseret News*, together with paintings of Mormon martyrs Joseph and Hyrum Smith, and dozens of photographs of early Mormon pioneers.[22]

Just as they had in Chicago in 1893, Latter-day Saint leaders also arranged for the Salt Lake Mormon Tabernacle Choir to perform at the 1909 Seattle Exposition. The well-known chorus performed sold-out concerts in Portland, Oregon, as well as Tacoma, Washington, before arriving in Seattle to compete in a Welsh choral contest. Choir officials had to turn away over five hundred people from their first concert. One Mormon observer noted that not even the president of the United States, who spoke days earlier in the same Seattle National Amphitheatre, attracted as many onlookers as did the Salt Lake City choir. The local press was likewise enamored by the Mormon singers. "Three thousand people were enraptured by three hundred voices in the exposition auditorium last night when the famous Mormon Tabernacle Choir gave a concert. The audience tired itself with encoring the numbers. Many musical treats have been offered the people attending the fair and others are to come, but there has not been, so far, any program, vocal or instrumental, that seemed to be received with the same satisfaction as that caused by the Tabernacle Choir," a reporter for Seattle's *Post Intelligencer* exclaimed.[23]

But controversy erupted on the night of the anticipated singing competition, after its Welsh organizers required the several-hundred-voice-strong Salt Lake chorus to pay 75 cents a head for admission to their own performance. Strong words were exchanged between the Mormon singers and the Welsh management resulting in the Utahns' boycotting the competition in protest. Seeking to placate the Mormon choir and exploit the singers' popularity, Seattle fair commissioners offered the chorus $500 and two days of free admission for the entire Utah singing party to the fair if they would perform again at the Natural Amphitheatre that Sunday evening, to which they agreed. Over twenty thousand fans of the choir showed up for the concert. "Nothing like it has ever been seen in the history of the city.

22. Ballard, "Church at the Seattle Exposition," 89–90.

23. As quoted in Melvin J. Ballard, in Conference Report, October 1909, 38.

Distinguished persons have come and gone, have had their hearing and been cheered by assembled thousands, but all these tributes sink into insignificance in comparison with the spectacle of last night," the same Seattle reporter documented.[24]

During the October 1909 Latter-day Saint general conference, Ballard described to his fellow Latter-day Saints gathered in the Tabernacle on Temple Square the positive airing the church was receiving at the Alaska-Yukon-Pacific Exposition. In his estimation, the church's involvement in the Seattle fair was among the most significant events in Mormon history. He excitedly shared that almost 3.25 million visitors had come to the Exposition and that 90 percent of those fare-paying guests made their way to the popular government building, where the Mormon exhibit was housed and staffed by Northwestern States missionaries and local church members. "We have by this means corrected many stories that would have been told by those who pretend to be well informed, and who would have related the old falsehoods. In this too we have enjoyed the friendship and good feelings of the crowds, and those in authority at the building, and they have told the truth with reference to our people. It has certainly done my heart good to see after long years of wanting, due appreciation of the Mormon pioneers, and though most of them have passed away and did not hear these words of praise," Ballard noted, "I am pleased that their children can listen to just eulogies, as they come from the thousands who now witness in its true light the work of the Latter-day Saints. One of the officials of the fair, in a reception given to the governor of this state, said that Oregon and Washington, and the other great states of the Western country, would never have been what they are today had it not been for the labors of the Mormon pioneers. I believe that is true, and I rejoice that, after all these years, recognition comes."[25]

Both the church and the state of Utah participated separately at the 1915 Panama–Pacific International Exposition in San Francisco during the Great War years, to celebrate the completion of the Panama Canal. Church periodicals kept members in Utah informed of the San Francisco exposition's milestones, including the opening-day events. "President Wilson at Washington touched a button, the great guns boomed, the fountains began to flow, the engines in the palace of machinery began to move, the people sang, 'The Star Spangled Banner,' and there were cheers, and tears, and

24. As quoted in Ballard, in Conference Report, October 1909, 39.

25. Ballard, in Conference Report, October 1909, 37–38.

laughter and exhilaration," one article described.[26] The state of Utah constructed an impressive stand-alone building in San Francisco for the fair, as did the other western neighboring states of California, Idaho, Montana, Nevada, Oregon, and Washington. "In the Utah building is a panoramic, working model of the famous Utah Copper mine, Bingham, showing actual processes of ore removal with miniature steam shovels, engines and cars in operation. The entire second floor of the south wing is occupied by the model of a typical Utah coal mine, showing exterior and underground workings and geological formations," one Utahn noted of his state's building. "The main floor is mostly occupied by officers' and reception rooms. Paintings and statuary of Utah artists and sculptors decorate the rooms. There is also a modest but interesting display of relics of pre-historic cliff-dwellers of southern Utah, loaned by the University of Utah. In most of the palaces of the Exposition, Utah is lost, but in the education palace she is well represented."[27] Utah church member Janette A. Hyde visited the Utah Building in San Francisco and was delighted with its offerings. "We have a beautiful state building, within and without. Everybody from the state is expected to go there and register, get programs, write letters, and rest in the luxurious rest-rooms; and if one is ill or overtired, a little light refreshment is served. Everybody meets everybody in the Utah Building, and we were exceedingly proud of our state and of the splendid manner in which we are represented in the building itself, and in the various departments where are exhibits are located."[28]

Hundreds of Latter-day Saints and other Utahns flocked to San Francisco to help celebrate "Utah Day" on July 24, or Pioneer Day back in Utah. Presidents Joseph F. Smith, Anthon H. Lund, and Charles W. Penrose of the First Presidency attended the "Utah Day" festivities and formally represented the church at the fairgrounds. They also participated in the other church-related events that July. During the formal state ceremony, President Smith spoke autobiographically about his pioneering experiences in Utah as a young man, including his visits to San Francisco during the 1850s while serving a church mission to the Sandwich (Hawaiian) Islands. He reflected on how much had changed in the American West in the intervening decades.

26. "Passing Events: The Panama Pacific Exposition," *Improvement Era* 18, no. 6 (April 1915): 562.

27. "Panama Pacific Exposition," *Improvement Era* 18, no. 10 (August 1915): 945.

28. Janette A. Hyde, "The Genealogical Convention at the Fair," *Relief Society Magazine* 2, no. 6 (June 1915): 257.

Days later, over 250 Mormon delegates, the majority from the Relief Society, participated in the three-day 1915 International Congress of Genealogy that was part of the world's fair program. For years the church had been one of the world's foremost family history organizations, based on its practice of vicarious ordinances of salvation for the dead. One Relief Society member expressed the Latter-day Saints' hope that the family history assembly would be a memorable event: "The Congress on Genealogy is certainly a feature which holds the attraction for the people of Utah; and those who are fortunate enough to attend it, may be sure of finding a wonderland at the Exposition, and an education in genealogy during the week of July 26."[29] The Genealogical Society of Utah, an entity of the church, was one of sixty-five participating genealogical societies at the California gathering. Exposition officials bestowed bronze medals on First Presidency member Anthon H. Lund and Relief Society President Emmeline B. Wells for the Mormon contribution to record keeping and genealogical research. In attendance were a number of Latter-day Saint luminaries and Utah government officials, including Governor William Spry.[30] The Ogden Mormon Tabernacle Choir also performed at the genealogical congress to great praise and positive press.

An affiliated Congress of Religious Philosophies was held in San Francisco between July 29 and 31, 1915, and the First Presidency appointed Elder James E. Talmage of the Quorum of the Twelve Apostles to represent the church at the spiritual gathering. "The invitation to The Church of Jesus Christ of Latter-day Saints to provide a speaker on the program of the Congress was in itself an event of note," Talmage's biographer points out, given the church's poor experience at the Chicago Parliament of Religions two decades earlier.[31] In fact, a few congress officials disclosed to Talmage that several members of their organizing committee had likewise "endeavored to exclude the Latter-day Saints from that year's program also, but had been forced to the conclusion that they could not honestly do so. The basis of Mormonism was a distinct and separate religious philosophy, and not just a variation in secular detail from some other." As a result, Talmage was

29. Hyde, "Genealogical Convention at the Fair," 259.

30. J. M. S., "The Church at the World's Fair," *Millennial Star* 77, no. 34 (August 26, 1915): 538; and James B. Allen, Jessie L. Embry, and Kahlile B. Mehr, *Hearts Turned to the Fathers* (Provo, Utah: BYU Studies Press, 1995), 79–80.

31. John R. Talmage, *The Talmage Story: Life of James E. Talmage—Educator, Scientist, Apostle* (Salt Lake City: Bookcraft, 1972), 180.

allowed to present alongside the Roman Catholic, Eastern Orthodox, and Protestant representatives at the Congress of Religious Philosophies on July 29. Talmage's paper, "The Philosophical Basis of Mormonism," was subsequently reprinted in the church's *Deseret News* and *Improvement Era* publications and later as a missionary brochure.[32] Latter-day Saints hailed the non-Mormon reception of Talmage in the Bay Area as a milestone. "The difference between the attitude of the managers of the San Francisco Congress and that shown at Chicago is very great. It indicates that the Church of Jesus Christ of Latter-day Saints, notwithstanding slander and abuse, misrepresentations and vilification, and all the tactics of the prince of darkness and his faithful 'anti-Mormon' tools, is on her way to victory and triumph over all adversaries, in the full daylight of truth," read one Mormon periodical editorial.[33] (It was fortunate that things went so well for Talmage in San Francisco because in 1919, at the Third World's Christian Citizenship Conference, held in Pittsburgh, Pennsylvania, a mob formed at the conclusion of his remarks on the church and threatened his life.[34]) Things were looking up for the Mormon image in America.

Celebrating a Mormon and an American "Century of Progress", 1933–1934

Following the two California expositions that opened to cosmopolitan crowds in 1915, the church did not participate in another world's fair until the early 1930s. The first week of April 1930 marked the centennial of the founding of the church in upstate New York. What had begun as a small religious movement, among a few families and their close associates in the burned-over district of New York, had grown within a century to be a major ecclesiastical organization headquartered in Utah. By April 1930, the church had 104 stakes, 930 wards, 75 independent branches, 27 dependent branches, for a total of 1,032 wards, branches, and stakes in North America (Canada, United States, and Mexico), together with 29 missions worldwide, and 800 branches in these scattered evangelistic outposts all over the world. Perhaps even more important than its impressive internal membership growth,

32. James E. Talmage, "The Philosophical Basis of 'Mormonism,'" *Improvement Era* 18, no. 11 (September 1915): 947–964.

33. J. M. S., "Church at the World's Fair," 539.

34. Talmage, *Talmage Story*, 196–200.

however, was its improving external image and relationship with its Christian neighbors. President Heber J. Grant rejoiced in the way many Americans were now viewing the Latter-day Saints: "I have never felt happier in my life than over the wonderful change that seems to have come all over the world in the attitude of people toward the Latter-day Saints. It has fallen to my lot now to labor for forty-seven and a half years as one of the General Authorities of the Church. In my early ministry as one of the officials, almost without exception as I traveled around the country, I found a spirit amounting almost to hatred in the hearts of people toward the Mormons." But Grant then discussed how the Mormons were now largely accepted in government, social, and political circles, in what he deemed a most welcome change. Even the president of the United States had become a friend to the Mormons, Grant declared.[35]

In keeping with the growing Latter-day Saint trend of holding commemorative celebrations for key events in church history, Mormon leaders determined to celebrate the achievements of the past one hundred years. These commemorative milestones included the centennial observance of the 1823 appearance of the Angel Moroni to Joseph Smith, the 1827 transfer of the golden plates to Joseph Smith, and the 1830 organization of the church. On April 6, 1930, more than one hundred thousand Latter-day Saints gathered in Salt Lake City, several thousand of whom filled the Tabernacle on Temple Square to capacity during the celebratory general conference sessions. All church members were able to participate remotely at 10 A.M. Mountain Standard Time over KSL Radio by listening to specially installed radios in church buildings across the United States. This enabled Latter-day Saints to join with their brothers and sisters in the Tabernacle in the Hosanna Shout, a sacred ritual generally limited to the climax of temple dedications. The conference sessions continued for another two days, with several speakers waxing eloquent and nostalgic on the church's centennial and its achievements. During the conference Mormonism's blacksmith orator Brigham H. Roberts introduced his six-volume *Comprehensive History of the Church*, which chronicled the first century of the church. The week following the general conference weekend, thousands of church members attended the "Message of the Ages" pageant presented in the Tabernacle, in which dozens of Latter-day Saints contributed their acting, singing, and musical talents to tell the story of Mormonism.

---

35. Heber J. Grant, in Conference Report, April 1930, 181.

During this time, the church's temples were illuminated at night to help add to the festivities.[36]

In the wake of their own successful 1930 centennial celebration, Latter-day Saints were anxious to participate in the approaching 1933 Century of Progress International Exposition, planned to commemorate the centennial of Chicago's founding. Nearly two decades had passed since the church had formally participated in a world's fair or international exposition. In the years following the 1915 Panama–Pacific International Exposition in San Francisco, the Great War had come and gone and five international expositions, including fairs in England and France, had dazzled the senses of world fairgoers. For whatever reason, the Latter-day Saints were not involved in the 1926 Philadelphia Sesquicentennial Exposition, which celebrated America's sesquicentennial. Nevertheless, the Mormons were hopeful that Chicago would again provide their religionists with another providential moment to improve their image and help move beyond the shadows of plural marriage.[37]

In his April 1932 general conference address, Apostle Melvin J. Ballard, who had served as a president of the Northwestern States Mission during the 1909 Alaska-Yukon-Pacific Exposition in Seattle, Washington, voiced the Mormon enthusiasm to participate in Chicago's "Century of Progress" fair. Like many other Latter-day Saints who were still reflecting on the achievements of the first century of the church, Ballard viewed the 1933–1934 Chicago fair as evidence of God's outpouring of light and truth on the darkened world, both spiritually and temporally. "Next year, in the city of Chicago, there will be an exposition celebrating the hundredth anniversary of the founding of that great city, for it was established three years after this Church was organized." He then noted that the exposition was to be called "A Century of Progress," bearing the same title of the church's Young Men's and Young Ladies' Mutual Improvement Association's 1930 manual. "The exposition will set forth what has happened in human progress during the past hundred years."[38]

By the second Chicago World's Fair, church officials confidently went about assembling an exhibits team to display Mormonism on the fairgrounds.

---

36. Steven L. Olsen, "Centennial Observances," in *Encyclopedia of Mormonism*, ed. Daniel H. Ludlow, 4 vols. (New York: Macmillan, 1992), 1:261; Thomas G. Alexander, *Mormonism in Transition: A History of the Latter-day Saints, 1890–1930* (Urbana: University of Illinois Press, 1986), 309–310; and James B. Allen and Glen M. Leonard, *The Story of the Latter-day Saints*, 2nd ed. (Salt Lake City: Deseret Book, 1992), 514–515.

37. Peterson, "History of Mormon Exhibits," 39–40.

38. Melvin J. Ballard, in Conference Report, April 1932, 57–58.

Bishop David A. Smith acted as general chairman and George D. Pyper worked as chairman of the exhibit committee, while church auxiliary leaders Marcia K. Howells, Oscar A. Kirkham, Clarissa Beesley, and May Anderson served on the planning committee. These men and women relied on the artistic vision and implementation of major Mormon artists, including Avard Fairbanks, a professor of art at the University of Michigan; J. Leo Fairbanks, a professor of art at the University of Oregon; and their artist-father J. B. Fairbanks from Salt Lake City. Acting president of the Chicago-based Northern States Mission, George S. Romney, oversaw the staffing of the church's exhibit, thanks to the tireless efforts of his young missionaries. The overall Latter-day Saint display was the combination of a series of paintings, sculptures, and texts that told the story of the church and defined church doctrine at a level non-Mormons could readily understand.[39]

In a pamphlet produced by the Northern States Mission, the Latter-day Saints attempted to summarize what their church's exhibit was attempting to display in the context of the larger secular theme of progress. "The revelations of science and the ingenuity and accomplishment of modern man have changed the old familiar conditions that we stand amazed, wondering what further miracles will come to transform our civilization. Yet, startling as is the story, the Mormon exhibit reveals something more ambitious. It is told in the Hall of Religions. It, too, is a story of a hundred years, and also the story of progress. Not only a hundred years of progress but of 'Eternal Progress.'"[40]

While the fair's gates were open, nearly thirty-nine million people visited the exposition in Chicago. One Latter-day Saint in Chicago excitedly noted that about seventy thousand people were daily visiting the overarching Century of Progress Exposition, including about four thousand individuals who toured the Mormon exhibit in the Hall of Religions each day. "One hundred and ninety-five days of constant recital of the accomplishments of the Church during the last Century!" he exclaimed when he thought about the incredible missionary opportunity the Exposition offered his fellow Mormons, who were used to going out among the people, rather than having the people come to them. "Twenty-three hundred forty pulsating hours of human contact! One hundred and forty thousand precious minutes of continuous revealment! Hundreds of thousands of tracts and pamphlets

---

39. "The Church Century of Progress Display," *Improvement Era* 36, no. 14 (December 1933): 864–865; and "The Mormon Exhibit at the Century of Progress Exposition at Chicago," *Improvement Era* 37, no. 10 (October 1934): 579–581, 608–609.

40. *Century of Progress Exhibition, Chicago, 1933* (Chicago: Northern States Mission, 1933), 1.

distributed to truth seekers!"[41] Other leading Latter-day Saints shared his enthusiasm for the Mormon participation at the Chicago event. "The miniature replica of the Salt Lake Tabernacle and Organ seemed to be the magnet that first attracted the crowds. It was an excellent example of the effectiveness of visual education. As heads peered around heads and over shoulders to look at that model, almost invariably someone in the group would begin to tell of his visit to the renowned edifice," Elder David O. McKay of the Quorum of the Twelve Apostles shared after visiting the Hall of Religions. "With the attention of the observers thus centered the missionaries found willing listeners to the story of the Pioneers and to the explanation of principles and ideas of the Church as depicted in artistic paintings and bas-reliefs on the walls of the booth." The visiting apostle commended the young elders for their manners and skill in discoursing on the history and doctrines of the church, and he praised the artists and craftsmen who designed the Latter-day Saint exhibit.[42]

Mission President George S. Romney likewise spoke in glowing terms regarding the Mormon evangelistic success in Chicago. "I wish you could go into the booth and see the exhibit in the Hall of Religions that has been made by the Church to which we belong, and listen to your young men and young women who are there working," he related during his October 1933 general conference remarks. "Our booth is in the Hall of Religions where many other religious faiths have made exhibits, and it is outstanding on account of the spirit of it. The figures in the paintings and the sculpture work seem to be living individuals—they look as if they could speak. They are outstanding. They are different. They are symbolical of the work that is done in the Church. They tell the story of the work of our Relief Society, our Sunday Schools, our missionary work, our Young Men's and Young Ladies' Mutual Improvement work." Romney was especially pleased how his church's exhibit showcased the "ideals" of Mormon family life, which by this time was almost as entirely monogamous and American as their neighbors. The mission president finished with a tribute to his young missionaries who staffed the Mormon exhibit for twelve hours each day of the week. He expressed his feelings that these young men were "filled with the spirit and enthusiasm of missionary work" and that the visiting public was "hungry" for the message of Mormonism. "The people stop and listen, and you may go into that booth any time of the

41. "Church Century of Progress Display," 864.
42. Quoted in "Church Century of Progress Display," 865.

day, when the rest of the hall is filled or when there are but few there, and
there will always be a group filling that booth of ours," Romney concluded.[43]

In addition to an official Latter-day Saint exhibit in the Hall of Religions,
Mormon women represented their faith in Chicago. Just as the planners of
the 1893 Chicago World's Fair sponsored meetings specifically for female visitors through their World's Congress of Representative Women, organizers of
the 1933 exposition determined to host a similar gathering. To show their
support, the National Council of Women produced exhibits to be housed on
the fairgrounds in the Hall of Social Sciences. "What a contrast between the
fair of 1893 and the fair of 1933, when modern inventions have freed women
from much of their household drudgery! No pickles and preserves are on
display nowadays," one Mormon observer noted of the changes in both technology and the activities women over the past four decades. Instead their displays "indicate the wide range of beneficial activities in which the modern
woman indulges—activities which read out into every phase of community,
state and national life."[44] The church's Young Ladies' Mutual Improvement
Association and National Woman's Relief Society were two of the many
female-led organizations that participated in the 1933 fair in Chicago. Once
again, Mormon women helped sponsor and manage another International
Congress of Women at the Palmer House, the site of the 1893 triumphs of
Mormon matriarchs.

As well as attending the 1933 Women's Congress, the Latter-day Saint
female leadership orchestrated a special tribute, with the help of radio technology, for all of the women gathered in Chicago. Since the presidency of
Bathsheba W. Smith in the early twentieth century, members of the Relief
Society were asked to organize local female church choirs to help bring a
better spirit to the meetings and to give women another creative outlet for
their vocal talents. In time, these choral groups became known within the
church as the "singing mothers." During the International Congress of Women
in Chicago, Relief Society President Louise Y. Robison arranged for 250 of
these choir members to gather in the Salt Lake Tabernacle and serenade via
radio broadcast the hundreds of women seated in the Chicago exposition's
Hall of Science. Their remote performance was led by conductor Charlotte
O. Sackett and accompanied by Frank W. Asper on the celebrated Tabernacle

43. Romney, in Conference Report, October 1933, 39–41.

44. David Kinley, "Our Century of Progress in Industry," *Improvement Era* 36, no. 5 (March
1933): 280, 294.

organ. Elder Richard L. Evans of the Quorum of the Twelve Apostles and the announcer for the weekly Mormon Tabernacle Choir radio broadcast, *Music and the Spoken Word*, was on hand to offer some introductory remarks on the role of women in society. "Hundreds of women, officers, delegates, and members of the Council, distinguished and representative women from many foreign lands, as well as the United States, were gathered in the beautiful Hall of Science as the Utah delegates, in breathless anticipation, awaited the first announcement, but when the voices of 250 women burst into clear, melodious song, they saw the success of the venture clearly expressed in the pleased smiles on many faces," Relief Society leader Annie Wells Cannon recalled of the event.[45] Once again music proved to be an effective method of introducing the church to this gathering of largely non-Mormons in Chicago.

Mormon women were pleased how their religion and gender had once again been represented in Chicago. They were delighted to receive complimentary notes from the organizers of the International Congress of Women following the meetings. Frances P. Parks, vice president of the National Council of Women and director of the organization's exhibit in Chicago, wrote YLMIA President Ruth May Fox that November and expressed her appreciation of how well the Mormon women functioned in Chicago. "Organized 'according to a plan' with Mrs. Lucetta Reese [as] efficient chairman, a committee of four hostesses upheld the fine name of the Young Ladies' Mutual Improvement Association. Whatever the weather might be—and we've had all varieties!—your hostesses reported on dot for duty. Visitors to the exhibit booth were welcomed, given a comprehensive lesson in the part organized women have played in the onward march of American women and an inspiration for the future," her letter read. Parks continued to praise the Mormon ladies for their "uniform courtesy and kindness."[46] Moreover, the Mormon sisters were delighted to learn that one of their own, Mrs. W. C. Wessel, former field secretary of the YLMIA, had been subsequently elected by the membership of the National Council of Women to serve as the organization's corresponding secretary thereafter.[47]

Although separated by four decades, similarities between the two Chicago world's fairs continued beyond the celebrated Woman's Congresses. Forty

---

45. Annie Wells Cannon, "The Relief Society Singing Mothers," *Improvement Era* 42, no. 3 (March 1939): 154–155, 162.

46. "Note of Appreciation," *Improvement Era* 37, no 1. (January 1934): 45–46.

47. "Note of Appreciation," *Improvement Era* 37, no 1. (January 1934): 45–46.

years after the 1893 World's Parliament of Religions convened to great fanfare, American religious leaders organized the First International Congress of the World Fellowship of Faiths, in conjunction with the 1933 exposition. Its ecclesiastical managers were anxious to recapture the energy and excitement of the earlier religious gathering. This interfaith assembly lasted from August 27 to September 17, 1933, providing twenty-two days of sessions on the world's religious traditions. In attendance were nearly two hundred representatives from different global faiths, who offered nearly 250 public addresses on the world's various religious traditions. In contrast to the original Parliament of Religions, this congress's planning committee went out of its way to include Mormonism in the larger conversation. Decades after Brigham H. Roberts was prevented from speaking on behalf of the church in the Hall of Religion during the Columbian Exposition, the organizers of the World Fellowship of Faiths (who were aware of Roberts's previous exclusion) invited Roberts to address their interfaith assembly. Roberts, then seventy-six years old and crippled by diabetes, accepted their request and traveled to Chicago by train to participate. There he presented to the religious congress delegates two papers entitled "The Standard of Peace" and the "Economics of the New Age."[48]

Roberts was pleased to be included in such an auspicious gathering in Chicago, especially given his earlier treatment, and delighted that his church was finally being given a place at the conversation table. Yet he was also aware that his participation did not mean as much in 1933 as it would have in 1893. The Latter-day Saint representative "came away from the World Fellowship encouraged at the great feeling of tolerance and goodwill and at the number of Asians Orientals who had come to the session, but he was troubled that the veneer of goodwill arose less from a confluence of conviction than from its absence, a lack of assurance," his biographer Truman G. Madsen notes. "He was troubled that not just the world, but Christianity itself, had 'ceased to believe that the redemption of the world will be through Christ.' He observed and rejoiced in the marvels of technology in the hall of science but lamented its contrast to the great decline in religious understanding." Moreover, Roberts pointed out that the 1933

---

48. Charles Fredrick Weller, ed., *World Fellowship: Address and Messages by Leading Spokesmen of All Faiths, Races and Countries* (New York: Liverlight Publishing Corporation, 1935), v–vi, 870–882; Marcus Braybrooke, *Pilgrimage of Hope: One Hundred Yeas of Global Interfaith Dialogue* (London: SCM Press, 1992), 114–116; and Truman G. Madsen, *Defender of the Faith: The B. H. Roberts Story* (Salt Lake City: Bookcraft, 1980), 378.

religious congress "was not as adequately housed or as properly publicized" as the 1893 Parliament and also lamented that "the press gave only brief account of the sessions" of the 1933 congress, unlike the 1893 Parliament. Clearly people were not as interested and the platform upon which he stood was no longer as contested. Roberts died weeks later, on September 27, 1933, having lived to see his church finally represented at an American Parliament of Religions.[49]

Not surprisingly, Latter-day Saints celebrated that one of their own had been invited to address the religious congress in Chicago. During the church's October 1933 general conference, Apostle Melvin J. Ballard suggested that Brigham H. Roberts's participation in the Chicago religious gathering was a miracle: "Forty years ago, when we sent Brother Brigham H. Roberts to speak for the Church before the Parliament of Religions, he did not get a hearing except in a committee room. But today it is different, we stand with equal opportunity to every other Church in the land."[50] Furthermore, Mission President George S. Romney related that when Roberts was introduced to the general assembly in Chicago, congress organizers pointed out that his current involvement signaled the growing prestige of the church on the American religious landscape. "Roberts was honored, it seems to me, more than any other of the distinguished people who spoke in the many meetings of that organization. He gave to the people a message, in fact, two great messages. He spoke of the Prince of Peace, and how that peace might come to the world by giving justice, social and economic justice, to all mankind," Romney described.[51] And in a subsequent *Improvement Era* article titled "Changing Attitudes towards the Church," Apostle David O. McKay celebrated Robert's inclusion in the 1933 interfaith congress. "Forty years ago the Mohammedan, the Jew, the Turk, the Shinto priest, and every other religious creed was permitted its representative to speak in the Hall of Religions at the World's Fair in Chicago," the only exception being a delegate from the church. "However, at the last religious conference held in Chicago," McKay pointed out, "Roberts, who was refused the opportunity to speak on the occasion to which I have just referred, represented the Mormon Church, although he was suffering very

---

49. Madsen, *Defender of the Faith*, 378; and "Tolerance Marks Religious Session," *Deseret News*, September 7, 1933.

50. Ballard, in Conference Report, October 1933, 20.

51. Romney, in Conference Report, October 1933, 40.

severely and had to go on crutches." From a public relations standpoint, the church had come a long way by 1933.[52]

Months after Brigham H. Roberts addressed the First International Congress of the World Fellowship of Faiths, the Salt Lake Mormon Tabernacle Choir prepared to once again serenade the city of Chicago, just as it had at the Columbian Exposition. During the summer of 1934, exposition organizers announced that the 250-voice Mormon choir would perform two concerts daily between September 11 and September 16, at the Ford Symphony Gardens. The Tabernacle Choir, at the invitation and with the financial sponsorship of industrialist Henry Ford, made its way to Chicago during that autumn to participate in the global extravaganza. A number of the choir's concerts were to be broadcasted over the Columbia Broadcasting System's radio station network. Their culminating performance was to be on Sunday, September 16, when CBS had arranged for five million Americans to hear the Tabernacle Choir broadcast live from Chicago in their homes across America. Many Americans were already used to hearing the one-hour *Music and the Spoken Word* broadcast on each Sunday morning via the radio, beginning in July 1929 (and continuing into the twenty-first century).[53] "Having prepared an astonishing sixteen concerts with no duplication of pieces, the group attracted the largest crowds of any of the exhibitors' guest artists. They also received invitations to sing at the Chicago Daily News Plaza, where they jammed traffic for blocks, and at the University of Chicago chapel, where after the singing Heber J. Grant gave a weighty speech on the political loyalty of Mormons," historian Michael Hicks writes.[54] Although rain broke up a few of the concerts, there is no question that the Mormon choral sensation won the hearts of fairgoers in Chicago.

Forty years after first performing at the Columbian Exposition, the now-seasoned Mormon Tabernacle Choir and its leadership were well aware of the significance of their involvement from a public relations viewpoint. "Honours that come to the Choir are reflected, of course, upon the Church which maintains the Choir and of which the singers are members. Now the Choir is

---

52. David O. Mckay quoted in Heber J. Grant, "Changing Attitudes toward the Church," *Improvement Era* 39, no. 10 (October 1936): 857.

53. Merrill, "Tabernacle Choir at Chicago Fair," 568; and Jeffrey Calman, *The Mormon Tabernacle Choir* (New York: Harper & Row, 1979), 84–89.

54. Michael Hicks, *Mormonism and Music: A History* (Urbana: University of Illinois Press, 2003), 160.

recognized as one of the finest organizations of the kind in America. Logically, then, the Church and its people cannot have the character formerly ascribed to them," Elder Joseph F. Merrill of the Quorum of the Twelve wrote from his mission presidency assignment in Great Britain: "Since a tree is known by its fruit how natural it is to come to this conclusion. Likewise, the Church cannot be a wicked institution if its members are an upright, honourable people of proven integrity." The apostle continued by explaining why the church had been so anxious to generate "favourable publicity" through unconventional means like its Tabernacle Choir, which could improve the church's image to audiences typically turned off by the theological messages of the church, beginning with the 1893 Columbian Exposition through the 1933–1934 Century of Progress Exposition. "This is the key to a variety of activities engaged in by officials and organizations of the Church. With what results?—a better understanding by the people generally of the principles and objectives of the Church. Evil-minded people had spread abroad so much intense prejudice against them that the delivery of the Gospel message through our missionary methods has been seriously handicapped. In defense the Church has been forced to use available publicity means, with excellent results."[55] The choir and Mormon officials knew, through personal and institutional experience, that their chorus was uniquely suited to exhibit Mormonism to the outside world, in a manner that was palatable to even the most jaded of their church's critics.

Exhibiting Mormonism in America

The sprawling fairgrounds of the Century of Progress International Exposition closed six weeks after the Mormon Tabernacle Choir performed in Chicago. On the evening of October 31, 1934, the fair's conclusion was marked by a spectacular final ceremony complete with over two thousand fireworks that illuminated the Chicago skyline. The fair had set new attendance records and had turned enormous profits for its organizers and its host city, not an easy accomplishment during the Great Depression. Nearly fifty million visitors had made their way to the Chicago fair during the months it was open to the general public. "The fair offered Chicagoans and Americans of different races and ethnicities, religions, regions, classes, and genders an opportunity to meet, interact, and face the challenges of their times," historian Cheryl

---

55. Merrill, "Tabernacle Choir at Chicago Fair," 568–569.

R. Ganz writes.[56] While most fairgoers viewed the progress of the last century displayed in Chicago as evidence of human intellect and abilities, the Latter-day Saints offered a different perspective. During a general conference address, Apostle Melvin J. Ballard reflected on how much had changed in the world over the past century. He described how in 1823 the Angel Moroni visited Joseph Smith and quoted ancient prophecies from the Old Testament book of Joel that were about to be fulfilled in the last days: "And it shall come to pass afterward, that I will pour out my spirit upon all flesh; and your sons and your daughters shall prophesy, your old men shall dream dreams, your young men shall see visions:...And I will show wonders in the heavens and in the earth."[57]

Apostle Ballard then declared that Joel's prophecy was being fulfilled at the very moment, as evidenced by the progress of humankind on display at the Chicago fairgrounds. "As I stood in the World's Fair a few days ago, A Century of Progress, in Chicago, witnessing the marvelous growth that has occurred in the hundred years that have just passed, I could not help but think of this prophecy of Joel," he shared with his Mormon audience. "In the hall of transportation and communication I saw what was the condition of the world one hundred years ago, so far as their means of communication or travel was concerned, and it had made almost no progress since the days of ancient Egypt." Ballard then pointed out that how the latter-day Restoration, which commenced with the First Vision in 1820, continued with the coming forth of the Book of Mormon in the late 1820s, and culminated with the organization of The Church of Jesus Christ of Latter-day Saints in 1830, miraculously coincided with what prominent social reformer Jane Addams described as "the beginning day of the emancipation and hope, opening paths of progress in all directions." To bolster his argument, he rattled off modern innovations, including the locomotive (1829), the sewing machine (1830), the telegraph (1832), the mechanized reaper (1833), the steam engine (1849), the elevator (1852), and steel (1856), all of which came after Joseph Smith's initial theophany. "Then followed internal combination engines, electric generators, automobiles, airplanes, typewriters, motion pictures, the telephone, the radio, the electric lamp, and a thousand other marvelous inventions."[58]

---

56. Cheryl R. Ganz, *The 1933 Chicago World's Fair: A Century of Progress* (Urbana: University of Illinois Press, 2008), 156.

57. Ballard, in Conference Report, October 1933, 16–17.

58. Ballard, in Conference Report, October 1933, 17.

The Mormon apostle then offered his own thoughts on the source of these many innovations: it was God's work, not that of man. From Ballard's vantage point, the leaps in communication and transportation technologies over the past century were the direct result of divine inspiration, and the latter-day Restoration had opened the floodgates for these types of achievements and advancements. "The Lord has sent into the world in this day choice men who can be used to accomplish these marvelous things, but even their smartness would not have succeeded had it not been the good pleasure of God to unlock and open the windows of heaven and pour his Spirit out upon all flesh, and we have made greater progress in the last hundred years than was made in all the ages of time. Surely God has done it." But to Ballard, the most important marvel of the latter days was the public relations progress the church had made with the outside world in such a short time in recent decades, as evident in Chicago. "In our booth at Chicago the elders of our Church are calling the attention of the thousands who pause there to the wonderful Gospel message. That to me is a miracle.... [Today] we stand with equal opportunity to every other Church in the land, with a display that is in many respects far more interesting, and more people pause to listen to our story. Mormonism is solving the problems of the day, and I thought as I witnessed these things, how God is moving."[59]

There is no question that from the 1890 Wilford Woodruff Manifesto until the 1930s, the church and its followers navigated their way through an era of dramatic transition and assimilation. To begin with, Latter-day Saints moved beyond their church's own political organization and into the ranks of both national parties, holding a wide variety of views on a multiplicity of economic, political, and social issues. Moreover, church members largely left the practice of polygamy for mainstream monogamy, although a few aging patriarchs still supported multiple wives from decades-earlier marriages. Renewed adherence to the church's Word of Wisdom or health code, coupled with a heightened emphasis on family history and temple work, supplanted theocracy and polygamy as the touchstones of the church in the minds of many outsiders during this same era. And since the 1893 Chicago World's Fair, the Latter-day Saints had engaged in a number of important building projects, including the erection of three temples beyond the Mormon corridor and a number of stake tabernacles and ward chapels, which had raised the profile of the church beyond Utah. During this same time period, the church

59. Ballard, in Conference Report, October 1933, 18, 20.

began to purchase historic sites, including the Smith family farm, in Palmyra, New York, near the Sacred Grove; the Hill Cumorah; and the Carthage jail where Joseph and Hyrum Smith were martyred in 1844. And they were starting to put up monuments to document their past.[60]

The church had also evolved administratively over the four decades between 1893 and 1934. Male priesthood leaders had reorganized general and local quorums and clarified each groups' responsibilities. There was also an increased emphasis on missionary service for young men, and young women were now allowed to serve alongside as sister missionaries. The church's auxiliary organizations had also transformed over these years. The National Relief Society had helped create and shape the church's welfare program and the Young Men's and Young Ladies' Mutual Improvement Association had broadened their program to encompass both cultural and leisure endeavors. As part of its continued efforts to help ensure a separation of church and state in the Mormon cultural region, the church divested its secondary schools to the communities of western states in which they were located while at the same time focusing on church curriculum through better organized seminary, primary, and Sunday School programs. And the Mormons relinquished their quasi-monopoly on the Mountain West economy. Increasingly, Latter-day Saints worked with members of other faiths in joint ventures and were accepting of non-Mormon capital for a number of undertakings. "In view of the relative isolation of church members in the nineteenth century from the currents of social change in the remainder of the nation, the alteration of Mormon society by 1930 was nothing less than miraculous," Thomas G. Alexander writes of these cultural sea changes. "Mormons and Gentiles were now working together in social and community betterment causes such as prohibition, nonpartisan government, the development of parks, and a multitude of other social and cultural causes."[61]

The church was in the process of transforming itself from a provincial American religion into an international religious tradition. By the early 1930s, things had changed for the Mormons and the way they were viewed by outsiders. "The acceptance of the church by outsiders and the good will enjoyed by church members were indicated by the events which surrounded these proceedings," Alexander points out. The historically anti-Mormon Salt Lake Tribune, for example, willingly published a series of even-handed articles on

---

60. Alexander, *Mormonism in Transition*, 307–308.

61. Alexander, *Mormonism in Transition*, 307–308.

the history of Mormonism, written by Elder Levi Edgar Young, who was both a professor of history at the University of Utah and a General Authority of the church. And Pathe Pictures, a non-Mormon production company, captured "The Message of Mormonism," the church's official centennial pageant with Utah's capitol building as its backdrop. "In many ways, the centennial observance was characteristic of the change which had taken place," Alexander continues. "Mormons could now freely reflect upon both the similarities and the differences between their beliefs and those of others. Gentiles too were interested in the development of the church and could read about and work with their Mormon neighbors with much less rancor than had existed before."[62] The church had made major progress over the past century, just like the city of Chicago.

Between the 1893 Columbian Exposition and the 1933–1934 Century of Progress International Exposition, the image of Mormonism evolved in the minds of the American and international public. The church went from being constantly reviled to being occasionally praised. During the four-decade interim, Latter-day Saints experimented at a number of world's fairs and expositions on how best to exhibit their religious tradition and cultural contributions. One of the biggest contributions of the Latter-day Saint involvement was more serious and thoughtful ways in how they portrayed the church to the larger world from a public relations and even a missionary perspective. These cosmopolitan events helped the Latter-day Saints determine how they wanted to tell their own story to the interested public, who would now start coming to Mormons, in addition to Latter-day Saint missionaries going out to them. The resulting public relations coups convinced church leaders and laity that they had come across a great mixture for future world's fairs to improve the Mormon image. This was a remarkable shift in strategy and vision that has continued unabated into the twenty-first century. Thus, these two Chicago world's fairs act as convenient bookends to tell a larger story of the church's accommodation and assimilation into the larger American religious mainstream.

---

62. Alexander, *Mormonism in Transition*, 256–258, 310.

Index